DISCONNECTED
AMERICA

MEDIA, COMMUNICATION, AND CULTURE IN AMERICA

Michael C. Keith and Donald A. Fishman, Series Editors

WAVES OF RANCOR
Tuning in the Radical Right
Robert L. Hilliard and Michael C. Keith

SCREENED OUT
How the Media Control Us and What We Can Do About It
Carla Brooks Johnston

DISCONNECTED AMERICA
The Consequences of Mass Media in a Narcissistic World
Ed Shane

INVISIBLE STARS
A Social History of Women in American Broadcasting
Donna L. Halper
(forthcoming)

QUEER AIRWAVES
The Story of Gay and Lesbian Broadcasting
Phylis Johnson
(forthcoming)

DISCONNECTED AMERICA

The Consequences
of Mass Media
in a Narcissistic World

ED SHANE

M.E. Sharpe
Armonk, New York
London, England

Excerpts from *Reality Isn't What It Used to Be* by Walter Truett Anderson,
Copyright © 1990 by Walter Truett Anderson.
Reprinted by permission of HarperCollins Publishers, Inc.

Selections from *The Age of Missing Information* by Bill McKibben,
Copyright © 1992 by Bill McKibben.
Reprinted by permission of Random House, Inc.

Excerpts from *Amusing Ourselves to Death* by Neil Postman,
Copyright © 1985 by Neil Postman.
Used by permission of Viking Penguin, a division of Penguin Putnam Inc.

Library of Congress Cataloging-in-Publication Data

Shane, Ed.
Disconnected America: the consequences of mass media in a narcissistic world / Ed
Shane.
      p. cm. — (Media, communication, and culture in America)
   Includes bibliographical references and index.
   ISBN 0–7656–0526–0 (hardcover : alk. paper) – ISBN 0–7656–0527–9 (pbk. : alk. paper)
1. Mass media—United States. I. Title. II. Series.

P92.U5 S48 2001
302.23´0973—dc21   00–059503

Printed in the United States of America

BM (c)   10   9   8   7   6   5   4   3   2   1
BM (p)   10   9   8   7   6   5   4   3   2   1

To Pamela

Thanks for a terrific connection

Table of Contents

Foreword

One of the recurrent topics of contemporary life in America is the fraying of community standards, the erosion of face-to-face interaction, and the detachment of individuals from participation in civic affairs. The villain in this societal drama is a multifaceted monster: Two-career families, suburbanization and residential sprawl, greater job insecurity, the breakdown of religious authority, increased time pressures, failing school systems, and the harmful effects of television.

Ed Shane's book synthesizes the most salient problems, or "disconnections," that individuals experience as a result of the rapidly evolving changes in the technologies of communication. Moreover, Shane places these disconnections into a broader framework: That the development of the information society has not only brought a "new dawn" of instantaneous communication, but it has been accompanied by a "darkening shadow" as individuals find themselves in a world of voyeuristic television programs, attention-getting stunts, trivialized information, and glorified crisis events. Shane contends that there is an inherent but unfortunate bias within the media against offering complex interpretations that provide history and meaning to the reporting of news events.

Many of the topics that Shane examines have been discussed elsewhere. Shane draws upon the theories of Robert Putnam, Christopher Lasch, and Daniel Boorstin to create an interpretive structure for his observations. But Shane has the ability to synthesize abstract trends, summarize lengthy research articles, and place them into a context that provides meaning to everyday events. His conclusion that we are moving closer to the narcotic-like trance depicted by Adolph Huxley in *Brave New World* than grim prison-like atmosphere created by George Orwell in *Nineteen Eighty-Four* is an astute interpretation of the growing dependence by the public upon communication technologies for work, entertainment, and even conducting and maintaining "caring" relationships.

There are three major virtues to this book. First, it is written clearly. Shane has a good eye for language, and the organization of materials is compelling. Second, Shane has the ability to identify major trends that will impact society. For instance, Shane writes: "The internet allows the general public to tap into sources once used only by journalists and government officials. That's democracy at its best when there are no mistakes. Yet misinformation and disinformation are aided and abetted by unsuspecting web surfers who pass along stories that interest them to long lists of e-mail correspondents." There is a multiplier effect to these e-mail messages as recipients further send them to friends and family members. Thus, what starts off as an advantage for society—direct access to information—ends up as a liability because of the absence of responsible gatekeepers to help the public sort out the information and distinguish the trivial from the important. Unfortunately, the "new dawn" of information is accompanied by a lengthy "darkening shadow."

The third virtue of this book is more intangible than the other two. Shane's thesis—that the evolving information society produces as many drawbacks as alleged benefits—is developed gradually and persuasively in each chapter. By the end of the book, the whole is larger than the sum of its parts. Yet each of the parts contains astute observations, and Shane's examples are riveting. The mixture of information, entertainment, and digital reality has created a new world—but not necessarily a brave one; "unsettling" would be a more appropriate term.

This book is likely to be widely read. Information has become the "economic capital" of the twenty-first century, and there are a growing number of books that describe digital property, the information economy, and the culture of the internet. But Shane's book provides a coherent and compelling interpretation, bringing together ideas and concepts being explored in many disciplines but that previously have remained "disconnected." This is work that provides insight and analysis into America's increasing immersion into instantaneous communication.

Donald A. Fishman
Boston College

Preface

Reading this book before sending it to the publisher made me appreciate Walter Cronkite's address to the Radio Television News Directors' Association meeting in Miami Beach in 1976. Cronkite had been misquoted by the press and by his own medium, and he sought to set the record straight in front of his newsroom colleagues. He began, "If we this morning were operating under the same strictures which bind you and me in doing our daily jobs, I now would have finished my speech—eleven seconds after starting it."

If the same conventions that are imposed on TV news applied to this book, you couldn't have read this far. You'd have no chance to discover that I believe there's a parallel between the problem that Cronkite pointed out more than a quarter of a century ago and disconnectedness in America today. You wouldn't learn why I feel that way, who else agrees with my premise, why it matters, or *if* it matters. If this were the evening news, you'd be lucky to get as much information about this book as you got from the cover. Oh, you may hear something about how many textbooks I've sold and that I'm a media consultant. Chances are, you wouldn't be told what that means, either. I'd get the conventional time allotment: a few seconds of introduction to set up the story, a graphic with my name superimposed over my picture, and a 9.8–second piece of video—a few precious seconds less than the time Cronkite used in his indictment of his industry.

Let's consider another set of television conventions—the morning-show interview. The 9.8–second average of the evening news clip expands to almost four full minutes! That may be enough time to steam a half pound of bay scallops in a microwave oven or to listen to a song on the radio, but it's not enough time to develop the theme of a book beyond a sentence or two to support the initial allegation. The morning-show interview would set up some sort of introduction. I imagine it would be a produced piece on videotape showing sequences of violent behavior from the news archives and parallels in major motion pictures. Television people have a sense of cause and effect about these things. The show's producers would be horrified to hear my suggestions for their introduction: Instead of television as a catalyst for violence, I'd suggest an edited sequence of the "news" stories I saw on Channel 7 in Los Angeles in late 1999 about "taste tests" between pizza and snack products. "That's the disconnect," I'd say. "Some reporter's response to a pizza snack from the grocery store trivializes my need for information about how to interact with my neighbors."

Nonetheless, the initial four minutes is now reduced to less than three. That time will be devoted to the premise of the book and will accommodate a few questions from the interviewer, which may or may not illuminate my subject matter. At least the morning-show format offers more than the 9.8–second sound bite. You'd discover that TV isn't the sole culprit; it only accelerated the disconnectedness. Further, you'd hear that there are remedies for the condition, although you wouldn't hear any of them because of time constraints. Oh, and you'd learn that I'm from Houston.

Then you'd see some commercials, and I'd be gone. The next segment would explore water on the surface of Mars, Ricky Martin's malleable hips, or a domestic dispute turned into a national soap opera. In the words of Monty Python's Flying Circus, it would be time for something completely different.

If we were using the morning TV convention, you'd have to stop reading about now. Television is happy with that amount of time. I'm not. After all, I've done considerable thinking on this subject, and I've supported it with research, some of it as I advise my media clients about their businesses. I want you to hear what I have to say, not just a synopsis of my premise. I also want you to draw some conclusions as I flesh out my arguments and—if you agree with the idea—work with me toward the remedies.

My aim is to reduce the bias against understanding caused by a bias toward brevity. There is such a bias, and it creates a disconnect:

- When TV spends more time on pizza snacks than on city government, we are disconnected from city government.
- When TV spends more time on the president's breakfast than on his philosophy, we're disconnected from national government.
- When TV spends more time on the journalist than on the story, we are disconnected from the story.

The net effect is disconnection from issues, from meaning, and—ultimately—from each other.

When Christopher Lasch's *The Culture of Narcissism* was released in 1979, it was a report on the American psyche faced with diminished expectations. We now know it was a warning about self-absorption with eyes so internalized that nothing outside matters. Television and electronic media exacerbated Lasch's narcissistic man. In *Technopoly*, Neil Postman documents the surrender of culture to technology and laments the equalization of ideas, symbols, and icons. This book is somewhere between Postman and Lasch.

✺   ✺   ✺

Disconnected America is written as warning, but call it complaint instead. Its message: that we have allowed the cabaret of the information explosion to lull us into thinking we know what's happening around us, that we have internalized the experience of electronic media to such a point that we diminish interpersonal contact or, as Harvard's Robert Putnam describes it, we've diminished "social capital."

Disconnected America explores the ever shortening distance between disconnectivity and alienation and offers a scenario about how we arrived here. Together, we'll examine the change from pervasive mass media that disseminate information quickly to de-massified individual media that incubate a new electronic narcissism. The result is an inwardly focused individual who sees all information—all stimuli, for that matter—in one context: the context of self, totally disconnected from other individuals, other ideas, other collected imagery. The new narcissist seeks shelter from information. The context is no context at all.

Disconnected America is a book of social criticism, so it asks more questions than it answers because there are no easy answers. Difficult solutions run counter to technologies that create their own culture. Once media take hold, there's no way to reverse the process. If there were, progress would also be reversed. So I'm not advocating a halt to progress.

✺   ✺   ✺

My fear, of course, is that no one will read this book. This message requires a new vehicle. The best venue for this material would be a video hacker's interruption into *Who Wants to Be a Millionaire,* into *Monday Night Football,* or into a news program where the last vestiges of a mass audience still attend.

In my mind's eye, I see the screen now: close camera shot. Very close. So close it's distorted. The nose of the commentator bulges unnaturally, and detail of the face tapers away—that's how close the camera is. The video intruder is unable to be recognized because the angle is so close, so distorted.

The shot is made with a cheap home camera, one of those slow-scan digi-tal cameras designed for grandma to see the grandkids via e-mail. The light-ing is harsh, so backgrounds are dark in contrast. Images flicker. It may as well be in black and white because of the contrast. In fact, black and white suits the message perfectly.

The messenger is an evangelist of sorts, preaching the gospel of disen-gagement and the erosion of social contact. His messages are a warning to the users of the very system that created disassociation in the first place. The messages are for the very people comfortably informed by electronic media and amused to distraction by an overload of what they have been told is "choice" in programming.

Of course, the intruder doesn't exist. Who, after all, would interrupt popu-lar media with a message the viewer doesn't want to hear? Better to tell the same story in this book—that is, if you have more than 9.8 seconds.

Acknowledgments

Undertaking a project like this book is a reminder that it cannot happen on its own. Michael Keith at Boston College began this process long ago by engaging me in several of his book projects. Then he interrupted the progress of this book by urging me to write a textbook for undergraduate media and marketing courses. As series editor, Michael offered the book a guiding hand from the idea stages through final text. I often thank him in person; now I can do so in print.

Peter Coveney at M.E. Sharpe was kind enough to see the merits of my previous books and to give his go-ahead to the project. His keen reading focused the thinking process. Thanks also to project editor Susan Rescigno and the inhouse and freelance production staff.

A rewarding, three-decade working relationship with media consultant George A. Burns is the genesis of many of the thoughts about the speedup caused by electronic media.

The Shane Media Services staff once again exhibited patience while I focused more on a book and less on them. A special word to the "style police," Lizzy Waggoner and Myrna Brasie. Their patient reading was a great safety net for fact errors, double keystrokes, and stray spaces.

If there's a theme in book acknowledgements, it's the appreciation that authors heap on their spouses. In my case, there would be no book otherwise. My wife and business partner, Pam Shane, made direct contributions by reviewing text and by challenging my assumptions. Her true contribution is years of allowing me to test philosophy and theory on her before exposing them to less sympathetic outsiders. Since she doesn't feel that patience is a virtue, I won't thank her for being patient. Instead, my sincere thanks for her encouragement and enthusiasm.

DISCONNECTED AMERICA

Chapter 1

The Illusion of Connectivity

Plato warned us. He was the first to call our attention to the perceptual alteration that media caused. In his day, however, the issue was writing.

Plato knew that writing would bring a shift from the ear to the eye as an organ of language processing. In *Phaedrus*, Plato recounts a conversation between Phaedrus and Socrates about an Egyptian divinity, Theuth, the god of writing (you may know Theuth as "Thoth" or "Hermes"). The divinity claimed that his invention would improve memories and make the Egyptians wiser.

Not so quick, said Pharaoh, responding to Theuth:

> The fact is that this invention will produce forgetfulness in the souls of those who have learned it. They will not need to exercise their memories, being able to rely on what is written, calling things to mind no longer from within themselves by their own unaided powers, but under the stimulus of external marks that are alien to themselves. So it's not a recipe for memory, but for reminding, that you have discovered.[1]

In Socrates' reply to Phaedrus, Plato cautioned the world about the written word: "Once a thing is put in writing, it rolls about all over the place, falling into the hands of those who have no concern with it just as easily as under the notice of those who comprehend; it has no notion of whom to address or whom to avoid."

Let people begin writing, Plato said, and they won't deal with truth, only a semblance of truth. Writing was detachment from self, especially from the self of the aural, storytelling tradition.

Plato's story is ironic, because he committed his argument to writing, but put it into the words of Socrates, who did not write. Plato expressed a fear about writing that obviously existed in his day. You can only wonder what

Plato would think of Western culture today. He could not have imagined what Gutenberg would do to writing, what the photograph would do to reading, what the Lumière brothers' motion pictures would do to perceptions he held so dear.

All our technological innovations have added, one upon another, to accelerate a media landscape, thus accelerating our own pace.

A Dominant Cultural Force

In the wake of Hurricane Andrew, which devastated southern Florida in 1992, Sears stores used radio to advertise television antennas as part of the "cleanup" after the storm. A Sears executive explained the campaign by saying, "Television is so much a part of life that people probably think about it before they get their roof back on."[2]

That's a provocative statement about a pervasive medium. There's no question that American television is a dominant cultural force. As Neil Postman puts it, "There is no audience so young that it is barred from television. There is no poverty so abject that it must forgo television. There is no education so exalted that it is not modified by television."[3]

Think of your own experiences with television. Where were you when . . .

- President Kennedy was felled in Dallas?
- the Woodstock festival created a cosmic moment?
- Neil Armstrong took one giant step for mankind onto the moon?
- Richard Nixon resigned the presidency?
- Protests were crushed in Tiananmen Square?
- the Berlin Wall was toppled?
- President Bush launched the Persian Gulf War?
- the Russian parliament building burned during a coup?
- the earth welcomed the new millennium in the year 2000?

Depending on your age, one of these events may have been a defining moment that caused you to share a community experience. Not touched directly by the experiences, some of us may have simply watched on TV.

"Did anyone get any work done yesterday?" asked the *Wall Street Journal* the day after the verdict was announced in the O.J. Simpson murder trial.[4]

Millions watched the event on television—51 million viewers by Nielsen Ratings estimates, or 49.4 percent of the nation's 96 million television households. A CNN survey projected that number to 100 million adults at a television set between 1:00 and 1:30 P.M. Eastern time that day.

AT&T's nationwide telephone network saw a 60 percent drop in traffic during the five-minute period while the verdict was being read. Traders experienced a lull on the New York Stock Exchange. At the Chicago Board of Trade, the world's busiest futures exchange, trading was at a standstill.

That's connectivity!

The first day of the Persian Gulf War in 1991, an estimated 85.6 million viewers tuned in. It was one of the highest ratings levels ever, although it is to be remembered that Gulf War coverage began during the evening hours when viewing levels are usually higher anyway because of prime time programming.

Princess Diana's death in a Paris underpass brought viewers around the world together for a weekend of shared grief. The same occurred in 1986 when the explosion of the space shuttle *Challenger* gathered millions around TV sets to share in the experience.[5]

The murder of John Kennedy was our first cathartic television connection. So vivid are the pictures lodged in the minds of those who watched TV that weekend in 1963 that most think they saw the bullets fly and watched the president fall, even though films were not released until thirteen years later! They did watch the swearing in of a somber Lyndon Johnson. They did watch the ambush of Lee Harvey Oswald by Jack Ruby. They did watch tears well in Walter Cronkite's eyes. They did hear NBC's Frank McGee choking back emotions in a display of humanity that defied his training as a journalist. They did hear the muffled drums as the catafalque was drawn through the gray streets of Washington.

It's difficult to imagine that a story could travel any faster through a nation of 200 million people. According to follow-up research studies, nine out of ten Americans knew of Kennedy's assassination within an hour of its being announced. About half received the news directly from broadcast media; the rest heard it from neighbors or co-workers.

Television was the preferred medium, according to researchers William Mindak and Gerald Hursh. "The reasons people spent so much time watching television," they say, "are to be found in the uniqueness of the coverage. Neither radio nor newspapers could match television's facility for realism and psychological proximity."[6] The problem with television is that it brings us together when we need it, as it did when President Kennedy was felled, but it also unites us in the trivialities of *Who Wants to Be a Millionaire* and the soap opera of the O.J. Simpson trial.

Television. Neil Postman calls it "the command center" of American culture.[7]

It wasn't always the center.

Community of Understanding

Since the dawn of time, we humans have constructed a community of understanding based on shared information. It must have been nice at the dawn of time because there was a scarcity of information. Our ancestors could take all the time they needed to assimilate information and to pass it along, usually verbally.

Agricultural and handicraft communities were better able to handle language than we are. Their decisions were simple: which fear was a demon and which was "God" speaking in strange ways; which old lady to burn at the stake for witchcraft or which old steak not to burn because it was holy bull. In the main, firsthand experience was the check against unprovable statements. The priests mediated, delivering and interpreting the information. Messengers from afar sang the folktales they heard in their travels, adding to their songs and to the local lexicon.

Then came the typographers, delivering information that could be examined at leisure and interpreted by the reader, which led to journalists who filter information and interpret for the reader.

Over too brief a time, information became abundant. "The information glut," it was called. Some went so far as to call ours "the information economy," even though an economic system is seldom based on surplus, but rather on scarcity. Everybody seems to *add* information, but no one attempts to reduce it.

In the context of glut, information is more diversion than contribution. The constant flow of data, the twenty-four-hour news cycle, and the easy access to "news" (whatever that word means anymore) are terrific for the insomniac and pretty good for Ted Turner and Bill Gates, but lousy for the rest of us.

We have lost control of our information in spite of "information management" resources that seem as abundant as the data they manipulate. Inundated, data consumers resort to clever ways to avoid the onslaught.

The teenager on the bus is oblivious to the passengers around him. The incessant tsch-tsch-tsch-tsch escaping from his headphones annoys those around him while simultaneously wrapping him in cocoon-like selfness.

The cell-phone user walking down Fifty-second Street is connected to the distant voice yet focused only on her own personal and innermost response to that voice. She's disconnected from the throngs walking her way on the street. She makes no eye contact and indicates no awareness of the passerby. Look at her and the distance of her gaze tells you she looks through you, not at you.

Marshall McLuhan might say that the teenager on the bus and the woman with the cell phone are examples of aural man rising from the ruins of visual man or that the next wave of cultural interaction will be the return to the aural tradition. He gave us, after all, those images of the "global village" and the "tribes" around the electronic campfire.

However, the global village as it manifests itself to date is quite visual, hardly aural. The split-second video image, the illusory montages that create our television fare, and the interaction via Internet are steeped in visuals, even if they have an audio soundtrack.

McLuhan gave us the full report on the original shift—Gutenberg's revolution from the aural, storytelling, priest-interpreted culture. Gutenberg's type was as linear and sequential as the aural tradition stories that preceded it. Yet its impact was nonlinear. "Typography cracked the voices of silence," says McLuhan, using a phrase traditionally used to describe sculptures: "As the Gutenberg typography filled the world the human voice closed down. People began to read silently and passively as consumers."[8]

By introducing wide distribution of literature, Gutenberg opened the written word to self-interpretation. Via Gutenberg, man became the center of the universe. As McLuhan put it:

> Printing from moveable type created a quite unexpected new environment— it created the PUBLIC. . . . The unique character of the "public" created by the printed word was an intense and visually oriented self-consciousness, both of the individual and the group.[9]

Much of early print output was the Bible, which was the primary reading matter in most households. In some homes, it was the *only* reading matter. So impressed was Martin Luther with the distribution of printing that he called the new technology "God's highest and extremist act of grace, whereby the business of the Gospel is driven forward."[10]

Self-Interpretation

While the business of the gospel propagated, so did individual interpretation. Distribution of Bibles allowed a variety of publics to form their own conclusions about whether the Word was God or only with God. Splitting hairs led to divergent beliefs and ultimately to peeling away new denominations, each empowered by interpretation.

Postman reminds us of an exchange between Benjamin Franklin and Michael Welfare, a founder of a New England sect called the Dunkers. Welfare complained to Franklin that lies were being spread about his group, so Franklin suggested that the Dunkers write and distribute their doctrines to let their critics know what they stood for. They had been thinking about their beliefs, Welfare told Franklin, but they hadn't quite settled on all the issues. Dunker doctrine was, so to speak, a work in progress. If they wrote it down, he said, they might feel "bound and confined by it, and perhaps be unwilling to receive further improvement." The Dunkers arrived at a surprising (and, possibly, unique) position, as Postman phrased it: "Thou shalt not write down thy principles, still less print them, lest thou shall be entrapped by them for all time."[11]

Newly colonized America was a remarkably literate place. As early as the voyage of the *Mayflower,* there's evidence of books and stipends for libraries. From 1650 onward, almost all New England towns created laws requiring schools for reading and writing.

So many settlers arrived from Great Britain that books in the local language were already available. All the colonists needed was a steady stream of ships, and that they had. Some vessels brought new neighbors; all brought copies of books that "deluged" England, according to Timothy Dwight, the president of Yale.

New England was a settlement of readers, but not writers. It was sufficient to read the imports. And books proliferated. Thomas Paine's *Common Sense* (full title: *Common Sense, Written by an Englishman*) sold about a half million copies. That's a conservative estimate, but let's assume it's correct. That means 16.7 percent of the population of three million bought the book. That's a truly mass medium. In today's television, that percentage would equate to a 16 share, and network television covets half that number.

In the colonies, reading was classless. No aristocracy grew up around the distribution of literature, and every citizen of the new land was a reader. Freedom of interpretation would do to British rule of the colonies what it had done to religion (thus creating the colonies). It offered the new Americans a sense of freedom and motivated their fight for independence.

Literacy and a passion for reading were the glue that held the new United States together. Newspapers sprang up from the beginning, but with expansion of the number of colonies—now officially "states"—newspapers extended the culture and created a community of understanding about the noble experiment in democracy.

By the 1850s, this well-read population would think nothing of spending an entire day listening to political debates (of which the seven Lincoln-Douglas debates of 1858 and 1859 are the most famous). After a two-hour verbal opus, the crowd would disperse for lunch, return for a rebuttal of another two hours, go home to dinner, and return yet again for the night's final speeches of an hour or more each.

There was sufficient understanding of the working of government that the audience was informed during the process. The debates were also mass entertainments, worthy of conversation for days after. The language of the debates fit the other mass media of the time—linear and sequential, just like books and newspapers.

There were other mass entertainments in America's second century: the traveling wagon show selling patent medicines and the circus tent that could hold all the town's children. They were diversions. They didn't hold the power or the unifying quality of print. Only the pulpit was stronger, yet preachers of every style and nuance relied on print for their theses. Their interpretation of the Bible was key to their popularity and to their success. Words were their most important products.

Not until America's third century was mass consciousness—the quilt of community understanding—to be frayed by the shift in media based in words to media steeped in an all-new language, the language of the eye and the image. Everyone knew how to "speak" the new way, but the ability to self-interpret would be beyond anything seen before. The photograph and the motion picture were to create uniquely American media that would not only engage the masses but also alter the culture.

Bigger Than Life

Have you ever seen Jack Nicholson on TV? Eliminate the quick glimpse of Nicholson courtside at a Lakers' basketball game. Forget the gangly, youthful actor with minor roles in *The Twilight Zone* or other early TV episodes. The answer is "no." Nicholson won't do television—no starring roles, no talk shows—"because once you shrink, you can never really get big again."

Norma Desmond knew about shrinkage. "I am big," said the aging screen siren in the movie *Sunset Boulevard*. "It's the pictures that got small."

And once the pictures—the movies—commingled the images of their stars with television, the stars themselves got small, too. Television invented the small star.

"They're all big stars," writes Taylor Latham in *Swing*, "but they aren't giants the way Cary Grant and Gary Cooper were. Instead of the traditional movie star aura, they have the irregular faces that television loves."[12] The television star is an image that's comfortable to have around the house, more like family than those bigger-than-life characters who engulfed us from the movie screen.

In *Life the Movie*, Neal Gabler cites the transition from print literature to the new language of the cinema:

> The movies' cultural power resided in the fact that they had not just appeared as a result of technology; they had arrived as a kind of fulfillment of American dreams and longings. Almost from the country's inception, American men of letters had been calling for a sinewy native art shorn of "any ultramarine, full-dress formulas of culture, polish, caste, etc.," as

Whitman put it. Whitman had expected this new art to come from literature, particularly poetry, and while his own work certainly qualified, it would
not be poetry but the movies that would be America's own native form.
Here was a medium free of any traditions whatsoever, much less the taint
of European culture.

As the most powerful form of entertainment, the movies were also the
most powerful agents of its cosmology, and long before television they had
become the central metaphor for American life. What the movies provided,
early critics like Jane Addams realized, was a tangible model to which one
could conform life and a standard against which one could measure it, both
in seemingly trivial ways, like fashion or behavior, and in more serious
ways, like the movie-induced expectations one had about the course of
one's own life or the value of one's deeds. "Why can't life be more like the
movies?" viewers asked, and then answered that it could.[13]

Movies and life were inexorably intertwined from the beginning. The brothers Auguste and Louis Lumière invented the cinema camera in France in
1895. A few days after Christmas in 1898, their father, a Lyon industrialist,
invited friends and family to the basement of a Paris café to watch lantern
slides projected on the wall.

It's the friends who are important to this story: the elder Lumière invited
impresarios and Paris theater people. Present over the few days' exhibition
were Léon Gaumont, Charles Pathé, and George Méliès. None would be
impressed with a lantern show. They had seen enough such exhibitions to
consider them routine.

But then a projected street scene began to move! Trams, cars, and, yes,
even *people* began to move across the screen. Later projections showed roll-
ing waves and bathers at the seaside. Newspapers used words like "astonishing" to describe this "marvelous realism." Méliès called it "jaw dropping."

Méliès knew from his own experience how important the Lumière brothers' invention was. He was a magician and illusionist by trade who presented
himself and others in feats of prestidigitation at his Théâtre Robert Houdin.
In spring 1898, Méliès was working with photographic equipment, shooting
images of the Place de l'Opéra to project on the screen at Houdin. As he
worked, the camera jammed. About a minute passed as he cleared the problem and resumed photography.

Only when projecting the images did Méliès discover that he happened
upon an accident that would change language, culture, and perception for all
time. The Place de l'Opéra remained stationary, but an omnibus in view when
the filmstrip began transformed magically into a hearse, which was in the same
place after the minute's delay. Passers-by, of course, passed by in the same
minute. The result was what appeared to be a man changing into a woman.

The New Illusion

Méliès did not invent the cinema, yet he discovered what Matt Matsuda calls "the language of discontinuity and deceptive persistence" and exploited it first as impresario and later as a filmmaker in his own right. When the Lumière brothers would not sell their new contrivance, Méliès developed his own motion picture camera. From short films showing babies, trains, steamboats, and other slices of life, Méliès turned to staged plays and developed, using Matsuda's words, "a body of original works which both replicated and extended the detailed, fantastic spectacles of his magic acts."[14]

For Méliès, the new cinema was not objective witnessing of daily life. Rather, cinema was illusion. His reality was tricks and simulation. He produced fanciful tales on film, including his signature *Un voyage dans la lune* (*A Trip to the Moon*) in which a gigantic cannon throws a bullet-shaped ship into space to plant itself nose first in the surface soil of the moon. Méliès was the first to re-create scenes for the camera. His version of the coronation of England's King Edward VII in 1902 was praised by the impersonated king himself.

Matt Matsuda calls the invention of the cinema camera "the invention of a memory machine" in *The Memory of the Modern:*

> Yet the machine did more than preserve the past; the authenticity of the moving image was so authoritative, so *real*, that filmed subjects seemed to exist not as records of a point in time, but in the present of projection. Sensibilities of temporal depth and sequence which gave reality to the past were dominated by the spectacular immediacy of the image. Striking images would become the viewer's memory of events, shaping recollections to the measure of filmed and projected scenes. Citing physiology, ethics, and the impressionable nature of what [Henri] Bergson called "the masses," critics of the new medium debated the accuracy and morality of the cinema, and raised questions about the virtues of screen memories, as opposed to those of the printed page.[15]

If television and electronic media create their own sense of time and memory, they owe their heritage to the movies' mix of light and shadow in action. All of perception would be shaken if not conquered by the new medium. Matsuda continues:

> With its ability to capture and collapse time, the cinema camera was an utterly modern marker for the accelerated memory of the late nineteenth century, a machine which generated superbly real living records while si-

multaneously creating its own fantastically unsettling perceptual and temporal frameworks. If the inventors of the machine—the brothers Lumière—thought of their creation principally as a scientific and documentary instrument, artists like Méliès saw it as part of a mechanism of dreams, a chance to capture absolute unreality and create effects and visions far beyond what his theater could imagine.[16]

As Méliès and his contemporaries discovered, the motion picture camera did not simply record; it created a new concept of time and vision. Events could be filmed in one part of the world and viewed not many days after in another. No longer did the public have to wait for the newspaper to uncover the news or for visitors to bring a story on the rare trip from afar. Speed and immediacy overtook the interpretation usually afforded events by historians and analysts. The public once again took the primary role in interpreting the world around them. Moreover, watching the new moving pictures, the viewer felt a part of the action.

Cinema received praise and awe at its inception and very little negative criticism. That it did not use language was the worst that could be said for it, and soon enough that would be solved by technicians who added sound to the movies. The vision, however, was the most compelling element of the motion picture.

Cinema accelerated the transition from words and language to what critic E.L. Godkin calls "chromo-civilization." Even venerable Shakespeare fell out of favor in the late nineteenth century. The Bard's writings were thought to hark back to a tradition rendered passé, "an aural anachronism in a society that opted for the visual," says Neal Gabler, paraphrasing the *New York Times*. The turn of the twentieth century made the *Atlantic Monthly* fret that images would eventually replace words and that visual symbols would become the primary form of discourse.[17]

There's no need here for a history of the rise of Hollywood and the image makers who honed the craft of moviemaking. It is necessary to remember the growth of the movie industry and its parallel with the Great Depression. While the Depression was global, the response was uniquely American. Traditional entertainment functions as a distraction from problems, and the movies were no different in that regard. In *America in the Movies*, Michael Wood describes our films as a "rearrangement of our problems into shapes which tame them, which disperse them to the margins of our attention."[18]

Movies of the 1930s and 1940s weren't just romantic, benign interactions with a dream reality. They were experiences that deeply shaped who the viewers were, how they grew up, and what they expected from life. That echoes Matsuda's point that movies are the stuff of collective memory, creating a living portrait instead of the cold, languid images of the painting or the still photograph.

Life imitates art, even though it sounds cliché. And the opposite is true, as well: Art imitates life, as we see from novels, movies, and television programs.

Neal Gabler sees a combination of the two:

> After decades of public-relations contrivances and media hype, and after decades more of steady pounding by an array of social forces that have alerted each of us personally to the power of performance, life has become art, so that the two are now indistinguishable from each other. Or, to re-work an aphorism of the poet Stéphane Mallarmé, the world doesn't exist to end in a book; when life is a medium, books and every other imaginative form exist to end in a world.[19]

Gabler suggests that, whether we know it or not, we create our own world every day in what he calls "lifies"—"movies written in the medium of life, projected on the screen of life."[20] The screen of life is a combination of ourselves and the television screen.

New Realities

It wasn't too many centuries ago that most societies—including ours in those founding days of America—recognized and accepted a single, "official" reality. Members of society dedicated themselves and their resources to defending their reality and destroying any opposition.

Official realities seemed to be permanent fixtures. Symbols were universal—at least for those in the immediate universe: the tribe, the town, the kingdom. No one knew they followed a reality or that they held a worldview. They just did.

Today there's little consensus about the official reality, including whether there is such a thing. As Alvin Toffler describes it in *The Third Wave*:

> Each of us creates in his skull a mind-model of reality—a warehouse of images. Some of these are visual, others auditory, even tactile. Some are only "percepts"—traces of information about our environment, like a glimpse of blue sky seen from the corner of the eye. Others are "linkages" that define relationships, like the two words "mother" and "child." Some are simple, others complex and conceptual, like the idea that "inflation is caused by rising wages." Together such images add up to our picture of the world—locating us in time, space, and the network of personal relationships around us.[21]

Toffler calls the changes "Second Wave" and "Third Wave." The "First Wave" was the mostly agricultural society of the distant past, punctuated occasionally by advances like the Greek and Roman cultures. The Second Wave was the sea change brought about by the industrial revolution that reordered the world and brought it work-saving devices and communication tools that altered the landscape, both cultural and agricultural.

The Third Wave is what Toffler terms today's "blip culture" of electronic media. We're caught between the worldview of the recent past and the future that has yet to become totally clear. Some embrace it; some reject it.

For anyone seeking an anchor for their own worldview, there's little solid ground. In *Reality Isn't What It Used to Be*, Walter Truett Anderson calls today's environment an "unregulated marketplace of realities." We are not so much believers, but "possessors of belief" constructed by "entrepreneurs of reality."[22]

And that's where television enters the story. Television took the mass medium and distributed shadow pictures into every home, allowing viewers to weave magic with the shadows. The audience for television increased because the population itself increased, thanks to the post–World War II baby boom, an important element, says Michael J. Wolf in *The Entertainment Economy:*

> Modern mass media—that is, television—were born with the baby-boom generation. From its first formative years, the evolution of media impacted the development of this generation and was in turn influenced by wants and desires of this new economic colossus—a whole generation of consumers who were socialized by what they saw on the tube. A common consumer culture leapfrogged national and cultural boundaries and then, as boomers had children and now grandchildren, the process has, if anything, been accelerated.[23]

Television is a great equalizer. The family whose apartment is destroyed by the overnight fire is equal to the budget bill on Capitol Hill. The budget bill is equal to the fallen jetliner. The Houston retailer who jumps into the air at the end of his commercials, flashing a handful of dollar bills and vowing to "SAVE YOU MONEY!!!" is equal to the dysfunctional family complaining to Jerry Springer about their children having sex with adults, or kids dressing in macabre black clothing and calling themselves "Goths."

How many more examples are there? Hundreds. Bill McKibben gives us a book full of them. In *The Age of Missing Information*, he describes twenty-four hours on the Fairfax, Virginia, cable system, chosen because it delivered at the time almost 100 channels. With the assistance of friends and relatives, McKibben recorded an entire day of the effluent of the cable system and compared it to a camping trip to Crow Mountain in the Adirondacks—two and a half hours from his back door.

The mountain, he says, reminded him of the "vital knowledge that humans have always possessed about who we are and where we live." The myriad cable channels did not, even though the 7:00 A.M. hour required four pages of verbal description and phrases from dialogue to conjure the effect of surfing all the available channels. The cable fare reflected what McKibben calls "a moment of deep ignorance," a disconnect from our senses that robs us of information:

> By virtue of its omnipresence [television] constantly reinforces certain ideas. It is less an art form than the outlet for a utility—like the faucet on a sink that connects you to the river, the TV links you to a ceaselessly flowing stream of information, and that very ceaselessness makes it different from a play or a movie. Television is the chief way that most of us partake of the larger world, of the information age, and so, though none of us owe our personalities and habits entirely to the tube and the world it shows, none of us completely escape its influence either.[24]

The first age of television, from the late 1940s through the 1970s, was characterized by a scarcity of channels and dominance by three national networks. Like earlier media, television offered a semblance of national culture and a shared information base. Who we were was what we saw in common, and consensus was indispensable to national unity. Consensus, however, came at the price of uniformity.

No more. Television's multichannel era of rapid clicks of the remote revolutionized our habits as viewers, as consumers, and as citizens. Toffler warns: "An information bomb is exploding in our midst, showering us with a shrapnel of images and drastically changing the way each of us perceives and acts upon our private world."[25]

Politics confused with show business. Reaction confused with opinion. Information confused with understanding. Spin-doctored statements to the media confused with the truth. Postings on the Internet confused with connectedness. Electronic images confused with experience.

Persistence of Vision

Images. That's what TV is all about. More specifically, television is about the creation of images in the viewer's consciousness. The image projected onto a human eye remains visible briefly after it disappears, a phenomenon called "persistence of vision." Thus, when the cathode ray tube in your television set paints thirty separate and distinct images on your retinas every second, the flashes move faster than your eye's ability to sort them out. Each image replaces the one before and lingers just long enough as it's replaced by the one that follows. Because of persistence of vision, you think you see constant motion. That's the principle that makes television possible.[26]

The operation of the eye is key here. Eye movements that help us to select what we see are combinations of automatic and willful responses. In *Visual Thinking*, Rudolf Arnheim explains the movements this way:

> They must direct the eyes in such a way that the area of the visual field to be scrutinized comes within the narrow range of sharpest vision. Sharpness falls off so rapidly that at a deviation of ten degrees from the axis of fixation, where it is at a maximum, it is already reduced to one fifth. Because retinal sensitivity is so restricted, the eye can and must single out some particular spot, which becomes isolated, dominant, central. This means taking up one thing at a time and distinguishing the primary objective from its surroundings.[27]

The twenty-one-inch (diagonal) television screen is perfectly suited for the eye. Its height is approximately fifteen inches. At a distance of four feet, the viewer's field of vision focusing exactly on the center of the screen matches Arnheim's ten-degree deviation of sharpness at all four of the screen's edges. Enlarged projection screens overwhelm the eyes, adding to the sense of experience. Because of persistence of vision, we think we see motion. Because we see motion, we think we see reality.

Marshall McLuhan knew the power of that phenomenon. From the millions of dots on the video screen, he surmised that the average viewer could accept only a few, so, to understand the image, the viewer had to plunge in fully. "Depth involvement," he called it.[28]

McLuhan warned us of "perceptual numbing," an insensitivity to all but the most extreme experiences in life. He predicted mass-produced fantasy and imaginings. He suggested that "depth involvement" would undermine our confidence in the possibilities for firsthand experiences and reliable knowledge about events in the world.

In the 1960s, McLuhan's warnings seemed plausible, and no businessman would open a presentation without quoting McLuhan on something. McLuhan was in demand as lecturer and prophet, which made him a rich man, particularly in comparison to his job as professor of literature.[29]

By the 1970s, McLuhan's predictions fell out of favor. His university colleagues picked holes in his theories. Recession set in and dampened the fervor businesspeople felt for McLuhan's pronouncements. If the medium were truly the message, the medium became overwhelmed by the message of the war in Vietnam and the unsettling stories from the Nixon White House.

Through the mid-1980s, McLuhan's message lay dormant until the now-defunct *Channels* magazine said flatly, "We need to start listening to McLuhan again."[30] After all, McLuhan had written at a time when the average TV set was turned on for less than four hours a day. In the mid-1980s, that figure approached seven hours a day and remains at that level today.

Ideas that were at first only plausible became impossible and now come full circle to the commonplace. The keyboard of a computer, the handheld controls of a video game, and the headset of a Walkman bring us to a level of media immersion or depth involvement not available in McLuhan's lifetime.

You'll remember that McLuhan saw an explosion of media spawning two possible outcomes, one utopian, the other dystopian. McLuhan's utopia had our depth involvement with television doing away with obsolete modes of perception, like reading this book. The reader does not become the book, but maintains a critical distance. The media user, on the other hand, becomes involved in the medium.

As we become accustomed to total experience through media, McLuhan predicted, we will learn to experience one another openly and completely. That's a McLuhan prediction that has not come to fruition. If anything, we're losing experiences with each other, at least positive experiences. There's a decline in civic engagement that tracks with the proliferation of media. There's evidence of a decline in civility and a corresponding redefinition and diminution of the concept of shame.

How could McLuhan miss these important points? He would have explained by saying we had not prepared ourselves for the media revolution. The question is whether it's too late to prepare. Have we gone too far in disconnecting ourselves, and is our lot only to react and to cope?

McLuhan's thesis boils down to a few words: The achievements of technology from the wheel to electricity are media, extensions of ourselves. Over the course of history, these media changed our way of perceiving the world. Movable type, followed by engraved drawing, the photograph, the motion picture, and television—each exaggerated the visual as the basis of understanding and culture. Each in turn moved us to a sensory perceptual world no longer linear and sequential like the person-to-person language that preceded Gutenberg's intervention.

Virtual Abandonment

The opening scene of a television commercial shows a hospital delivery room. The camera doesn't watch the baby emerge, but we hear its first cries and we see it wrapped in its first blanket. A doctor says "Congratulations" to a young man attending the birth. "Oh, I'm not the father," he responds and nods to the mother: "We met in the hall." The scene shifts to another young man at a computer, shouting to an empty room that he'll be along as soon as directions to the hospital download.

It's a humorous slice of life, but all too real given increasing self-absorption with personal electronic media. There's evidence from family law practices in Tennessee, Minnesota, North Carolina, and Pennsylvania: The Internet is blamed for divorces and playing a key role in custody fights. Internet addicts could find themselves in court.

Typical is a 1998 case in which a divorced woman who shared custody with her husband lost her custody rights. Attorney Kate Vetrano of King of Prussia, Pennsylvania, proved that the woman's plan to move to a new city was based on a "tenuous relationship" that started on the Internet. Though the relationship spanned a year, the woman had seen her cyberfriend only twenty-three days during that year. The judge awarded custody to the woman's ex-husband.

In 1995, Linda Olup, of Olup & Associates in Edina, Minnesota, began asking lawyers attending her seminars whether Internet issues were involved in their cases. The 1995 answer was "No." Within three years, she reported, just about every attorney she questioned said "Yes."

The *Kiplinger Washington Letter* editors coined the phrase "virtual abandonment" after finding anecdotal evidence of divorce and custody cases in which the Internet played a part. Lawyers told *Kiplinger* that, while adultery does not affect distribution of property in no-fault states, some states could interpret Web surfing and Internet addiction as "abandonment."[31]

As Internet use grows, Americans report spending less time with friends, family, and other people. Research by the Stanford Institute for the Quantitative Study of Society shows this key finding: "The more hours people use the Internet, the less time they spend with real human beings." Stanford's Norman Nie, the principal investigator in the research, called it "an early trend that, as a society, we really need to monitor carefully." The 36 percent of people in the study who use the Internet five or more hours per week reported significant changes in their daily lives. For example:

- The more years that people have been using the Internet, the more hours they spend on the Internet.
- A quarter of those who use the Internet more than five hours a week feel it reduces their time with family and friends or attending events outside the home.
- A quarter of regular Internet users who are employed say the Internet has increased the time they spend working at home for their employer without cutting back time at the office.[32]

The changes in the lives of Internet users are real, but the implications are unclear. Nie emphasized that heavy Internet users were only a small fraction of the total population when the study was released in early 2000, but "that fraction is steadily growing."

Another study wasn't so ambiguous, calling six percent of Internet users "addicted." Dr. David Greenfield, a West Hartford, Connecticut, psychologist, claims that, once online, Internet addicts quickly progress from mild flirtations with e-mail and chat rooms to making the Internet the neurotic nexus of their lives.

Greenfield studied 18,000 people in an online survey on the ABC-TV news Web site in 1999 using a thirty-six-item questionnaire designed to measure addiction. He adapted criteria for addiction and abuse used for problem gambling—questions about changes in daily life, alteration of mood, neglect of obligations, legal and financial problems, loss of job or family.[33]

One significant finding in Greenfield's research was that people who get into trouble with Web usage often have underlying psychiatric conditions such as depression or bipolar disorder, for which there are treatments.

The Internet can't shoulder the blame for fraying the quilt of community understanding. It's just the latest extension of a media industry that creates the atmosphere for disconnect. Stanford's Nie puts it this way:

> The Internet could be the ultimate isolating technology that further reduces our participation in communities even more than television did before. It's not like TV, which you can treat as background noise. It requires more engagement and more attention.

Greenfield was more direct: "The Internet is like television on steroids. But the thing about TV is that shows end. On the Internet, the sense of 'boundarylessness' can suck you in. . . . When people stare at a screen, they experience a trancelike dissociative quality, a hypnotic effect."

That's what people have always said about television. And it still is. Other words associated with television viewing are "glazed" and "zonked" and "catatonic."

First Alert

As early as television's introduction, there were misgivings. Author E.B. White's reaction when first exposed to the new medium in 1938 rings too true today:

> I believe that television is going to be the test of the modern world and that in this new opportunity to see beyond our range of vision we shall discover either a new and unbearable disturbance of the general peace or a saving radiance from the sky. We shall stand or fall by television, of that I am quite sure.[34]

The following year, television was demonstrated to the general public for the first time at the World's Fair. The new medium was retired for a few years during World War II, while technology fed the war effort. Edward R. Murrow's voice broke through the crackle and hiss of the 1940s radio to bring word pictures of the conflict. Radio unified the response by the U.S. government, embodied in President Franklin Roosevelt's calm and reassuring talks to the American people.

The same Ed Murrow later became known for television in a variety of news and interview roles. His history as the man who brought the news of World War II and the on-screen opponent of Senator Joseph McCarthy's witch hunt against supposed Communists in America made him television's most important nonentertainment figure. His medium's constant bent toward entertainment and escape made him a bitter man. He hoped to use radio and television for more noble purposes than song and comedy.

Against the wishes of his superiors at CBS, Murrow issued his own warning about the media at the 1958 meeting of his peers, the Radio Television News Directors' Association, in Chicago:

> It is my desire, if not my duty, to try to talk to you journeymen with some candor about what is happening to radio and television. . . . I am seized with an abiding fear regarding what these two instruments are doing to our society, our culture and our heritage.

Murrow accused the television networks' prime-time schedules of insulating audiences from the realities of the world. He suggested that major corporations, instead of selling automobiles and cigarettes, contribute to special programming that indicates our "belief in the importance of ideas." (In his speech, Murrow said "tithe," not "contribute.") He concluded his scathing indictment:

> This instrument can teach, it can illuminate; yes, and it can even inspire. But it can do so only to the extent that humans are determined to use it to those ends. Otherwise, it is merely wires and lights in a box.[35]

The speech was unsettling, even devastating, because it came from the most visible and credible newsperson in television at the time, not from a social critic.

A decade later, Walter Cronkite, who had replaced Murrow as the face and voice of CBS and would become the nation's calm and reassuring father figure, also took television to task, but in a more diplomatic way. In the foreword to a book for students called *TV Covers the Action*, Cronkite said he wanted the readers to know the limitations of television as a source of knowledge:

"Television is the most powerful communications medium yet devised."
This has become a cliché because it is a simple statement of a simple truth.
Yet, for all its power and its impact, television is not a complete news medium. It lacks two essentials to so qualify: time and permanence. Television can do *most* communication chores far better than print or unidimen-
sional radio. Better than any other medium it can familiarize the public
with the people who make the news and the places where news is made. It
achieves the ultimate through its ability to transport the chairborne viewer
to the scene where news is being made. It can background the news with
all the visual aids that ingenuity of man can provide—and thus capture the
interest of the otherwise uncommitted. But for all these advantages, television still can only take its place *alongside* print media as a prime source of
the news.

Cronkite's words were not so steeped in bitterness as Murrow's.
Cronkite held out hope for the medium and for the students who would
read the little book he introduced. Part of his foreword became prophetic,
however:

So completely have we been accepted by the public as a prime source of
news (as established by qualified surveys), that we are in increasing danger
of being charged with a responsibility we cannot discharge. It would be a
tragedy if either the public on the outside or some of us on the inside should
be deluded into believing that, simply because we are powerful, we can do
the whole job of news communication alone. Or if the public should lose
confidence in television news because it failed to understand our limitations and mistook them for indolence or worse.[36]

As the 1960s came to a close, Americans watched television more than
ever, and 50 percent of them considered TV programming "extremely enjoy-
able," said a survey by Robert T. Bower, funded by CBS. The percentage
was lower when viewers were asked about their overall satisfaction with
TV—only 37 percent.[37]

In Congress, however, the satisfaction with television seemed lower,
although no percentages exist to compare to the public's average. The social upheavals of the previous few years—rebellion on campus, reaction
against the war in Vietnam, riots in the streets of major cities—spurred
interest in some sort of investigation of the causes. Funds flowed freely for
experiments and research into the question: Does televised violence have a
harmful effect on children? In 1970, Senator Joseph Pastore, a Rhode Island Democrat, charged the office of the Surgeon General with determin-
ing the answer.

When the study was released in early 1972, the findings were ambiguous at best. Surgeon General Jesse Steinfeld said that the experimental findings were weak and not consistent from one study to another. His official statement was carefully crafted:

> Nevertheless, they provide the suggestive evidence in favor of the interpretation that viewing violence on TV is conducive to an increase in aggressive behavior, although it must be emphasized that the causal sequence is very likely applicable to some children who are predisposed in this direction, and TV is only one of the many factors which in time may precede aggressive behavior.[38]

There were no hints of the numbers of children predisposed, nor were other factors examined. The string of words like "suggestive" and "although" and "some" added to the sense of equivocation.

Fast forward to 1999, the year of shootings at Littleton, Colorado's, Columbine High School. The United States Congress was putting together a juvenile justice bill in answer to the horrors of students with firearms and bombs. In the United States, per capita aggravated assaults were up sixfold since 1957, and the blame was being placed on visual media—television, computer games, and the like. Surgeon General David Satcher, a guest on NBC's *Meet the Press,* was asked if he could do a report on media violence. "Sure, I can do another Surgeon General's report," he answered, "but why don't we start by reading the 1972 Surgeon General's report?"

Ironically, a central theme of the ensuing years was a now-famous report on the link between cigarettes and cancer, written by the same Surgeon General who had issued the report on kids and violence. The years between the first report and the Columbine shootings made the findings of the 1972 investigation less ambiguous.[39]

Nonetheless, it would be some years before television's impact could be studied with any certainty. In the meantime, anecdotal evidence mounted.

Emerging Evidence

Television was perceived by some to cause problems with relationships. As early as 1980, a Roper poll called television one of the leading causes of friction among married couples. The question: "Which of the following do you and your spouse most frequently disagree about?"

Television wasn't the first answer mentioned: 30 percent said money was the root of their evils, followed by 22 percent who said that children caused friction. Just behind children, however, 21 percent said there was something about watching television that upset their relationship with their spouse.

A high-tech and value-free culture is the problem, says Mary Pipher, a Lincoln, Nebraska, mother of two: "It's tough for a functional child to grow up in a dysfunctional community." Pipher argues that old-fashioned communities, which once sheltered and nurtured families, are superseded today by electronic villages that divide and isolate. She claims that computers, video games, and VCRs separate families from each other and from their neighbors and friends.

For hundreds of parents who attend Pipher's lectures, she's the Dr. Spock of a new generation. Her fame began in 1994 with a book about troubled teenaged girls called *Reviving Ophelia*. She added to her rallying cry for parents with *The Shelter of Each Other* in 1996.

"For the first time in the history of the human race, children don't sit around and have a meal with their parents and talk about the day," she told the Associated Press. Instead, Pipher said, children are socialized by Power Rangers and Jerry Seinfeld's oddball friends rather than by grandparents, neighbors, and Scout leaders:

> People are not connected by real relations. They're connected by personas. We might think we know Susan Sarandon or Whoopi Goldberg, but they don't know us. And if our car doesn't start in the morning, Whoopi Goldberg isn't going to help.[40]

The American Society of Pediatrics in 1999 recommended to parents that children under two should not watch television and that parents and doctors alike should take a greater interest in what children watch.[41] It says volumes about parents that any organization is moved to make such a pronouncement. It's unfortunate that Americans need an academy of experts to help us bring up our children.

The pediatricians weren't the first to issue a warning about television.

A member of the Federal Communications Commission from 1966 to 1973, Nicholas Johnson addressed in an interview what he called "a most serious subject":

> That is what commercial television is doing to mess up our heads in the way we perceive ourselves, and the world about us, and our lives, and preaching at us constantly standards of conspicuous consumption, and hedonism as the sole salvation; a sense of one's worth as an individual to be measured by the number of products he buys; the suggestion that all of life's problems can be immediately dispensed [with] by taking a chemical into the body, or spraying one on the outside of the body.[42]

In the late 1970s, advertising executive Jerry Mander offered *Four Arguments for the Elimination of Television*. The book said television was not reformable, that the medium's problems were inherent in the technology, and that TV was a danger to your health and sanity. It became a familiar message through the end of the twentieth century. Mander's four "arguments" were clearly defined as he watched television—some of it his own creation—shape the American psyche:

- The Mediation of Experience. As humans have moved into totally artificial environments, our direct contact with and knowledge of the planet has been snapped. Disconnected, like astronauts floating in space, we cannot know up from down or truth from fiction. Conditions are appropriate for the implantation of arbitrary realities. Television is one recent example of this, a serious one, since it greatly accelerates the problem.

- The Colonization of Experience. It is no accident that television has been dominated by a handful of corporate powers. Neither is it accidental that television has been used to re-create human beings into a new form that matches the artificial, commercial environment. A conspiracy of technological and economic factors made this inevitable and continue[s] to [do so].

- Effects of Television on the Human Being. Television technology produces neuro-physiological responses in the people who watch it. It may create illness; it certainly produces confusion and submission to external imagery. Taken together, the effects amount to conditioning for autocratic control.

- The Inherent Biases of Television. Along with the venality of its controllers, the technology of television predetermines the boundaries of its content. Some information can be conveyed completely, some partially, some not at all. The most effective telecommunications are the gross, simplified, linear messages and programs which conveniently fit the purposes of the medium's commercial controllers. Television's highest potential is advertising. This cannot be changed. The bias is inherent in the technology.

Mander's ad agency, San Francisco-based Freeman, Mander & Gossage, created award-winning commercials for its clients before Mander left in 1974 to work on public service and public affairs campaigns. Obviously, Mander's thesis bit the hand that fed him, especially when he took on television's corporate leadership:

To have only businessmen in charge of the most powerful mind-implanting instrument in history naturally creates a boundary to what is selected for dissemination to nearly 250 million people. There can be little disagreement with the point that if other categories of people had control, then the choices would be different. If television is a medium of brainwash, then a more diverse brainwash would surely be an improvement over the sort we get at present.

The overriding bias of television, then, the bias which contains all the other biases, is that it offers pre-selected material, which excludes whatever is not selected.[43]

Mander's early warning drew a parallel between life with television and sensory deprivation: The viewer sits in a darkened room; only two senses operate, and only within a narrow range; bodily functions are stilled. "Television isolates people from the environment, from each other, and from their own senses," he said.

Johnson and Mander may not have been heeded, but they were heard and, in many cases, derided. A professor at the University of Houston called both men "media snobs." Jib Fowles lumped Johnson and Mander with other critics of TV and claimed they all had been "repulsed by the swift incursion of television."

Fowles claimed that the public was in charge, that the public controlled television as forcefully as Mander's businessmen did, and that the ratings proved it:

[Snobs] find it convenient to ignore that the senders and receivers of television programming are very much in tune with each other, just as senders and receivers are in any successful communication situation. Snobs would be right to infer that the networks and the viewers were not linked together by a two-way flow of communication if the audience turned away to paperbacks, movies, radio shows, live sports, comic books, or other fantasy sources, and if the television system collapsed as a result. But since the system has endured, then the feedback which brings stability must be pumping through it.[44]

Fowles justified his defense of the television industry because it was not as big as other industries—tobacco, for example. That's an interesting choice for comparison, given big tobacco's admissions of manipulations and the court judgments that resulted.

You might forgive Fowles for his opinions on both television and tobacco, given that they were written in 1982. However, if he had paid attention to his 1982 environment, he would have had a hint about what was to come from electronic media.

A casual reading of magazines and newspapers of the time would have alerted Fowles to something more than "media snobbery" on the part of those concerned about TV. George Gerbner, dean of the University of Pennsylvania's Annenberg School of Communications, was quoted widely from a 1980 *Parents* magazine article that crime and violence occur ten times more often on TV than in life:

> We found that by junior high, children who are heavy viewers have already developed the "mean world" syndrome.
> They are more likely to be anxious and insecure, and more likely to think of people as mean and selfish and the world as a mean, cruel place in which they must protect themselves.

Citing other studies, Gerbner said that, by the time most kids finish high school, they have spent 25 percent more time watching television than attending class and they have seen more than 13,000 violent deaths on screen. He feared a dramatic result:

> Television has indirectly changed child-rearing practices, family relationships and the way our culture is passed on to the young. Often TV viewing occupies so many hours that genuine communication is almost absent from many families. A number of researchers have begun to worry that children now receive their outlook on life, their picture of the world and their values from what is portrayed on TV rather than from their families.[45]

A 1980 study of California public school students indicated that the more a student watched TV, the poorer the performance in school. The same survey—of 500,000 students—showed a decline in reading, language, and math scores for each hour of television watched per day.[46]

The same year, *Family Circle* magazine published "A Four-week Program to Turn Off the Tube." Author Joan Anderson Wilkins described the adjustment her family made when the TV set was knocked off the table onto the floor and they had to live in a home without television:

> My husband and I soon found ourselves reading to the boys at night...and the kids loved it! I took out my dusty collection of records and played Beethoven sonatas. We suddenly found a lot of substitute activities to enjoy and extra time that made our lives fuller and more satisfying. Most surprising, within a short time—just a few weeks—the Wilkins family was enjoying life without the tube.

Family Circle printed a daily time chart for parents who wanted to break their kids of the TV habit and outlined what steps to take for each week of withdrawal.

The magazine also added evidence of television's power and indications of its danger to kids:

> The Surgeon General's report on TV viewing concludes that television watching has contributed to the disappearance of conversation, correspondence and visits with friends.
>
> TV children, the report adds, tend to be passive, bashful and easily distracted.
>
> Physicians responding to a poll sponsored by the American Medical Association blame exposure to TV violence for heightened aggression in children, injuries resulting from emulating TV incidents and nightmares.
>
> Teachers are also beginning to see disturbing symptoms in the television child. From conversations with teachers all along the Eastern Seaboard, Nancy Larrick reported in a recent *New York Times* article that: "Television children are either hyperactive or apathetic, both to extremes.
>
> Children exposed to excessive television at a young age have difficulty entertaining themselves, have short attention-spans and often have a glassy, daze-like stare."[47]

An early reference to the glassy daze of the young TV viewer came from Marie Winn in her 1977 book, *The Plug-In Drug*. Some years before she wrote this warning about TV's power, Winn parked her two preschoolers in front of the TV set each day and let *The Flintstones* and *I Love Lucy* act as electronic babysitter.

She told the story of taking a closer look one day—not at the TV set, but at the kids. "They seemed zonked out," she said, "almost like zombies. I thought, 'This is a little weird. This isn't the way they look in normal life.'" She said that the one-way nature of television bothered her:

> The kind of attention you pay is different from two-way activities. There are a variety of children with a variety of vulnerabilities. Obviously not every child gets hooked. But often you find at least one of these in a family—the child who seems to zero in with excessive attention on the tube. The child who wants to watch too much, who is hard to distract while watching.[48]

From what were at first casual observations, Winn mounted research on the subject that resulted in her first book and a follow-up ten years later. *Unplugging the Plug-In Drug* was a guidebook that urged parents to turn off the TV and seek alternate entertainment for their families. Entire communities adopted the idea and staged "TV Turnoff Week" and "No-TV November."

How could Jib Fowles miss the message? How could anybody miss it? Headlines about the dangers of television were everywhere in 1981:

- "Each Family Should Make TV Decision," said the *Houston Chronicle* as it printed letters from concerned parents.
- "Is TV Turning Off Our Children?" asked *Redbook* magazine.
- The Associated Press asked, "Is there life after television?" in a story about fifty families who pledged to turn off the set in Providence, Rhode Island.
- *Friendly Exchange*, an insurance industry publication, advised parents to "Take Control of Your TV."
- The airline magazines got into the discussion, too: "TV or Not TV?" appeared in Hughes Airwest's *Sundancer* magazine.[49]

Producer Norman Lear, the man who developed *All In the Family* and other hit TV sitcoms, sensed danger, too. In 1981 he appeared before the House telecommunications subcommittee and told the members that he saw as much potential for harm as good in the proliferation of television channels on the horizon:

> Does this, then, mean that the average television viewer, who already watches from four to six hours of TV per day, according to most recent studies, will be drawn to even more television viewing? Common sense would indicate that that is possible. And common sense would also dictate that such passivity cannot be good for the human spirit. It makes for a lessening of interpersonal relationships and for a diminishing desire to explore life outside one's self. It may be 50 or more years before we actually know the results of all this encouragement to catatonia in the living room. But it does not bode well, in my opinion.[50]

Lear called the apathy of vast numbers of TV-viewing Americans "antithetical to the needs of the nation, whose elected officials govern with the consent of the governed, presumably alert and involved."

It's the nature of electronic media to accelerate time between cause and effect, and the proliferation of channels and entertainment options sped up the timetable of Lear's prediction. It didn't take fifty years to learn the impact of television; it took less than twenty. By 1997, half of American households could receive more than fifty TV channels, and 85 percent received seventy or more. And the average viewer watched more than seven hours of TV each day.

The warnings became louder, yet no better heard. In a 1997 editorial, Al Vecchione, retired president of MacNeil Lehrer Productions, called television "a challenge to our society's mental and physical health." After forty-three years in the field, Vecchione said, "trash continues to dominate." He accused his medium of transforming everything it touches:

Television has fed into the distortion of our values and standards and shaped the minds of two generations of children, with much evidence that the shaping has been largely negative. Research dating back more than 20 years, including the surgeon general's landmark study of television violence, has identified and underscored the negative impact of television on our society. As these studies suggest, television's contribution to the increase in violence in our everyday lives registers somewhere between significant and enormous. At the very least, it has desensitized children and adults to the true effects of violent behavior. And there is new evidence that heavy viewership can lead to a decline in physical fitness, leading to growing rates of obesity among young and old alike. All this is due, in large part, to the sheer volume of time spent sitting in front of the tube.[51]

The world we know is "The World According to Television," says John Perry Barlow in *Wired* magazine's Netizen column. We live in a processed world without context. In that world, voters are more concerned with imaginary threats than real ones, just as they are concerned with crime magnified on the screen. Responding to their anxiety, they elect representatives to address the problems whether or not they exist. Barlow creates this all-too-believable scenario:

> Looking to raise share and beat back the future, the media raise an imaginary problem, say, a cyber-tsunami of online kiddie porn. Out in Televisionland, parents who have already been driven into a state of omniphobia by TV depictions of kidnappers, child molesters, and Calvin Klein commercials, freak out and call their congressperson.
>
> Of course, the congressperson doesn't actually know whether or not there's a flood of kiddie porn online. He (or she) has never been online and isn't about to go there. But he does know that his constituents have seized on An Issue that they are truly passionate about. Under such circumstances, it takes a brave man to do nothing. So he gets together with his colleagues and passes a law that effectively addresses a problem almost no one has ever actually experienced, while issuing forth a whole new set of real ones.

Barlow calls it "government by hallucinating mob," a mob detached from anything he would call "real." In Barlow's assessment is the most telling indictment of television: Nothing seems more real than television.[52]

Television Feeds Our Anxieties

Watch most local newscasts, and stories of random shootings and domestic violence seem to be the only thing happening in town. Even though those stories happened across town, they feed the fear that the next time the violence might happen next door. After all, the report invaded the living room; surely those criminals could invade the neighborhood. If they did, we may not know about it until we see it on TV, we're so detached from our neighbors.

Television Feeds Our Disdain for Our Fellow Man

Why else would we sit mesmerized as dysfunctional families parade across the stage to enrage Jerry Springer or engage Maury Povich? We simply want to compare them to our lives and assure ourselves that our families are neither so chaotic nor so depressing. Yet our anxiety is exacerbated because we know we could be the victims of crime. Our family could be next.

Television Encourages the Solitary Viewer and Separates Us from Our Fellow Man

In winter 1986, half of prime-time TV viewing was done alone, up from 45 percent in 1981. In 1961 the percentage viewing alone was only 29 percent. The Television Information Office attributed the figures to more TV sets, TV sets in more personal sizes and shapes, and more Americans living alone.

Television Internalizes the Viewer and Excludes Outside Stimuli

Bill McKibben, the man who contrasted 100 channels of TV to a day in the Adirondacks, calls television a distortion of both time and space:

> TV restricts the use of our senses—that's one of the ways it robs us of information. It asks us to use our eyes and ears, and only our eyes and ears. If it is doing its job "correctly," you lose consciousness of your body, at least until a sort of achy torpor begins to assert itself, and maybe after some hours a dull headache, and of course the insatiable hunger that you never really notice but that somehow demands a constant stream of chips and soda.
>
> TV chops away perspective, too. On the mountain, even if your eye is drawn to something in particular, your peripheral vision fills in all sorts of detail, constantly. When you watch TV your peripheral vision ceases to function—you stare at the screen like a pitcher staring in at the catcher's mitt. You no longer even notice the *set*—the frame, the knobs, the antenna (if you're still backward enough to need an antenna). Your vision is cut down to maybe 10 degrees of the horizon—on a large screen maybe 15 degrees. What we see, we see sharply—the images have been edited so that peripheral vision is unnecessary. In the "Cosby" living room there is a

staircase, and in front of it a sofa, and the family is sitting on the sofa. No one is off in the corner making faces—it's fantastically stripped down, uncomplicated, and as a consequence whoever is in the foreground assumes vaster importance than he'd be granted under an open sky.[53]

Visual perception is a multidimensional network. A viewer might be able to tell you with language what is seen at any given moment, but language doesn't show what the viewer sees. The words will not have the interconnection of the events that they have in the visual field. Looking, for instance, at McKibben's mountain, you could begin to assemble a series of words that might communicate the idea to someone else. You'd be working with the *idea,* not a picture, not an experience.

Nor could the words about the majesty of the mountain operate in their linear sequence quickly enough to replicate the space-time relationship of each blade of bright green grass to the next. The words wouldn't provide the change of hue from the grass to the crown of trees on the mountain, nor the sense of depth as the shadows wander from west to east.

More time, more words, would be spent on the viewer's emotional state at seeing the mountainscape. Assume for a moment that it's a warm, dry day that brings contrast from spring rains of a week before. The viewer may add response that doesn't exist in the scene: a memory, for example, of a cool breeze felt on the same spot or fears that summer's heat will come only too quickly and spring is all too brief.

A Language of Its Own

No matter how well those words are chosen, emotional and physical attributes of the perception cannot be communicated exactly. The words may evoke emotion, but that's from the reading, the description, not from the viewer's perception. By transferring the perception to words, the network of visual, aural, emotional, tactile, and olfactory experiences is disconnected from the original. The reader or listener then reassembles the parts and fills in any blanks.

Unfortunately, when confronted with reassembling the picture from video, the brain does not have the leisure to ponder words or phrases and to let the imagination fill in details like the crown of trees or the wandering shadows. To fill in the blanks left by video, the estimated 250 million sight receptors in the brain must collect data from 525 lines of scanning video, then assemble it all as a meaningful "picture" in the mind.

A half second after the first picture is complete, the brain begins again on the next picture, depending on persistence of vision to trick itself into "seeing" a moving image. Once the lines and shadows are assembled comes the problem of adding aural information from a relatively understaffed group of only 50 thousand hearing receptors. Putting the final image together is hard, tiring work, and the brain knows it.

The mosaic of video breaks down the visual experience into segments and symbols that change the object-to-eye pattern of the original, much the same as the verbal description did.

Like words, the video-mosaic is a language unto itself.

Interpreting the rapid-scan language of video leaves the viewer in a state some call "passive." A set of studies in 1990 by psychologists Robert Kubey of Rutgers University and Mihaly Csikszentmihaly of the University of Chicago showed that television left viewers passive. But there was more: People were tense and unable to concentrate after watching TV. The studies claimed that most viewers believed that television offered relaxation and escape from their problems. In actuality, the researchers said, watching TV left people in worse moods than when they began.[54]

Research by Kubey and Csikszentmihaly reinforced the fact that assembling the images from video is anything but a passive activity. Defending the television industry, the National Association of Broadcasters (NAB) responded with a statement that television "is more often the symptom and not the cause of many so-called societal ills."

The NAB mounted the following argument: "Other spectator activities, such as attending the ballet or watching the Mets play at Shea Stadium, at times produce similar types of fatigue, boredom and general lack of concentration." That seems to confirm that TV is hard work for the busy brain. The broadcasters missed the point, trying to prove that TV was okay.

The word "passive" is generally used by those who watch only the body of the viewer in the "achy torpor" described by McKibben. Passivity is beside the point.

Psychologist Bruno Bettelheim said his concern was "less with content and much more with what persistent watching does to a child's ability to relate to real people, to become self-activated, to think on the basis of his own life experience instead of in stereotypes out of shows."[55]

Bettelheim was closer to the mark than those who cry "passive," because he hinted at an erosion of the ability to discern reality against media projection. It's the hard work that the brain has to do to assimilate video-mosaic language that sets this language apart from "English" or "French" or "mathematics" or "cuneiform" as language media. After the hard work of reception and assembly, the brain honestly believes that more has happened to it than the simple completion of an image. So much neural energy passes through the brain during video-mosaic assembly, that the poor, tired unit cannot believe that it has not participated in perception of a real experience. Certainly the brain has a right to confuse the hard work of video-mosaic assembly with the similar stimulation of perception experience that includes visual, aural, emotional, olfactory, tactile, and kinetic assembly.

Experiments published in *Psychology Today* and *Scientific American* indicate that sight actually dominates the sense of touch.[56] When a person views his own hand distorted by a prism, he believes his hand is where his eyes tell him, not where his hand tells him it is. In addition, subjects were asked to feel a square block that, viewed through a prism, looked rectangular. In each case, the subjects claimed that the block was rectangular, even though their sense of touch told them otherwise.[57]

The brain loves visual stimulus, and the video screen supplies the visuals. In *Remote Control*, Frank Mankiewicz and Joel Swerdlow cite several nonscientific studies conducted by author Jerzy Kozinski while he was a school teacher. In one, Kozinski invited a number of seven- to ten-year-olds to a room where he would tell a story. The room was equipped with video camera and monitors, so the children could watch either Kozinski or a video screen.

By prearrangement, another adult burst into the room and began a loud argument with Kozinski, at one point turning the verbal abuse to violence, striking Kozinski. There was neither sound nor protest from the children, except that those watching the "live" Kozinski joined the others in watching the video version.

"You looked so scared and he was so mean," said one child after the argument was over. "You could see *everything* on those screens!" exclaimed another; "How much does it cost to buy one?"[58]

Kozinski's conclusion was that the screens transformed a violent action into an aesthetic happening. The video screens created distance between the event and the audience, even though all of it happened in the same room.

In another case, Kozinski interviewed ten- to fourteen-year-olds, asking them private and personal questions. "Do you steal?" he asked, and "Do you masturbate?" Alone with Kozinski in the room, each child hesitated and seemed shocked and embarrassed.

Kozinski then asked his respondents if they'd mind if a television camera recorded the conversations, reminding them that parents, friends, and "the whole country" might see the tapes. Most of the twenty-five children lost their embarrassment and confessed to minor sexual offences, picking pockets, shoplifting, and other wrongdoing, all while playing to the camera.[59]

The first instance supports arguments about desensitization to violence. The second underscores legitimization by television. It's the same phenomenon that prompts audiences to hold signs for the camera outside the *Today Show* or wave their arms behind reporters at otherwise serious news events.

Not only does the brain seem to prefer the visual stimulus, but in the experiments by Kozinski, the video screen reference was much more in tune with the language of the students watching the attack on Kozinski than was the actual event. Perception of the event on the screen was perception in a language they could understand, given their experience with the medium.

Mankiewicz and Swerdlow quote the work of John L. Debes III, coordinator of visual learning for Eastman Kodak:

> If so large a portion of the population is inclined to the visual, and if that portion of the population is exposed to television from infancy until they finish school, how can we expect such youngsters to prefer anything except a sequential visual language with which to learn or to communicate?[60]

One of the commandments of the age of television, according to Mankiewicz and Swerdlow, is that if people believe an event has occurred, they believe they've seen it on television:

> Thus, something over 70 percent of Americans believe they saw John F. Kennedy's assassination live on their home screens. In truth, no one saw it live on television; and the general public did not even see it on film until the 1976 showing of closely edited portions of the Zapruder film.

Mankiewicz and Swerdlow call television "the great certifying agent of our time." Borrowing the idea of certification from Walker Percy's novel, *The Moviegoer*, they said:

> Nowadays when a person lives somewhere, in a neighborhood, the place is not certified for him. More than likely he will live there sadly and the emptiness which is inside him will expand until it evacuates the entire neighborhood. But if he sees a movie which shows his very neighborhood, it becomes possible for him to live, for a time at least, as a person who is Somewhere and not Anywhere.[61]

Television expands the self-certification process. We don't just live Somewhere; we're *Somebody* living Somewhere. Television validates our very Somebody-ness by reflecting what we think is ourselves. We see our neighbors, or at least we see people who seem like us. We also see people not at all like us who are transformed by being in our living rooms. The politician, the pope, and the performer seem so much more accessible when they're in the same room.

The same device also separates us from our sense of place. The age-old connection between location and experience is broken by television and other electronic media. The politician, the pope, and the performer would not have been in our presence without media. There's a disconnect between where we are and what we see and hear, between our access to them and their accessibility to us.

The old components of place, whether physical location or station in life, are undermined by television and further fractured by new, personal, one-on-one media. The new world is relatively placeless.

Television's view of the world is nonlinear and nonsequential. There's no skill set available to read the images television delivers amid the glut of stimuli. With no code of interpretation, all messages are not only nonsequential but also non sequitur. They exist in a vacuum to be interpreted by the individual receiving the message. Worse, they can be selectively ignored by that same individual. Add the personal, private online experience and the vacuum expands. Self-interpretation becomes self-absorption. The challenge for media is to break through self-absorption to be heard.

Chapter 2

The Attention Economy

A Christmas card: The character on the front is plump and bald. He's got a reddish nose and rosy cheeks. He's dressed in red and has a candy cane by his side.

Santa Claus?

No, a radio talk show host, pounding the desk and shouting: "No, Virginia, there is no Santa Claus. Grow up, honeybunch. You're the victim of this country's liberal media, who convince you that you can get something for nothing!"

The character's phrase "liberal media" is a response trigger designed to get the attention of his audience. He expects his trigger to make somebody's blood boil and to make his phone ring.

"Triggering" is what talk hosts do when they use highly charged words and phrases to stimulate calls, comments, and controversy. The most notorious hosts poke at their listeners' resonating chords, hoping to find a "hot button" sensitive enough to prompt response. When the phones ring, the show gets interesting, and the ratings might increase.[1]

Host G. Gordon Liddy thinks nothing of calling Ross Perot "the goatscrew from Texas" just to position himself in his listeners' minds as a person who speaks his own mind.

A caller on the Talk America radio network asked why the P.T.A. was involved in an investigation. The host's answer: "Probably a bunch of liberals." It had less to do with the question than it did with the host's attempt to position himself as antiliberal.

A right-wing talk station in suburban Pittsburgh peppers its shows with highly charged words: "trilateralists," "the new world order," "Communists." A caller to one of its programs said in a conspiratorial voice to a local host, "There's a meeting about the new world order. What can we find out about it?" The host urged his listeners to be their own reporters and find out more.

Every time Rush Limbaugh refers to Al Gore as the "Vice Perpetrator," he used radio's equivalent to the bumper sticker. When Limbaugh says, "there are no soccer moms in this poll," he's pushing hot buttons. When he berates "tax-and-spend liberals," he's found a trip wire that will set off listener opinion.

When Limbaugh's listeners greet him with "dittos," "100 percent dittos," and "mega-dittos," they're doing the same thing in return—offering adulation and support in shorthand. Because he's the most successful of the radio talk hosts, Limbaugh's brand of shorthand became the standard.

Why does radio do this? The easy answer is ratings. Radio is a mass medium that survives when ratings are high enough to stimulate sufficient advertising revenues. As much as talk radio may position itself as the bastion of democracy, the real purpose is to entertain and to sell advertising. It cannot achieve that unless it attracts—and holds—your attention.

Hosts carom from topic to topic, usually easy-to-digest topics. The danger of the bumper sticker mentality is that profound and complex issues are too much for either host or caller to grasp. Poking listener hot buttons is a staple of radio because it reduces complex issues into easy-to-grasp words, phrases, and sentences. Notice I said "radio" and not just "talk radio." Talk radio puts the idea to greatest use because its spoken word base requires rapid listener response. The more conservative the talk show, the more likely the host will use hot button statements to trigger immediate response.

Call it "positioning," the word coined by Al Ries and Jack Trout in their landmark advertising book of the same name.[2] "Positioning is not what you do to a product. [It's] what you do to the mind of the prospect. That is, you position the product in the mind of the prospect" and maintain the prospect's attention.

Ries and Trout refer to "those little ladders in your head" as they describe the effects of positioning. If you don't think of yourself as having ladders in your head, think metaphorically. The authors suggest a mental ladder with a product or brand on each step. Some people have a lot of steps, some only a few. It's a way to deal with the explosion of products and information about them.

To get a product onto a mental ladder, a marketer has to identify the brand in some way, and that's positioning. When Avis Car Rental said, "We're Number 2, we try harder," it positioned itself against Hertz, which was acknowledged as the leader in car rentals. Avis was successful because it borrowed Hertz's ladder and took a place on step number two. (Success came from being the underdog, not from trying harder.)

Another classic example of product positioning is 7-Up's "uncola" campaign. A lemon-lime drink actually captured a place on the cola ladder by telling the world how much it wasn't like Coke or Pepsi. As Ries and Trout pointed out, "You won't find an 'uncola' idea inside a 7–Up can. You find it inside the cola drinker's head."[3]

Radio relies on positioning to get programming messages to its listeners: Good Time Oldies. The Best and Most Country. Today's New Rock Alternative. All Rock and Roll Classics. Smooth Jazz. Such quick phrases identify the station well enough for a listener to make a quick choice.

Using a brief word or phrase on the radio is the same as big business using corporate logo icons. Think of the images that give you instant recall of a company or product. Nike's swoosh. Coca-Cola's white script in the red circle. IBM's blue square. The CBS eye. The NBC peacock. The red and white Campbell's soup can. Each provides immediate communication of complex concepts to cut through the clutter of an overcommunicated world.

Michael Wolf reinforces the mental ladder metaphor with a high-tech image of his own in *The Entertainment Economy*:

> I have an image of people walking around with a little hologram of Times Square playing inside their heads: giant billboards and full-motion video screens ten stories tall, moving text messages, phalanxes of sexy models all enticing, seducing, and hawking their wares. You can't turn your head without being bombarded with a message: buy me, love my brand, be fulfilled! One is almost paralyzed by the sheer magnitude and variety of what is being offered.[4]

You don't have to be a corporate entity to simplify communication. Think of the choices you're confronted with every day, and how much easier they become if they're offered as choices of two:

- Paper or plastic
- Ranch dressing or honey mustard
- Regular or decaf
- Rap or pop
- Liberal or conservative
- Democrat or Republican

Should all of life be reduced to easy, binary choices? No, but Americans prefer the idea as they grasp for some handle on complex concepts in an environment of information overload or what Richard Saul Wurman termed "information anxiety."

What are the telltale signs of information anxiety? A few of the symptoms, according to Wurman:

- Chronically talking about not keeping up with what's going on around you.
- Feeling guilty about that ever higher stack of periodicals waiting to be read.
- Nodding your head knowingly when someone mentions a book, an artist, or a news story that you have actually never heard of before.
- Refusing to buy a new appliance or piece of equipment just because you are afraid you won't be able to operate it.
- Giving time and attention to news that has no cultural, economic, or scientific impact on your life.[5]

Who can keep up with it all? Unfortunately, more data does not equal more information. Nonetheless, we are asked to sift through data and make sense of it. As Wurman puts it, "Information anxiety is produced by the ever-widening gap between what we understand and what we think we should understand . . . the black hole between data and knowledge."

That's what brings us to instant communication by logo icon, instant selection between binary choices, instant response to language that cuts through the clutter, instant attempts to attract attention.

Bumper stickers, for example. They cut through. Bumper stickers are designed to communicate in three to five seconds just like a roadside billboard does. The bumper sticker distills a complex issue into instant communication:

- In Boston: "Doing my part to piss off the radical right."
- In Houston: "Proud member, Vast Right-Wing Conspiracy."
- In Columbus, Ohio, a sticker that exhibits pride and affiliation: "My daughter and my money go to O.S.U."
- In northern California, a sticker that exhibits self-esteem: "If you're not living on the edge, you're taking up too much space."
- In southern California, the lack thereof: "We are all dysfunctional. Get over it."
- In Key West, a sign of the times: "Remember when driving was dangerous and sex was safe?"
- In Buffalo: "Stamp out bumper sticker mentality!"[6]

The talk show trigger and the bumper sticker communicate quickly. They stand out amid the clutter. They help us make sense of the information explosion. In spite of the flood of data that engulfs us every day, the phenomenon of information overload is barely in its infancy. Futurist Richard Worzel outlines this scenario:

> If, according to some estimates, the amount of information doubles every eighteen months, then by 2015 there will be 1,000 bits of data for every

fact in existence. But we will not necessarily be better informed. Meaning-ful facts—those that have reliable and relevant information—will become our most valuable resource.[7]

A greater resource will be the time and attention necessary to ferret mean-ingful or relevant facts from the Niagara of data to come.

Paying Attention

Attention is so basic it's almost too obvious to comment on, that is to say, "to pay attention to." We are normally not aware of our attention unless it's inter-rupted in some way, when we're surprised by a loud noise, for example.

But surprise assumes a contrast. Imagine yourself outside a restaurant on the peaceful square of the town of Sonoma in California's wine country, sipping the local output. If a passing truck backfires, it would probably startle you. On the other hand, if you were sitting outside on Fifth Avenue in New York, you'd hardly notice the same backfiring truck amid the din of the city.

Attention, therefore, is relative to its external challenges. In today's media environment, the challenges to attention are enormous. Most messages have to penetrate Michael Wolf's Times Square hologram or climb Ries and Trout's ladder of the mind.

The mind rejects some information because "it doesn't compute," that is, the information doesn't fit a preconceived set of patterns we use to filter our input. Maybe the information doesn't meet our expectations or it just doesn't get heard.

That's why the single most valuable commodity in the media environ-ment is attention—that set of intellectual processes that converts raw data into something useful. Attention is becoming so scarce that it resembles the classic definition of an economy. When bread is scarce, the price of a loaf rises until production meets demand.

As the American economy was being forged in the 1800s, natural resources and raw materials were at a premium. Tycoons who tied up access to the materials needed to cook, sew, and build housing made huge profits by cor-nering the market on scarce resources.

The industrial revolution shifted markets from raw materials to finished goods, and a new breed of entrepreneurs created goods that consumers de-manded. In our economy of abundance, supply outstrips demand even more so when we consider "intellectual property"—an increasing number of people work not to produce or transport goods, but to manage information.

Former Yahoo! marketer Seth Godin uses the setting of a tropical island to make his point about the attention economy in *Permission Marketing*:

Imagine a tropical island, populated by people with simple needs and plenty of resources. You won't find a bustling economy there. That's because you need two things in order to have an economy: people who want things, and a scarcity of things they want. Without scarcity, there's no basis for an economy.

When there's an abundance of any commodity, the value of that commodity plummets. If a commodity can be produced at will and costs little or nothing to create, it's not likely to be scarce, either. That's the situation with information and services today. They're abundant and cheap. Information on the web, for example, is plentiful and free.

Software provides another example. The most popular web server is not made by Microsoft or Netscape. And it doesn't cost $1,000 or $10,000. It's called Apache, and it's created by a loosely knit consortium of programmers and it's totally free. Free to download, free to use. As resources go, information is not scarce.[8]

There's no shortage of information. But time to deal with the flood of information is another matter. That requires attention, and attention is in short supply. Bill Gates has just as much as you do. And even Warren Buffett can't buy any more than you can. The combined shortage of time and attention is unique to today's information glut. Consumers are willing to pay handsomely to save time, and marketers are just as eager to pay handsomely to get consumers' attention.

"Information glut." "Information explosion." You've heard those and other terms. Call it what you will, but don't call it "the information economy." That's a misnomer if you define economics as the study of how a society uses scarce resources. In our lives, there's certainly no scarcity!

The glut is multiplied exponentially in cyberspace, where information is more than abundant—it absolutely overflows. Call it "data" rather than "information," because the word "data" doesn't conjure useful content, just a jumble of symbols that need interpretation to become "information."

It overflows, whatever you call it.

Boon or Bane?

Is the overflow good or bad? The World Future Society tackled that question at its General Assembly in Washington in 1996, using the theme "Boon or Bane?"

"Bane," said panelist Kirkpatrick Sale, claiming that information technology was "shattering our economy, shriveling our society, and shredding our environment."

"Boon," said former ambassador Harlan Cleveland, because the human species for the first time becomes the "lead actor in its own evolution" thanks to information.

"Boon," echoed Stewart Brand, who claimed, "Information technology has done what the New Left never actually accomplished, which is give power to the people."

"Bane," said Michael Marien, editor of *Future Survey*, who expressed "considerable doubt about whether the positive impacts outweigh the negative impacts, both now and in the future." Marien outlined a "Top 10 List" of reasons why the information revolution is bad for us. Here are a few that are pertinent to this discussion:

- It's bad for quality of life. It speeds the pace of life and makes time increasingly scarce.
- It's bad for democracy—so far, at least. Of course, there's the promise of enhanced citizen participation and electronic town meetings, but don't confuse the potential with the reality. Marien cited a poll in which only 33 percent of adults could name their member of congress, let alone for what he or she stands. Ironically, as a society becomes more complex, people are turned off of politics and turned on to an expanding variety of electronic entertainment.
- It's bad for the future. There seems to be a decline in the quantity and quality of serious futures thinking. Why? Quite possibly because infotech and infosociety have made the future unappealing and created a reaction against the future by those who, unconsciously or not, want to stop the world and get off.

The number one negative on Marien's list is that having much more information is bad for our heads:

> It is bad because it produces "infoglut," which may well be the greatest under-studied problem of our time. Infoglut is not a static matter. Scientific information doubles about every twelve years and general information more quickly. Useful knowledge, however, is in short supply, especially compared to information devoted to entertainment and commercial interests.[9]

Marien echoes what Worzel said about information doubling every eighteen months. It's a phenomenal number. Information assaults us by the ton. What's needed is an ounce of useful knowledge or relevant information and the ability to sort through the excess to find it.

What is scarce is enough attention to deal with all the information that tempts us. "Attention has its own behavior, its own dynamics, its own consequences," says Michael Goldhaber of the University of California at Berkeley. Attention is scarce, Goldhaber writes in *Wired*, "and the total amount per capita is strictly limited. . . . The size of the attention pie can grow as more and more people join the world audience, but the size of the average slice can't."

Goldhaber says the attention economy changes advertising, too, since ads will exist only to attract and direct attention:

> The key point about the various forms and avenues of attention is that while we each want it to some extent, it does not arrive in equal measure. This explains why many of us are working harder and harder to get some, and why we eagerly latch onto technologies such as the Internet and the Web. Cyberspace affords new opportunities for capturing attention that might otherwise dissipate. It promises nearly everyone a chance at attention from millions, the potential to be noticed by the largest possible audience—or by an audience of peers whose attention we value most. But the Net also ups the ante, increasing the relentless pressure to get some fraction of this limited resource. At the same time, it generates ever greater demands on each of us to pay what scarce attention we can to others.
>
> And here's where it gets interesting: attention can't be bought. When advertisers pay for an ad, for example, they are guaranteed only a chance at an audience's notice. Audience members learn to ignore or turn off all but the most interesting ads, and even then they may not focus on what's being advertised. In fact, as the attention economy becomes dominant, the advertising industry won't exist as it does today, since its point is to induce people to spend money.[10]

Advertising's Assault

The enormous expenditure by advertisers to attract our attention shows just how influential commercials really are. Even in the face of declining viewership, national television networks command huge prices for commercials on the most popular shows. Once comedian Jerry Seinfeld decided to end production of his hit show *Seinfeld* on NBC-TV in 1998, rates skyrocketed to as high as $2 million per thirty seconds for the farewell episode.

Each year before the Super Bowl, media outlets tout the prices paid for access to that audience's attention. The nightly news on your hometown TV station is most likely the costliest local advertising buy available, even if the dollars pale next to network figures. And what does that money buy?

"Half the money I spend on advertising is wasted, and the trouble is I don't know which half," said Lord Leverhulme (later quoted by department store magnate John Wanamaker, who now gets the credit for the phrase). Each of those men would be comforted by today's media measurement. They would have seen the cause-and-effect relationship between advertising and purchase levels. Even today, neither would know which half of his budget was wasted.[11]

Advertising is impossible to separate from the economy as a whole, especially the uniquely American economy of abundance. In an economy based on scarcity, total demand is usually equal to or in excess of total supply, so every producer sells everything that's produced. When supply outstrips demand—as in the U.S. economic system, for example—advertising fulfills an essential function: moving merchandise from the manufacturer to consumer, creating a need or desire for something that may be unnecessary.

In a 1953 lecture at the University of Chicago, Yale University's David M. Potter explained his views on the role of advertising:

> In a society of abundance, the productive capacity can supply new kinds of goods faster than society in the mass learns to crave these goods or to regard them as necessities. If this new capacity is to be used, the imperative must fall upon consumption, and the society must be adjusted to a new set of drives and values in which consumption is paramount . . . Clearly it must be educated, and the only institution we have for instilling new needs, for training people to act as consumers, for altering men's values and thus for hastening their adjustment to potential abundance, is advertising.[12]

Advertising existed long before the United States did, yet the United States took an early and commanding lead in using advertising to fuel the nation's economic growth. Popular forms of media have a rich history of subsidy by advertisers who want access to consumers who use those media. An NBC-TV executive expressed it this way: "We deliver eyeballs to advertisers."

In terms of attracting your eyeballs, the television commercial is a most pervasive form of communication, as Neil Postman demonstrates in *Amusing Ourselves to Death*:

> An American who has reached the age of forty will have seen well over one million television commercials in his or her lifetime, and has close to another million to go before the first Social Security check arrives. We may safely assume, therefore, that the television commercial has profoundly influenced American habits of thought. Certainly, there is no difficulty in demonstrating that it has become an important paradigm for the structure of every type of public discourse.[13]

One thing to be said for the commercial: It cannot tell us what to do, in spite of those commercials that shout and cajole. Instead, commercials make us *feel* like doing something, buying a car, for example, or making a long-distance call.

Yet we wouldn't feel like buying if the commercial were not couched in the context of our own self-reflection. Advertisers from the beginning have made appeals on behalf of their products. Not until the 1950s and the advent of the television commercial did they substitute images for claims. With the advent of TV, the commercial became an emotional appeal, not a test of truth.

Postman defines the television commercial as drama or mythology:

> The television commercial is not at all about the character of products to be consumed. It is about the character of the consumers of products. Images of movie stars and famous athletes, of serene lakes and macho fishing trips, of elegant dinners and romantic interludes, of happy families packing their station wagons for a picnic in the country—these tell nothing about the products being sold. But they tell everything about the fears, fancies and dreams of those who might buy them. What the advertiser needs to know is not what is right about the product but what is wrong about the buyer. And so, the balance of business expenditures shifts from *product* research to *market* research. The television commercial has oriented business away from making products of value and toward making consumers feel valuable, which means that the business of business has now become pseudo-therapy. The consumer is a patient assured by psycho-dramas.[14]

If television is the electric mirror, then each commercial is a magnification mirror, showing us a larger-than-life reflection of ourselves. The commercials Postman calls "psycho-dramas" are about the viewer. They're aimed at the "cult of me," the specific person or type of person who will buy or be influenced by what is on the screen:

- "I want to hang with people as cool as me," said a commercial during a baseball playoff game. Was it for the Air Force or the Army? It doesn't matter. It attempted to cut through the clutter and reach potential recruits by catering to the self-concept of the target audience.
- "You're alone but you're strong," asserted a John Hancock Insurance commercial aimed at single mothers and screened during a miniseries.
- "How much does the world weigh? Ask a single mother," appeared for another advertiser in the same program.
- "I have a priceless kid" was the title of a marketing program developed by two Sacramento radio stations for a pharmacy chain.

When one or two advertisers address the cult of me, it seems personal and friendly. "Well, finally, they're talking to *me* and not the masses in general," the viewer says. However, after a flood of messages with "I am relaxation" (a travel commercial) or "I am the asset, not my money" (a brokerage house), the viewer comes to understand that he deserves a break from all the contrivances. There's a disconnect at work when copywriters strive for those words that break through the clutter and address the consumer directly. The collection of those messages becomes not personal, but impersonal, just another flood of words aimed at somebody else.

Resonance or Dissonance?

When advertisers discover they can't get your attention by connecting personally, they go deeper and aim for the spirit:

- A young woman sits in church and confesses. She's been miserly. She's a penny-pincher. Before her contrition takes hold, the preacher exclaims, "It's not a sin to be frugal!" The young woman rejoices in her prudence, ready to enjoy the cost savings of a Chevrolet Cavalier.
- Running through the mountains of Tibet, Michael Jordan meets a holy man who calls up the wisdom of the ages as it applies to Gatorade: "Life is a sport; drink it up."
- It's evening and time for vespers. As a community of Catholic nuns walks toward the chapel for their prayers, they talk in hushed tones about OS/2 networks, surfing the Net, and reading *Wired* magazine.
- The football team is in the locker room when the coach says they have to be more politically correct in the team prayer. "Hit it, padre," says the coach, who hands off to a Catholic priest for a short prayer. Next is a rabbi, then a Native American, then a Buddhist, then a whole line of spiritual leaders waiting to bless the team. The tag line: "Not going anywhere for a while? Grab a Snickers."

These ads are a response to a spiritual awakening happening across America, primarily manifested through books about religion, angels, and the quest for who we are and who brought us here. In the past, such periods were sparked by religious revivals, often based in a specific church or interpretation: the Pilgrims' arrival, for example, or Brigham Young's trek through the desert. Not this one. It's spiritual in the truest sense, and less religious, an examination of personal values rather than dogma or denomination.

Advertisers who attempt to make use of spirituality or religion undermine the effect they seek to achieve. They trivialize the very feeling that awakened the spirit. The Snickers team prayer, for example, makes light of the plurality of our religious beliefs even though it does not make light of any particular faith.

American Demographics warns advertisers that connecting with spiritual values "may also desecrate a bond of trust with the consumer." The magazine suggests that spiritual motives work for some companies and some products, "but you have to know what you're doing." The editor of a nonprofit religious magazine says that "ad makers are out of touch with mainstream America" and criticizes "creative types who don't believe in anything religious, so it's okay to make fun of those who do."[15]

The Colors of Bennetton used religious icons in an ad, but it was designed only for shock value: it showed a nun and a priest kissing. Most Bennetton ads have been criticized for their poor taste, and rightly so. The company continues the concept—a car burning in one series of ads, convicted murderers in another—knowing the controversy gets it the attention it needs for its stores.[16]

Yet another attempt at penetrating the cult of me is to tap those icons that trigger emotions. Sometimes the trigger is a song, sometimes a memory, sometimes a deep feeling. Consider the triggers in an automobile commercial that plays the "Star Spangled Banner" in the background, thus triggering a sense of national pride. However, the version used is the raw, edgy guitar rendition performed by Jimi Hendrix at the Woodstock festival. That triggers either nostalgia for a time of free love and happiness or a sense of outrage against such feelings, depending on the age and persuasion of the viewer. While creating a connection for one person, the commercial creates a disconnect for another.

Combine in your mind's eye U.S. government films of NASA space launches, both successful and unsuccessful, sweeping vistas of the earth and stars, and words from T.S. Eliot's "The Love Song of J. Alfred Prufrock." The commercial presents a mélange of triggers that both arouse and confuse. The NASA footage taps that pride in achievement that the United States gained in the space race, yet the billowing flames of one launch shock us into recognition of the risks of the pioneering spirit. Images of spaceship earth resonate with today's spiritual awakening, yet any picture of earth from space is as dissonant to religion as Copernicus's first descriptions of the heavens.

Then there's Prufrock: "Let us go then, you and I," says a female actor with a throaty, smoky voice. The words were chosen to match the pictures. The ad takes a few lines literally and fits them into a thirty-second frame. What of the person who is triggered not by the literal use, but by the reference to Prufrock, where a few lines of the poem conjure all 130?

It's easy enough to say that only an unusual few who see the commercial will know the depth of what Prufrock knew: the yellow fog, the eyes that fix you in a formulated phrase, the arms that are braceleted and white and bare, "To wonder, 'Do I dare?' and, 'Do I dare?'" Those who know the poem find it undermined, and even desecrated, in their minds. And would they dare do business with the sponsor, AIG, a financial institution, who has caused such a disconnect?

Not every television viewer's attention can be triggered by T.S. Eliot. Most, however, can be triggered by a piece of music, especially if it's a song that was evocative of some event in life. The high school prom. The first date. The party after the walk on the beach. You probably know a song like that, that conjures some warm feeling. If that song is turned into a commercial, you understand the same trivialization that happened to the poetry lover.

Poems and songs are the sound tracks to our lives. Once they are co-opted for selling, there's a disconnect from the product's message. As Prufrock would say (but not in a commercial) "That is not what I meant, at all."

Moving Targets

We expect advertisers to choose carefully the environment in which their messages will work most effectively. No company would pay millions for thirty seconds in the Super Bowl or a few hundred dollars for an endorsement by a local radio personality if the message mechanism did not bring consumers out to try the product advertised, would they? Some commercials are aimed at people who are not and will not be consumers of the product. They may not *buy* a $250 pair of athletic shoes, but they will reinforce the good taste or trendiness of their friends who do. It's no fun to pay $50,000 for a car if your friends have never heard of the make and model.[17]

A huge challenge for marketers is trying to follow the constant fragmentation of America's demassifying masses. Even when America was a more homogeneous audience, an awareness of targeting to differentiate what messages went to whom existed. A textbook published in 1915, *The Business of Advertising* by Ernest Elmo Calkins, showed a clear awareness of the use of different periodicals to target various populations: children, farmers, college students, and religious people. There were "trade" or "class" magazines, such as those aimed at plumbers or Masons.[18]

Joseph Turow at the University of Pennsylvania at Philadelphia studies Calkins and the work he pioneered: "He appreciated the targeting value of a small-town newspaper, saying that it gives local influence to the advertisements which it carries. And he suggested 'canvassing consumers' in different cities around the country in order to gather information for an ad campaign." Today we call it perceptual and attitudinal research, probing choices, habits, and motivations. The results are used to target you as a consumer and to get your attention.

In *Breaking Up America*, Turow uses General Motors as an example of targeting and segmentation to differentiate products. Trying to work out of a sales slump in the 1920s, General Motors reorganized its strategy based on price segments. Chevrolet, Pontiac, Buick, and Cadillac were priced differently and advertised to buyers with different incomes. The aim of today's targeting is to reach consumers with specific messages delivered in familiar, even specific language, about how products and services fit them personally.

Turow presented this analysis in *American Demographics* magazine after *Breaking Up America* was published:

> Target-minded media help advertisers do this by building primary media communities formed when viewers or readers feel that a magazine, radio station, or other medium resonates with their personal beliefs, and helps them chart their position in the larger world.
>
> Nickelodeon and MTV were pioneer attempts to establish this sort of ad-sponsored community on cable television. Owned by media giant Viacom, they are lifestyle parades that invite their target audiences (relatively upscale children and young adults, respectively) into a sense of belonging that ranges across a panoply of outlets, from cable to magazines, to books, videotapes, and outdoor events that their owners control or license.
>
> The idea of these sorts of 'programming services' is to cultivate a must-see, must-read, must-share mentality that makes the audience feel like they belong to a family, attached to the program hosts, other viewers, and sponsors. *Sports Illustrated* is no longer just a magazine; it is a cross-media brand that stands for a certain approach to life.
>
> Some media are going a step further by making an active effort to exclude people who do not fit the desired profile. This makes the community more 'pure' and thereby more efficient for advertisers. *Signaling* is one way to do this. Simply put, signaling makes it abundantly clear that "this is not for everyone." "Beavis and Butthead" filled this role for MTV during the mid-1990s, as did "The Howard Stern Show" for E! Entertainment Television. These programs had so much "attitude," they sparked controversy among people clearly removed from their "in" crowds. Executives involved with scheduling the shows hoped controversies surrounding them would crystallize the channels' images and guarantee sampling by the people they wanted to attract. The executives acknowledged they also expected "signature shows" would turn off viewers whom they didn't want in their audience.

Another form of targeting goes beyond chasing undesirables away. As Turow says, it simply excludes them in the first place. *Tailoring* is the capacity to aim media content and ads at particular individuals. "With just a little effort (habit, actually), people can listen to radio stations, read magazines, watch cable programs, surf the Web, and participate in loyalty programs that parade their self-images and clusters of concerns. With no seeming effort at all, they receive offers from marketers that complement their lifestyles."[19]

No one really lives a "lifestyle," yet we all lead lives that may or may not have enough similarity to be classified by an advertiser for targeting. Advertisers scramble to keep up with the rapidly expanding choices we make to entertain and amuse ourselves. No advertisers can keep up with our attempts to enhance our lifestyles and to develop a personal story that separates us from the lifestyle next door, no matter how hard they try. And they do try. They must, or they'll never get your attention.

"This new culture is there when we blink, it's there when we listen, it's there when we touch, it's even there to be smelled in scent strips when we open a magazine," says James Twitchell in *For Shame*. "There is barely an empty space in our culture not already carrying commercial messages."[20]

The Speedup

As we expand our personal information, wealth, and education, we expand also our daily menu of experiences without expanding the day itself. We compress our activities and then complain about a lack of time.

Do not anguish. There's no such thing as "lack of time." The whole of time is distributed equally for each of us, the same numbers of minutes each hour, each day, each week. Your millisecond is the same as your neighbor's. Back to Bill Gates and Warren Buffett: they have the same amount of time you do.

Time management books teach us to "multitask": to open the mail while the telephone's on hold; to dictate to a recorder while driving; to work on the laptop computer while commuting. And we've taken multitasking to an extreme. Cadillac, for example, introduced a car with a voice-activated computer that allows the driver to surf the Internet while driving. As *USA Today* lamented, "That means the yahoos will be speeding down the freeway, talking on the phone, putting on makeup, sending e-mail *and* checking their tech stocks."

Not to be outdone, Ford introduced a minivan with a built-in washer/dryer, microwave oven, freezer, TV/VCR combination, trash compactor, and vacuum cleaner. The accoutrements are for the convenience of the traveler, but the assortment takes the idea of multitasking to a new level.

So why are we so pressed for time if technology allows us so many conveniences? The conveniences themselves make us want to do more, thus the multiples of multitasking. Add the other onslaught, as well:

- In 1999, there were 10,000 more books published than just five years earlier.

- In that same year, 30,000 CDs and albums were released by the record industry.
- More than 900 new magazines were launched.
- The number of feature films released by major studios increased by almost 80 percent in 10 years.
- Cable and satellite TV have expanded the daily video choices. Internet access is growing at an astonishing rate.[21]

They all eat up time that does not expand as the choices do. And media distorts our concept of time. The speedup attributed to movies in the early 1900s was accelerated exponentially by television, especially the ability to edit scenes to one and two seconds each.

That led futurist Edward Cornish to call television "the great time-eating machine." Reviewing a study of the use of time, Cornish reports that the bulk of the free time that Americans gained since the 1960s ("a stupefying 40 percent," to use his words) is taken up with TV.[22]

"People's subjective feelings of time scarcity today may be related to the vast increase in the choices they face—at the supermarket, in the workplace, on television, and elsewhere," writes Cornish. He goes on to describe television as "the primary culprit in Americans' feelings about being overworked, overstressed, and victimized." We've seen so much, heard so much, and experienced so much that we're bored with anything that moves slowly. Including ourselves. So we speed ourselves to match the media that hastened our pace in the first place.

The average 9.8–second sound bite on TV is luxury compared to the impatience Web surfers exhibit when loading page views. If an e-commerce Web site takes longer than eight seconds to display a catalog page or to take a customer's order, the shopper is likely to look elsewhere for a speedier, less frustrating experience, according to Zona Research. (A cottage industry grew up around that fact: Web-based businesses pay $7,200 to $20,000 annually for simulations and real-world tests of their accessibility.)[23]

How did we get so impatient?

"Velocity," says David Marc. What we once called "pacing"—in writing, in theater, and in life—is now velocity:

> The lifetime it takes to master a mythologically or religiously based poetic gave way to the dozen hours it takes to read a novel . . . gave way to the two-hour feature film . . . gave way to the sixty- or thirty-minute broadcast episode . . . gave way to the three-minute video . . . gives way to the several seconds it takes to absorb an image, tire of it, and hit the remote control button for another.

Marc calls it an "ironic fulfillment of an early twentieth century avant-gardist dream" that linear narrative is no longer a power in mass communication. Instead, the montage is the focus of American popular culture, driven by the scarcity of attention. Television, Marc says, is both cause and effect in the movement toward montage, and he predicts a not-too-distant future in which "even the stodgiest English teachers may one day look back upon the shows of the Network Era with a respectful fondness." Nickelodeon's "Nick at Night" programming already feeds the nostalgia for the black-and-white sitcom era when Dick Van Dyke's pratfalls were additions to a story, not the story itself. As Marc describes the advance from the days of pacing, "Video games have already elevated traditional television genres into didactic, even pedagogical art forms."[24]

If television is too slow for our attention span, we can speed it up with the flick of a finger on the remote, voting for or against any image that might impose itself too long. We search relentlessly for something to remember, hoping all the while only to forget. The remote is the tool of our impatience and the metaphor for our eroding attention. Alvin Toffler says that we have accelerated because society has:

> New information reaches us and we are forced to revise our image-file continuously at a faster and faster rate. Older images based on past reality must be replaced, for, unless we update them, our actions become divorced from reality and we become progressively less competent. We find it impossible to cope. This speedup of image processing inside us means that images grow more and more temporary. Throwaway art, one-shot sitcoms, Polaroid snapshots, Xerox copies, and disposable graphics pop up and vanish. Ideas, beliefs and attitudes skyrocket into consciousness, are challenged, defied, and suddenly fade into nowhere-ness. Scientific and psychological theories are overthrown and superseded daily. Ideologies crack. Celebrities pirouette fleetingly across our awareness. Contradictory political and moral slogans assail us.[25]

That's the disconnect caused by the attention economy: time fragmentation and a reorientation of leisure patterns. In the past, leisure meant big blocks of free time. Today, nothing is free, especially time. Michael Wolf says that this belief results in fun that's not valuable unless we're paying for it:

> As time has become segmented and broken into variable-length blocks, it has become commoditized. The entertainment marketplace allows us to recapture some of the pleasure associated with free time by offering fun in big and small doses, as stand-alone fun, or as part of a more utilitarian activity, and it charges us as it does so. Furthermore, once people get used

to treating the enjoyment of free time as a commodity, not only will they spend their money on video games, movies, theme parks, and so on; formerly low-cost or no-cost activities such as gardening, flower arranging, or riding a bicycle now come with an attendant range of goods and services that you pay for: do-it-yourself kits, rose-pruning lessons, bicycle tours, basketball camps, cooking schools, instructional lovemaking tapes. Somehow, the idea is that if you don't pay for it, if it doesn't happen according to someone else's schedule, it isn't real and valuable fun.[26]

Meet Me in Monte Carlo

In the desert of southern Nevada is the ultimate example of paying for fun—the glitter and the glitz of a theme park whose sights and sounds beckon the attention of anyone who ventures nearby.

The Eiffel Tower is uncomfortably close to the Arc de Triomphe, an odd juxtaposition for those who know the city of Paris. The altered landscape doesn't seem to matter to the visitors to the Hotel Paris on the Las Vegas Strip. They're attracted by the new Las Vegas landmark, the tower, which can be seen for miles.

But then, everything can be seen for miles in Vegas because of the broad expanse of desert floor. Luxor's glass pyramid gleams in the sun by day and thrusts a beacon of light skyward by night from a point atop the structure. From across town, Luxor appears tantalizingly close, but even the pharaohs would have been surprised by the distance.

From architecture to advertising, Las Vegas is hyperbole, the perfect vehicle for the attention economy. Advertising for Las Vegas properties tout "the most luxurious high-rise enclave in the history of Las Vegas" and "service extraordinaire" as well as the more mundane "big, bountiful buffet." Other enticements in Vegas advertising:

- "Permission to misbehave granted." (New York, New York Hotel)
- "You'll find each other so much more fascinating away from home." (Monte Carlo Resort and Casino)
- "What was it like to live among untold riches and lavish indulgence?" (Luxor)
- "A world of fun is within your reach." (Circus Circus)[27]

As theme park, Vegas reassembles ideas from around the world, much as Epcot Center in Orlando reconfigures Beijing's Temple of Heaven or Montmartre as it looks in Paris. Well, almost as it looks. Epcot reduces the size by about a quarter, but at least there's a sense of copy and proportion.

Epcot doesn't stack the Eiffel Tower atop Caillebotte's rue de Turin and rue de Moscou as Las Vegas does.

Vegas doesn't mind that the representation is not exact. The New York City skyline is rendered atop a high-rise hotel and the streets of New York are juxtaposed on each other inside. Only at the New York, New York must you go *up* a flight of stairs to reach the subway.

Renaissance shopping along the Grand Canal in Venice was unlikely to offer golf shops, a Warner Brothers store, or Rockport shoes; however, the canals of the Venetian hotel in Vegas do. And more: Houdini's Magic Shop, Movado watches, Madame Tussaud's Celebrity Encounter (no longer a "wax museum"), Ann Taylor, and Banana Republic, to name just a few stores working for your attention, to say nothing of your dollar.

Would the Caesars marvel at the hotel that bears their name and the shops that line their forum? Likely not. Would the gods approach them in such an atmosphere? No, Las Vegas is a place for mortals.

Only the lavish Bellagio seems not to trivialize an original. The ornate Italian-style hotel is inspired by villas in Tuscany, but it is itself, not a desert knockoff. There's no Eiffel Tower, Empire State Building, or Grand Canal for comparison. It feels real, not fake like the others. Nonetheless, Bellagio screams for attention with careful appointments of opulence. Hundreds of blown glass flowers adorn the ceiling at the registration desk. The chairs in the lobby bar are expensive re-creations of northern Italian antiques. A gallery in the hotel displays real works by impressionist masters—Cézanne, Renoir, van Gogh, Degas, and Gauguin—plus works by Picasso, Matisse, and Miro.

Vegas is a mixture of two attention economies. Call the first one the "big attention economy"—desert moguls building ever more opulent, ever more lavish attractions to capture both attention and dollars. The "new" Las Vegas is designed for family entertainment. Gaming tables and slot machines are still there, but in the newer hotels the casinos are not at the front door. At the Luxor, for example, they're on a separate floor entirely. The "mob money" atmosphere of the old Vegas has given way to Sigfreid and Roy and their white tigers, a roller coaster circling the tower of the Stratosphere Hotel, and water parks for the kids to add to the blockbuster stage shows for mom and dad.

At the same time, a smaller, more personal attention economy is at work in the city. Hawkers on the streets hand out flyers encouraging passersby to take advantage of the pleasures of a select number of Las Vegas women, who, as a comedian once put it, "must need the money because they seem to own no clothes."

On the crowded Vegas streets, the two economies collide and create a disconnect. Hand a full-color photo of a hardly clad buxom blond to the wrong visitor and he drops it to the ground. Thus lurid come-ons from strippers and escorts litter some Vegas crosswalks. For the curious whose attention is drawn by the flyers, newspaper vending boxes offer free tabloid-sized versions of the same pictures.

Famous for Fifteen Minutes

Here's another take on Las Vegas, but the setting is almost coincidental in this story. People have been getting married in Las Vegas for years, so one more wedding is hardly worth notice. That is, until the wedding is staged on national television in the context of the ratings phenomenon *Who Wants to Be a Millionaire,* which revitalized a tepid ABC-TV network in late 1999 and became a nightly staple and a daily conversation piece for millions.

Fox TV's *Who Wants to Marry a Multi-Millionaire* was a surprise hit, although it ran only once. It was bizarre, to say the least, both during the show and long after the fact. And it was a promise of television voyeurism to come, a clear sign of disconnected America.

Who Wants to Marry a Multi-Millionaire, for anyone who may have missed the program or the media hype in the weeks after it, began with fifty women who had been chosen from more than 3,000 applicants who were willing to give up a Tuesday evening—and conceivably a lifetime—for a San Diego "multimillionaire" (Rick Rockwell, a sometime actor, sometime motivational speaker, sometime stand-up comedian whose net worth was in the neighborhood of $2 million, thanks to investments in real estate).

The ratings for the two-hour special climbed steadily from 10 million viewers during the first half hour to nearly 23 million by the time the list of hopefuls was winnowed to a happy few. A nation of voyeurs watched a combination beauty pageant and game show. It ended with the happy groom on bended knee proposing to the winner and a civil ceremony under an arch of flowers.[28]

The lucky bride is someone we all know now: Darva Conger, an emergency room nurse who walked away with more than $100,000 in prizes, including an Isuzu Trooper and a three-carat diamond ring worth $35,000. Oh, yes, and a husband.

That's how we know her so well. Darva had second thoughts during the honeymoon and spent the next several weeks telling the nation about them. "America's favorite made-for-television couple had a busy day in New York City yesterday," said the *Washington Post*, describing both husband and wife as "campaigning for Best Victim" in a string of TV interviews.[29]

Darva claimed that her reaction was not the joy she showed on the TV show, but something that "bordered on revulsion" when her new husband had the nerve to kiss her. Rick said he was "hurting today," having seen his wife's interview on *Good Morning America*. The interviews were pure theater from two people who were willing to put themselves in the Fox spotlight but not into each other's.

Each of the fifty women who were contestants for Rockwell's hand and fortune had been auditioned like actors in sessions that Fox clearly labeled as "tryouts," so how could either the winner or the losers claim they weren't aware of the potential outcome?

Fox wanted our attention and got it. Darva obviously wanted it even more. She also got it. Her interview with Diane Sawyer gave *Good Morning America* its best ratings performance in two years. Even after pledging to stop granting interviews, Darva was back on CNN's *Larry King Live* telling her story.[30] The following week it was NBC's *Today* and *Dateline*. Darva attempted to unwrite the story of her television marriage. She told *Today* host Matt Lauer that Rockwell made her feel "like he had won a toy on a prize show." Of course, the world knew very well that he had. Darva failed to realize that the story was already written and she couldn't change what people believed. She first "considered," then accepted an idea that extended her period of stardom—a *Playboy* centerfold.

Outside that same *Today* show studio there were people lined up at 5:00 A.M. waiting for their own stab at fame. Three women in bathrobes and hair rollers. A man in a frog costume. A teenager who said she'd wear a whipped cream bikini if she thought it would get her on the air. Why? "Because it would be so cool to be on national TV and have two seconds of fame," said seventeen-year-old Katie Runeari of Oswego, New York.[31] Two seconds? Andy Warhol's prediction of fifteen minutes of fame for every living soul is being eroded quickly.

Warhol's "fifteen minutes" is the central truth of the age of electronic media, and it began with Warhol himself: "well-known for his well-knownness," said art critic Robert Hughes. Warhol was celebrity for celebrity's sake and for little other. Now everybody can follow in his footsteps, because everybody wants the attention that a few minutes in the spotlight offers. Two seconds is more like it, especially for the audience that scrambles for position in Rockefeller Plaza to be seen ever so briefly during the *Today* show.

Why do they stand in the cold behind weatherman Al Roker and scream on cue when the cameras are on? Because they're on TV, that's why. TV gives them the attention they might not get otherwise. TV is the context in which their lives are lived. TV images are the collective memories they hold. With the transitory nature of accelerated life, TV is their myth, the common link to their common stories. TV molds their manners.

In other words, TV is their life.

It's a natural response to communicate with friends and family holding a sign on national TV. It's as if each American has the inalienable right to be on TV at some time in his or her life. If TV is the mirror that reflects the ultimate "me," then "me on TV" completes the equation. The new celebrity, based in Warhol, is us. We are the players in a big TV show, some of it on the screen, some of it in our own lives. Where one ends and the other begins is difficult to say, given the pressures on our attention.

Most attention is paid to people we know. The attention economy is a star system at its most efficient and productive. The relationship between stars and fans is essential to commerce in this new economy. The attribution "star" is not limited to the people we see in the movies or on sitcoms. Politicians are stars. So are business leaders like Bill Gates and Steve Case.

Celebrities accumulate attention the way an antique dealer accumulates bric-a-brac along with items of value. And some celebrities are celebrities for celebrity's sake. In *Hot Air*, Howard Kurtz describes "fledgling pundits" who start out on C-SPAN:

> They can practice their delivery in a low-pressure environment and the only compensation is a coffee mug emblazoned with the network logo. The talented ones work their way up to midlevel pontification on CNN, CNBC, or PBS. The glibbest of the glib might get a coveted invitation to appear on "Nightline," "Meet the Press," or "Face the Nation."[32]

The "pundits" Kurtz refers to are journalists who spend their time on TV talking about stories, leaving the viewer to wonder who's actually covering the stories. (Margaret Carlson of *Time*, a regular on *The Capital Gang* program, was quoted in the *Washington Post* about her simple rule for success on TV: "The less you know about something, the better off you are.")[33]

Another example of celebrity for celebrity's sake is the constant stream of column mentions for rapper Sean "The Puff Daddy" Combs. You'll see it written "Sean 'Puffy' Combs" and "Sean (Puffy) Combs," according to Randall Rothenberg of *Advertising Age*, who studies stylebooks—and, apparently, The Puff Daddy:

> Need a real-estate story? The Puff Daddy's got homes in Beverly Hills, the Hamptons and Park Avenue. A crime story? Some Puff Daddy associates have been charged with assaulting journalists of whose reporting they disapprove. A travel story? The Puff Daddy likes to winter in St. Bart's. A business story? The Puff Daddy is the publisher of the hip-hop magazine *Notorious*. A fashion story? The Puff Daddy likes to go to polo matches in Southampton.

Not that Puff Daddy doesn't get attention on his own. His rap albums sell millions. He owns his own record label and a restaurant or two. But he's also hungry for attention and gets it from the *New York Times'* Private Lives column, where, by Rothenberg's count, Puff Daddy was eclipsed only by Yankees' owner George Steinbrenner in mentions in a year's time.[34] During the same year, Puff Daddy's mentions surpassed those for Madonna and Donald Trump. That's the sign of a person who's famous for being famous.

But suppose you're not a celebrity or a star. Does that leave you out of the attention economy? Not if you're willing to take one of four courses of action:

- Do something outrageous
- Tell your story publicly and weave a thread of victimhood through it
- Tell your story as confession with redemption or recovery as the outcome
- Accept a smaller share of attention via the Internet, knowing you'll achieve a greater degree of intensity among your fan base.

The Outrageous

You don't need this book to explain "something outrageous." Watch any television newscast and you'll see an escalating definition. It makes you nostalgic for the "old days," the 1970s, for example, when streakers were shocking and outrageous. The passage of time and the parade of nude bodies since then make the notion of streaking quaint by today's measurement.

Can you pass a magazine rack—even in the grocery store—that doesn't display sexual references on the covers? Can you turn on a rock station without some shock jock using his penis as a measuring device? Can you surf the video channels without finding a shouting match disguised as a talk show?

In pursuit of the outrageous, we refuse to let our leaders hold secrets. Once presidential peccadilloes were just that, nothing that the public knew or cared to know. Veering off course was between the offender, a spouse, and God. Today, we have to know all the lurid and outrageous details. Ironically, the more we tell our secrets, the more we induce banality. The unusual becomes the commonplace.

In pursuit of the outrageous, we fill the nightly news with stories like the one from Salt Lake City about a troupe of modern sideshow performers who staple $5 bills to their foreheads, press their faces into hissing blowtorches, and allow assistants to throw darts at their backs. The audiences for the "geek shows" (taken from the old-time carnival sideshows) are twenty-somethings who are bored with rock bands.[35]

In pursuit of the outrageous, we've given up our sense of outrage. Television and electronic media have desensitized us to things that once caused shame, the basis of social decorum and decency. The very act of exposure excites us more than the secrets exposed.

The Culture of Complaint

As the Dark Ages lightened into the Renaissance, the church was the focus of attention. In an attempt to maintain that focus while the science of the day risked undermining the tenets of faith with new discovery, the leaders of the church created a roster of saints, formerly of this world, now members of an elite that the faithful should strive to emulate.

Our nineteenth-century ancestors had the same challenge. As the industrial revolution mechanized men's lives, leadership wanted to offer something to strive for. The solution was to embroider stories of the past into a roster of heroes to emulate. Christopher Columbus sailed the ocean blue in fourteen hundred and ninety-two. George Washington chopped down the cherry tree and threw a coin across the Potomac. Wyatt Earp and Doc Holliday fought a battle of self-defense. The stories gave America something to believe.

Today, we don't manufacture saints or heroes; we manufacture victims.[36]

At the Olympic Games in Atlanta in 1996, two Chinese women rowers blamed jet lag for their lack of medals. A Mexican cyclist blamed his bicycle. A British hurdler blamed the bad food and the chairs at Olympic Village. The Brazilian soccer team blamed the distance from their living quarters to the practice field AND the dimensions of the American football stadium they played in AND the fact that their star player was shy. So much for the old adage, "It's not whether you win or lose; it's how you play the game."

It's also how you report the game. A book called *Interference: How Organized Crime Influences Professional Football* looked like a touchdown for author Dan Moldea in 1989. *Good Morning America* called. So did *Nightline*. Appearances on those shows prompted other media outlets to seek interviews. That is, until the *New York Times Book Review* panned the book. Moldea sued and won, sending shudders through the publishing industry.[37]

McDonald's found itself in hot water in Albuquerque when an eighty-one-year-old woman spilled hot coffee and sued the company. No doubt she was scalded and hurt, but the product is called "hot coffee" for a reason. Even people who ordinarily side with the little guy supported McDonald's in public opinion polls and on radio talk shows when they heard that the little old lady had received a $2.9 million judgment.[38]

A Wisconsin lawyer threatened to file a wrongful-discharge suit for an employee who was fired after claiming to have finished several tasks she had not actually completed. Her defense: She was a pathological liar. Fortunately, and surprisingly, the suit was never filed.[39]

Atlanta Constitution editorial writer Marilyn Geewax called America "a nation of crybabies" when a woman called her to complain of sexual discrimination at a trade show in Atlanta. The offense: The trade show would not allow the woman to bring her seven-year-old daughter on the display floor. That prompted Geewax to publish a "complete Whiners' Checklist" to keep self-appointed victims off her phone:

> Step 1: When faced with a problem, call the news media immediately. Take no time to work with proper authorities to find solutions.
>
> Step 2: Make sure you use the words "victim" and "discrimination" as often as possible. That will absolve you of any responsibility for your situation.
>
> Step 3: Ignore the feelings of those around you. Remember, everything really is all about *you*.[40]

There's a fourth step if those aren't enough: Call the TV talk shows.

Kevin says he threatened to commit suicide to convince Margie to stay with him. Margie feels Kevin is obsessed with her and says she's afraid of him. That's why Margie stayed in Ann Arbor while Kevin traveled to the *Sally Jessy Raphael Show* to describe his profound love.

Chuck is a teenager whose parents say they are "horrified when he dresses gothic." In fact, they were so horrified, they told Maury Povich about it. Chuck appeared on the show, too, in black clothing, circles of black makeup under his eyes, and chains trailing behind him. Chuck's father is the victim in this story: "I have a vision of taking my son fishing," said the distraught man, who apparently thinks the fish will be as offended as he is.

Victims seek attention and viewers pay attention because, so often, the victims are in the mold of the viewers themselves. A study of participants in the *Donohue* program indicated that the opportunity to use the broad medium of television to pinpoint a small subgroup of viewers was paramount in the minds of those who appeared as guests. Patricia Joyner Priest wrote her doctoral dissertation about self-disclosure on television and used *Donohue* as her laboratory. The producers gave her access to interview the show's guests:

> The perception of legitimacy conferred from television treatment of a topic was affirming to members of the television audience who engaged in similar behaviors or held parallel interests or points of view. This notion of legitimization played a part in Charlotte's rationale for appearing on the show to discuss her efforts to come to terms with her lesbian identity in the

Priest's study led her to view the phenomenon of television disclosure as "a plaintive cry for inclusion in society via a medium which excludes marginalized groups except for rare treatments in which they are stereotyped or vilified."[41]

Redeeming Values

"If the Inner Child doesn't let you off the hook, the embrace of redemption will," said *Time*'s art critic and resident curmudgeon Robert Hughes, noting that the range of victims formerly available to us has expanded to include every permutation of "acronyms pursuing identity."[42]

Kevin, the man from the *Sally Jessy Raphael Show,* went beyond victimhood and made a bid for redemption. He told Sally that he knows he bottled things inside and built a wall between himself and Margie (he got serious enough to call her "Margaret" during that segment of the show), and he begged for forgiveness. He believes in love at first sight and Margie is his love.

Kevin's not the first to beg for forgiveness on TV. Richard Nixon was, in his "Checkers" speech, when he asked for a second chance the first time. After him came a long parade of confessions and apologies, too many of them indistinguishable from Kevin's on the talk show.

Presidential apologies began with Kennedy's in the aftermath of the Bay of Pigs invasion and gained some polish as Jimmy Carter reported the frustrations of dealing with Iran during the hostage crisis that captured attention during the last year of his administration.

If, as the song goes, "Love means never having to say you're sorry," then there's no love in politics. Meg Greenfield called it "The No-Fault Confession" in *Newsweek*:

> After waits of varying length that only heighten the suspense, a grim-faced president will come before the people and announce that he "accepts" responsibility for what happened. "PRESIDENT ACCEPTS RESPONSIBILITY" we will headline.
>
> What is so fascinating about this formulation is, first, that it implies that the assumption of responsibility, which is his whether he wants it or not, is somehow optional; it thus also suggests that his acknowledgment of this self-evident and inescapable fact is an act of statesmanship and valor.[43]

Our job, of course, is to express our relief that the president had the courage to do the right thing. Fortunately, television fogs our memory for the facts of the case, so the apology rings true.

Until the TV talk shows, this tactic was not available to lesser beings.

Now everybody can confess. Celebrities and politicians started it in a bow to ethics. Now, real people do it, too, in the name of self-disclosure. Whichever, we share with them some of our precious attention.

Attention Online

There was once a joke in media circles that the entertainment industry was fragmenting at such a rate that one day there would be a channel for nude skydivers. The radio people who made the joke said it would be a radio station; the TV people said it would be a cable channel.

The joke is now reality. An Internet search engine uncovered 954 Web links to nude skydiving.[44] While that's a large number, many of the listings are redundant, as Net searches tend to be. Nonetheless, the joke no longer makes media people laugh. Reality caught up.

In cyberspace, attention is paramount. And the focus can be as narrow as the surfer chooses. Who knows how many nude skydivers there are? When the nude skydiving community needs information, there's a Web presence ready to pay attention to them. And those who are interested in nude skydiving as a sport are no doubt ready to return the favor by offering attention to sites that serve them.

Mass media cannot afford to serve such a narrow community except in the most inconsequential way: a feature on a newscast; a nude skydiving demonstration in a series of extreme adventures. Online media are perfect for activities with limited interest or limited fan bases because they're not mass media. Rather, they're very specific, very narrow content providers.

Berkeley's Michael Goldhaber calls the people who follow an online community "fans" and "entourages." And every entourage needs a "star" to follow. Communities are centered on a single topic and attention flows from stars to the entourage and back. The larger the community, the more likely there will be "microstars," too, and they'll develop their own fan base.[45]

If you know the word "trapunto" and know that the phrase "Puffy Foam" is trademarked, then you have an idea of one online community that also exists offline. If you don't know these terms, it's because you're not a part of the community that uses them. Trapunto is a technique for creating padded embroidery. Puffy Foam™ is the brand name for the stuff that makes it padded. The growing embroidery community is an extension of "Club Ed," a newsletter for people who use their Hoop-It-Alls and their Giant Hoop-It-Alls to enhance clothing, quilts, and anything else that will stand still for a stitch or two.

More and more of the exchanges about bobbins and appliqués are taking place on the Web, as the star of the embroidery community, Deborah Jones, adds computer patterns to download and stitch. "All embroidery is created from three basic types of stitches. Do you know what they are?" asks www.embroiderydirect.com.

Tatiana Volkova of Laguna Hills, California, is another online star, with a worldwide community online. As a teenager in the former Soviet Union, Tatiana lost her left leg in an accident. As she grew into a slender and attractive adult, she noticed that men seemed attracted to her because she was an amputee. Over time, she realized that there is a "community" of admirers of female amputees, called "devotees."

A cottage industry developed when Tatiana collected photographs of other women she met in St. Petersburg who had also lost legs or arms and sold the pictures online. A package of color stills of a one-legged woman costs US$60.00. A videotape of schoolteacher Olga Poozanova vamping precociously for the camera while touring St. Petersburg on a black peg leg costs US$100.00. That is, until Olga changed her loyalty to another online community where her own star could shine more brightly. Yes, Tatiana is not the only online entrepreneur catering to an entourage of devotees, but she seems to have the largest collection of microstars in her stable.

As Michael Goldhaber defined the online star system in *Wired*:

> Attention flows not only from fan to star, but in a hyperlinked way it can be passed from star to star, or fan to fan. A growing variety of attention types can bounce along through cyberspace: personal advice, suggestions, connections, editing, assistance in self-expression, responses, acclaim, or new software designed especially for your purposes. More gets more.[46]

Yet more also means less. A study in the journal *Nature* indicated that even the most industrious search engine in 1999 couldn't find more than 16 percent of the sites on the World Wide Web. Two years earlier, that figure was 34 percent. With six trillion bytes of text alone—that doesn't include pictures or downloadable files—the Web is next to impossible to index or to measure.[47] Based on 1999 statistics, 10,270 new Web domains are added every hour!

According to Seth Godin, Alta Vista, one of the most complete and most visited search engines, claims 100 million pages indexed. That means when you do a search, you're looking through those 100 million pages. Alta Vista delivers about 900 million pages a month to people searching. Do the math: the average page is called up only nine times a month. Says Godin, "Imagine that. Millions of dollars invested in building snazzy corporate marketing sites and an average of nine people a month search for and find any given page of information on this search engine. This is a very, very big haystack."[48]

Anybody who creates a new online community is destined for a limited entourage of fans who have to search the haystack. The only exceptions are among those who can aggregate attention through mass media. That's why radio and television are jammed with commercials for enterprising "dot-com" companies hoping you'll find them.

That's more competition than your attention can attend to.

Chapter 3

The Bias Against Understanding

Question: True or False? Half of all U.S. marriages end in divorce.
Question: True or False? Crime is on the rise in the suburbs.
Question: True or False? New York's Broadway Theater at Broadway and Fifty-third Street sells more tickets than the Yankees and the Mets combined.

Answers: False. False. False.

Most people say "true" to the first two questions. They've read enough headlines and heard enough statistics on the TV news to answer confidently. In spite of the repetition of those statements, they're not true. Some say "false" to the last statement because it seems unlikely (and they're right). But it was widely published as being true.[1]

Let's take them one by one.

The Divorce Rate

The 50 percent figure for the U.S. divorce rate has been quoted, unchallenged, for over a decade. The figure is based in fact, but the conclusion is wrong.

In 1988, there were 2,389,000 weddings in the United States and 1,183,000 divorces. That's 49.5 percent, the source of the percentage so widely quoted. Viewed alone, those statistics might lead you to believe that all 1988 marriages ended up in divorce. Or that all the divorces that year were the result of 1988 marriages.

To get at the real percentage, take all the people who are currently married or who have ever been married (about 72 percent of adults, says the Census Bureau) and divide that by the number who are divorced (about 9 percent of U.S. adults). The real number is just under 13 percent.

True Crime

The worst crimes are increasing, but they're increasing in central cities, not in the suburbs.

Because of media attention to two incidents in widely separated areas of Florida, 90 percent of Floridians say their state is a dangerous or somewhat dangerous place to live. In September 1993, a German tourist was shot dead in a rental car near Miami International Airport. A few days later, a British tourist was murdered at a rest area in northern Florida, almost 500 miles away. Regardless of the distance between the two murders and the absolute lack of connection between them, they were linked inseparably by national TV coverage.

Only in New York and New Orleans did violent crime in the suburbs increase faster than central city crime (in an analysis done by *American Demographics* magazine). Murder rates in the suburbs were 81 percent lower than in the large central cities in 1992 statistics. The magazine concluded that "media attention contributes to Americans' common belief that no place is safe anymore—not even the sheltered, affluent suburbs."[2]

The public's concern with crime rises and falls with media reporting about crime. High-profile crimes create high-profile coverage. The greater the coverage, the larger the proportion of Americans who cite crime as the most important issue facing the nation.

A *Los Angeles Times* poll in 1994 asked Americans whether their feelings about crime were based on the media or on their personal experience: 65 percent named the media, 21 percent named personal experience, and 13 percent said both.

A Gallup study in 1993 asked Americans to rank cities according to their perceived danger of crime. People were correct about Miami (number one) and New York (number two), but missed totally the fact that Alexandria, Louisiana, was third in terms of violent crimes per 100,000 population. The public also ranked Washington, D.C., number four. The city was actually eighty-eighth on the list.[3]

Broadway vs. Baseball

"New York's Broadway Theater at Broadway and Fifty-third Street sells more tickets than the Yankees and the Mets combined," said John Naisbitt and Patricia Aburdene in *Megatrends 2000.* The statement seems unlikely. When it was first published, however, it was taken for fact because of its source. In their update of the best-seller *Megatrends,* Naisbitt and Aburdene used that statement—in bold print, mind you—to indicate a revival of the arts in America.[4]

The revival was real. Broadway's 1988–89 season was the biggest to date, and eight million theater-goers paid $262 million dollars to see performances of *The Phantom of the Opera, Les Misérables, Cats, Starlight Express,* and others. That figure is the combined total for all Broadway theaters. The one theater called "The Broadway Theater" alone sold slightly over 800,000 seats (for *Les Misérables*) during 1989. That same year, the Yankees sold just under two million tickets and the Mets sold just over two million. So the information was flat wrong, and it left an impression on the reader (and anyone who quoted Naisbitt and Aburdene) of a larger theatrical revival than the impressive one that was actually underway.

Like the other figures, there's a basis for the statistic: There were 416 performances in 1989 at The Broadway. There were 162 Yankees games and 162 Mets games, and half of each season is played at home. Sure enough, 416 is the higher number. However, The Broadway seats 1,752, Yankee Stadium 57,545, and Shea Stadium 55,601. Even factoring in a minimum number of baseball sellout crowds, do the math, and you can't explain how The Broadway "sells more tickets."

Eric Miller of the newsletter *Research Alert* discovered the error and used it in a speech the following year: "This is just one fact in one book. New trend-announcing books appear all the time, articles appear every day, and TV news creates similar hyped impressions."

There is not only a barrage of information, but of inflated and enhanced "facts"—some of it hype, some of it error. It's part of our lives. Whether we want it or not, we are overexposed to manufactured illusions. Most of what we read and hear is difficult, if not impossible, to check for accuracy. Richard Saul Wurman calculates that a typical weekday edition of the *New York Times* contains more information than the average person alive in the seventeenth century was likely to come across in a lifetime.[5] Add to that all the other papers, the traditional news media, and emerging electronic data sources, and keeping up with it all is the challenge, not checking for accuracy.

That creates a bias. It's not a bias against a person, a party, or a point of view. It's a bias against understanding. It's a by-product of the speedup of technology and the reduction of attention.

In the pre-electronic days, a story had to wait for development and distribution, which happened over time. The event occurred. A journalist reported on it either immediately or some time later, after investigating additional aspects of the story. An editor added information or created context for the presentation. Then the reader absorbed it at his or her own pace.

Today a dramatic event, the death of Princess Diana, for example, is broadcast instantly and globally. Information cultures, whether tabloid or mainstream, print or electronic, local or national, focus intensely on the event.

Instant access via the Internet spreads rumor and innuendo as quickly as it spreads legitimate, corroborated information.

In *Warp Speed*, Bill Kovach and Tom Rosenstiel blame lack of investigative reporting on the architecture of television: "In the mixed media age of the twenty-four-hour news cycle, the first impression the public gets is increasingly unedited and live. There is little opportunity for the reporter to leaven the lawyer's remarks by other reporting, or to juxtapose this lawyer's account with the opposing view. That will come at the next competing live event."[6]

The entire world heard unsubstantiated theories about the crash of TWA 800 into Long Island Sound. Conspiracies, terrorist plots, government cover-ups, nonexistent eyewitnesses—all surfaced as "stories" and were repeated without question or criticism. Even ABC's Pierre Salinger, a veteran of news organizations and the White House press office, was taken in by a "scoop" transmitted online. Investigators concluded that not one of the spurious theories was correct and that there was no evidence of foul play.

Writing in *Wired*, Jon Katz describes news reports as "unfiltered hysteria" because stories take on lives of their own:

> We are confronted with more information about a single subject than can possibly be lucid, coherent, or even digestible. Cable channels, stuck with many hours of airtime and little new information to fill them with, scramble for "experts" who present and argue these stories as if they were vast global sporting events.
>
> And as the [Louise] Woodward case [the so-called nanny murder case] revealed, it's no longer just major news that ignites these firestorms. Increasingly, smaller, regional stories are given the same intense international attention.[7]

For all the coverage, our understanding of the underlying issues rarely increases. The faster the stories bombard us, the slower the truth is to follow.

You'll recall the arrest of Rodney King by Los Angeles police officers and the videotape that showed officers subduing King by beating him. The short segment of the tape that showed the officers wielding their nightsticks was only a minor part of the testimony in the King trial. The entire tape was shown to jurors. What they saw offered a different perspective. Police first tried to subdue King with a "stun gun" called a Taser. That sequence lasted about two minutes. When King did not respond, the officers began to use their nightsticks.

The nightstick segment, and that segment only, played thousands of times on television, usually in a loop that showed the incident repeated in rapid succession. During NBC-TV's nightly news on the evening that the trial was over, the segment showing the beating played five times while Tom Brokaw told the outcome of the trial—the release of the officers.

Radio reports of rioting that followed the acquittal in the King case were more incendiary than the rioters themselves. "This area is out of control," shouted a Metro Networks reporter on KFMB, San Diego. "There are about thirty fires, some of them smoldering." Smoldering is hardly out of control! Later that evening, the fires did engulf Los Angeles neighborhoods, and looters ran with what they could.

San Diego was comfortably removed from the riots and the King case itself, yet businesses closed early, and downtown's Horton Plaza shopping center urged patrons to leave. The media reports scared San Diegans into believing that riots would spread southward.[8]

No News Is Still No News

In 1998, expecting a repeat of the Persian Gulf War, reporters flocked to Kuwait to catch the action for their networks. The United States threatened airstrikes against Iraq.

What viewers back home saw would hardly make the ratings soar. Three TV crews captured video of soldiers watching the Howard Stern movie *Private Parts*. Twelve reporters boarded a blue bus from the Sheraton Hotel to the Al-Jahra Hospital where they would see a drill designed to show tiny Kuwait's readiness in case Iraq launched an attack on it. The hospital had not been informed, so when the reporters arrived, embarrassed doctors scrambled to accommodate them with a staged "rescue."

There was lots of reporting, but no war. U.N. Secretary-General Kofi Annan reached a deal with Iraq's Saddam Hussein to prevent the confrontation. The Kuwait Ministry of Information did its best to provide something to show the folks back home—thus the hasty hospital drill.[9]

At the Republican Party's national convention in Dallas in 1984, Nancy Reagan waved from the podium. Her husband was to be nominated for his second run at the presidency at that convention. She was demonstrating the support and enthusiasm expected of first ladies. On NBC, the scene reflected Mrs. Reagan's exuberance. Republicans were applauding her, looking delighted, and jumping up and down. The home viewer would naturally believe that the Dallas Convention Center was undulating with enthusiasm.

On the convention floor at the same time, delegates and their guests were standing in small groups, some paying attention to the podium, some not. Many of those seated had their arms folded. Other were talking among themselves. The mood of the delegates was described as "tepid."[10]

The disparity between the events in the hall and what appeared on the home screen was significant. NBC had used ingenuity and careful camera shots to create a lively show. CBS anchor Dan Rather suggested that the GOP convention, because it lacked drama, obliged the networks to do more interpretive work than usual. In Rather's words, "The people in the living room see it for what it is, an event meticulously stage-managed to death." Television takes dull rhetoric and compresses it into sharp images and tidy sound bites.

The Stage Is Set

Simplification and trivialization are the enemies of understanding, and when it comes to coverage of political news, glib one-liners and bumper sticker rhetoric dominate.

When Ronald Reagan was president, there was a sign for reporters in the press secretary's office: "You don't tell us how to stage the news and we don't tell you how to cover it."[11] All administrations attempt to manage news coverage, at least to deliver the news in the most favorable or the least negative light. The Reagan administration took news management to high art.

Typical example: On the White House agenda in spring 1985, a report was to be released about aides using their diplomatic passports to buy foreign luxury cars at a discount. That same day, the White House needed to inform the press that doctors had discovered that President Reagan had two minor health problems.

The information was held for a day or two and good fortune intruded even though it came in the form of sad news: Soviet leader Konstantin Chernenko had died. Presidential spokesman Larry Speakes took advantage of Chernenko's passing to release the negative news nagging at his agenda. Few noticed. His news was overshadowed by the Chernenko story.

When it was announced in 1981 that the press briefing room was to be remodeled, reporters assumed that it was for their comfort and convenience. Instead, according to John Tebbel and Sarah Miles Watts, "It was Hollywood set-building carried into politics" and the new president was to be the star of the show:

> Permanent seats were installed in rows, and for the first time correspondents were assigned to these seats for press conferences. It was not a permanent arrangement, it was explained, except for the fact that the wire-service people and the television correspondents would always occupy the front row, where the cameras could be trained on the latter, and with the President also in view, so that Reagan could, in effect, carry on a direct dialog with the television audience, for whom the conferences were primarily designed.

Another renovation came in 1984 when the doors behind the president's podium were used as part of the show. A marine in full-dress uniform stood guard during the press conference. As the last question was answered, the doors swung open to reveal the long corridor that leads to the executive offices. The president moved to the door as it opened, and the TV cameras saw him stride away, down the long, broad corridor.[12]

The Reagan presidency certainly was not the first to spin stories and manipulate the press corps, and it surely was not to be the last. Reagan's, however, was the first White House to use media effectively to its own ends. Those that followed simply improved on the spin strategy.

In *Reality Isn't What It Used to Be*, Walter Truett Anderson called Reagan "the first postmodern politician" and included the Reagan presidency in his sweeping review of politics as theater:

> What the government did in the Reagan years was not always easy to discover, but what it *said* it did was put forth to the media—and through it to the public—with relentless clarity. Early in the morning of every White House working day came the "line of the day" meeting in which top strategists would decide what news would be fed to the press that day, how the story should be angled, and who would be primarily responsible for it. The word would go out via conference call to senior officials, who were expected to tailor their own comments to the press accordingly. This kind of coordination made it possible for the White House to put through the messages it most wanted the public to get, and to exercise "spin control"— which is really story control, shaping the context of meaning surrounding an event and giving it positive or negative connotations.[13]

Reagan's speeches were "paced, well-written, tightly written—ideal for sound cuts," said Brian Healy, a CBS News senior producer in Washington during the Reagan years. Reagan's off-the-cuff remarks were not nearly so useful to news organizations, Healy said. "He hesitates, halts, has a lot of dead space, and it's just much tougher to get a cogent idea than when he's doing a staged event."[14]

In other words, only those remarks slick enough to fit into the briefest sound bite were worthy of the American public's attention on the nightly news. The "Great Communicator," as Reagan became known, was only "great" when his comments were cogent. He was lucky. If he fumbled or stumbled (which he did often, especially on matters of foreign policy) his remark was left on the cutting room floor. America seldom knew. What the spin doctors didn't filter, the media operators did.

Shaping images and perceptions was an American phenomenon but was felt elsewhere in the world. Speaking at a Harvard commencement speech in 1995, Vaclav Havel, the president of the Czech Republic and that country's national hero, claimed that television distorted people's view of their neighbors and themselves. He shared his own reaction to the medium: "I never fail to be astonished at how much I am at the mercy of television directors and editors, at how my public image depends far more on them than it does on myself."[15]

Not just on the directors, but on the viewers themselves. Havel's "image" is something that's not actually his. It's difficult to think about images without thinking in the possessive. However, whose image is the "president's image"? Surely, he has an image of himself, but is that the image held by his countrymen, his constituents? Probably not.

The language of possession implies a theory of communication in which presidents move their message to the people. TV, however, not only distributes images, but also creates them. Television's most powerful images aren't invented by the directors and editors President Havel mentioned. They are drawn from us and by us as viewers.

In *Channels* magazine in 1986, Jay Rosen wrote that being president in the age of television is "an out-of-body experience." The specific remark had to do with the media's fascination with cancers removed from President Reagan's nose and colon. The basic question in journalistic circles was where the public's right to know intruded on the president's privacy.[16]

"Out of body experience" has deeper meaning in the television age. "Television makes the President the symbolic center of our national life," Rosen said. "But in a curious way it also dislodges him, allowing an image of him to float out over the culture and seep into consciousness until it belongs as much to the audience as it does to the President himself."

Rosen claimed that Reagan was our most popular president "not because most people agreed with his programs, but because he has allowed himself to be dissolved into our idea of what a president should be. This turns out to be a composite of father, leader, and regular guy. But it is our image not his. . . . Reagan the television President is everywhere. He has been dispersed."

President Jimmy Carter had the opposite problem: The TV audience found it difficult to create an image of him in their own patterns. "With his Southern roots and oddball brother," Rosen speculated, "Carter had too much that belonged to him specifically."

It's been said that John Kennedy was not the president on television but the president of television. That could be said more accurately of Ronald Reagan. Reagan's battles with cancer, Rosen theorized, "offer a new way of insisting that the President (and the Presidency) can still be *located*, fixed precisely, in the person of Ronald Reagan." Even if it had to be fixed on his nose or in his colon!

The Filter

Television's filter shapes our images, not only of presidents but also of the world around us. That filter creates a further bias against understanding. Try to get information on local political races on TV in large cities and you're likely to fight through house fires, police actions, and freeway chases before you hear a candidate's name mentioned. In one example that is typical of many large market situations, the *Houston Chronicle* reported that none of the commercial English-language TV stations in Houston used their regular news programs to report on proposals or backgrounds of the contenders for lieutenant governor or attorney general, two of the highest profile races in the state (sometimes higher than the governor's office, which achieved its own national profile with George W. Bush).

According to the *Chronicle*'s analysis of transcripts and videotapes, two stations—the local CBS affiliate and the local Fox-owned outlet—"mentioned" public appearances, poll results, and campaign advertising. Two others, the ABC-owned station and the local NBC affiliate, never mentioned the candidates in their campaign roles.[17]

The news director of the CBS-TV affiliate claimed that "politicians like to control their message to voters by restricting their newsworthy statements to the commercials they pay for." In fact, the issues in those specific campaigns were released by candidates at press conferences and speeches; their commercials were used more to attack opponents, not to define issues.

The news directors say they're only giving the public what the public wants. In their mind, that's house fires, police actions, freeway chases, and the like. Throw in a splash of celebrity news, some unabashed self-promotion and the occasional scandal, and not only is understanding undermined but so is information itself.

In the magazine *Brill's Content*, Eric Effron calls the bias against understanding "the big blur," a fuzzy area when "the lines between fiction and nonfiction, between editorial and advertising, between news and entertainment, become undecipherable." Effron wrote that his eight-year-old son saw Geraldo Rivera on CNBC one night and said, "Hey, it's the guy from *Seinfeld*." In the *Seinfeld* finale in 1998, Rivera "covered" the story of the fictional trial of Jerry Seinfeld and his neurotic sidekicks. Effron offered his son an explanation of sorts:

> So I explained that the guy Max remembered from *Seinfeld* was, in fact, Geraldo, but he was just playing "Geraldo" doing the fake news, while the Geraldo I was watching this night was doing the real news. Or something like that.[18]

Which Geraldo created the bias against understanding? Both of them. When NBC decided to use the huge audience of its leading sitcom to promote its new news hire, it blurred the line between the network's role as a provider of information and a provider of entertainment. NBC allowed the *Seinfeld* version of Geraldo to use the CNBC news set. Geraldo looked the same in both settings. "Not even Max should have to wonder which is which," says Effron. But we all do.

If Max had been old enough to respond in 1992, what would he have made of ABC's *Prime Time Live* investigation of Food Lion grocery stores? ABC reporters phonied resumes to gain employment by Food Lion, then launched an "insider's" expose with hidden cameras, showing what were purported to be health violations. The network did not conduct even the most cursory journalism. There was no check of health records, no review of lawsuits by disgruntled Food Lion patrons. In other words, no reporting, only videotape out of context.

The journalism community soundly denounced the ABC tactic. "The episode made me glad to be a print journalist," wrote Rance Crain in an editorial in *Advertising Age*. The prestigious Medill School of Journalism at Northwestern University used the ABC investigation as subject of a symposium to mark the school's seventy-fifth anniversary. Dean Mike Janeway referred to the "tense truce between art and commerce" becoming unenforceable as "the cult of entertainment is blurred by the cult of news."[19]

From time to time, even the cult of entertainment will pull a fast one on you. Take, for example, the story of Louisa May Alcott's *Little Men*. You probably remember reading it in school. It's the continuation of the story of the March family from *Little Women*, the most famous of Alcott's autobiographically based novels.

You probably don't remember any of the little men or their fathers and uncles working at a Welch's grape juice factory. That's a stretch of the truth imposed on the story by the Pax TV network in a late 1999 episode of the series based on Alcott's book.

Welch's was, indeed, founded sometime during the 1880s, the period of the novel. Welch's *is* headquartered in Concord, Massachusetts. And, yes, Louisa May Alcott lived in Concord and her books are set in Concord. Squish all that together like so many grapes going into Welch's juice and you've got a perfect opportunity for paid product placement in a new production for a struggling network.

It's okay, because it's entertainment, said advertising people. "When the label is entertainment, as it clearly is in *Little Men*, if Pax can feature the sponsor in this special way, that's fine," said Rich Hamilton of Zenith Media Services in New York. "If the label of the show was news," he went on, "it would not be fine." It won't surprise you that the presentation of *Little Men* on Pax TV kicked off a special in-store promotion for Welch's products at grocery chains in twelve cities.[20]

Product placement in programs and movies is a widely accepted practice, but this instance was excessive because the Alcott work is so well known. It's easier to forgive the Fox network and AT&T for their co-promotion during *New York Undercover* when a character in the show referred to 1-800-CALL-ATT as part of the story line. At least the script of the show is created for television and has neither historical background nor widespread exposure among the public. The Alcott novel is a fixture in American literature. Enhancing it with grape juice only demeans it.

Synergy

Another deceptive mix of art and commerce is a "newscast" you may have seen. "Movie News" was hosted by a desk-bound anchorman and featured celebrity interviews. One installment in 1994 took viewers behind the scenes of three films: *The Lion King*, the animated musical; *I Love Trouble*, a thriller with Nick Nolte and Julia Roberts; and *Renaissance Man*, directed by Penny Marshall.

Only the most astute film buff would catch the fact that the three films were all from the Walt Disney Company or one of its subsidiaries. *The Lion King* was a Disney release. The other two were from Touchstone Pictures and Hollywood Pictures, both Disney-affiliated companies. Only at the end of the slick sixty-second "newscast" was there a brief flash on the screen: "Paid for by Buena Vista"—Disney's distribution company.[21]

Would you have caught the fact that "Movie News" wasn't news at all but a commercial for Disney properties? Maybe, maybe not. Surely, Disney didn't want you to. "Movie News" was subtle and misleading.

There's no question, however, about the Disney message elsewhere. There's a constant barrage of Disneyisms on ABC-TV since Disney absorbed that network in 1995:

- Disney animated movies provide programming for ABC.
- ESPN provides a sports bar for the Disney cruise ship and for Disney's Baseball City spring training facility near Orlando.
- Disney's Lyric Street Records introduced the Country group SHeDAISY in special theater showings arranged with Buena Vista's entrée.
- Country radio station programmers received VHS copies of their favorite Disney cartoons along with SHeDAISY's first CD.
- Disney's investment in New York City's Theater District is promoted

every day by ABC's *Good Morning America* as it originates live from the company's Times Square studios.

Disney's not the only company taking advantage of the situation; it just has the most extensive reach, given theme parks, hotels, movies, toys, books, videos, records, magazines, clothing, just to name a few resources beyond ABC and ESPN. Because of the plethora of opportunities, Disney CEO Michael Eisner institutionalized synergy by creating a position for a senior vice president of corporate synergy to look for ways to further exploit the Disney brands.[22]

Synergy's good for Disney, but it makes everything on ABC seem like a promotion for the parent company. Synergy puts Mickey Mouse in your face when you'd rather have him in your memory and your experience of cartoons or a good time at Disney World. While Disney fights for your attention by tying the Magic Kingdom to everything in your path, it inadvertently creates a disconnect from what made the memories magic in the first place. (More on "Disneyfication" in Chapter Six.)

Paranews

Any company that can gain access to you under the guise of news will do so. In the 1980s, television news directors debated the use of prerecorded interviews with business leaders designed to be used by television stations in their newscasts.

The news directors were confronted with a credibility issue because the prerecorded materials their stations received featured known or respected journalists working on behalf of the companies that wanted to get their messages on the air. Sixty-two stations broadcast "Energy at the Crossroads," a program produced by Mobil Oil Company and featuring reporter Roger Sharp interviewing the president of Mobil and other energy "experts" arguing for government incentives for oil exploration and environmental tradeoffs. Sharp at the time was a reporter for WABC-TV in New York. Mobil also employed news anchors from Detroit and Philadelphia for the programs.

Robert Goralski, a former NBC White House correspondent, became information director for Gulf Oil Company and hosted interviews for that company.

Those early debates faded as TV stations, strapped for staff and resources, ultimately welcomed what came to be known as "video press releases." Instead of sending reporters to cover a story firsthand, stations would write their own copy around clips of video provided by corporations and public relations agencies. To preserve "journalistic purity," members of the Radio Television News Directors Association insisted that the video clips be labeled. The words "Courtesy Mobil" or a similar attribution was flashed briefly on the screen.[23]

Does airing video releases mean the news organization is trying to dupe you? No, but it may mean that it ignored (or, worse, missed entirely) another story because the video release filled the time sufficiently. It also may mean that what you saw spun the story in a way the diligent journalist would not have.

Scott Donaton, the editor of *Advertising Age*, says the use of what he calls "manufactured news" is spreading:

> A good chunk of the content on any given TV newscast represents either a calculated marketing effort by a third party or a TV station promotion masquerading as news. ("Next up, meet the real-life hero who inspired the made-for-TV movie we're about to show you.")[24]

Donaton used as examples three unrelated and subtle uses of TV news time to further marketing strategies: Michael Jordan's "retirement" from acting as a product endorser, John and Patsy Ramsey's book tour to defend themselves against those who say they killed daughter JonBenet, and the winter 2000 Twinkies shortage.

Jordan's announcement that he would not do endorsements without equity in the company he endorses put him in the spotlight that could have faded once he stopped sailing through the air with a basketball in his hands.

The Ramseys created a public relations coup with interviews by Barbara Walters on ABC and Katie Couric on NBC. The women conducting the interviews conjure family values and warmth, Walters as America's celebrity godmother and Couric as the nation's baby sister. In each case, the Ramseys portrayed themselves as the victims of JonBenet's murder and the botched investigation. NBC took the interview a step further into the marketing dimension by posting a transcript of Couric's interview on the *Today Show* Web site and allowing it to be accompanied by advertising from Barnes & Noble booksellers.

The ultimate proof of the bias against understanding came when a Teamsters Union labor dispute disrupted distribution of Twinkie snack cakes. When television and other mass media announced the dispute and a resulting shortage of Twinkies, consumers rushed the stores to buy what was left. Often above such trivial subjects, the *New York Times* must have obscured more meaningful news by devoting the better part of a page to the so-called strike. "Twinkies strike afflicts fans with snack famine," shouted the *Times* headline. The newspaper even published a recipe for homemade Twinkies. The makers of Twinkies couldn't have made a better advertising buy.

Attention for Sale

Sometimes the best advertising doesn't get bought in the traditional way. Instead it gets talked about. When advertising is the subject of news stories, there's a tendency to pay attention to the message that might otherwise be tuned out mentally if it appeared in a cluster of commercials.

Political advertisers know this very well. Produce a negative ad about a national opponent and the Sunday morning "news analysis" programs will run your commercial—free. Doug Bailey, the creator of Washington's daily newsletter *The Hotline*, was a political consultant when that line of work was practically unheard of. "Campaigns these days make many ads that will never or almost never run," Bailey said in a *Wired* interview:

> They are made in order to have a press conference about the ad, to show it to the media, hoping that the media will pick it up and put it on the nightly news. But the campaign doesn't put any dollars behind it. This frequently happens in Washington—they run the spot there and the media are supposed to assume that it's run throughout the world, which of course it never is.[25]

When Charlton Heston called President Clinton a liar in a National Rifle Association commercial, network newscasters fell all over themselves showing the spot. Then they'd interview a White House spin doctor, then Heston himself, then other NRA members, then other spin doctors. Who knows if the commercial ever actually ran? It did, but the coverage in newscasts and commentary was better than it would have been with a paid schedule.

The opposite happens, too. Ads take on a life of their own, regardless of attempts to counter them. Political strategists usually cite the 1988 commercials produced by the first Bush campaign that showed Democratic nominee Michael Dukakis in a military tank. Dukakis popped out of the hatch of the tank, attempting to strike a leadership pose. Instead he looked like an awkward prairie dog.

The film of the candidate was real. At some military exercise or another, Dukakis had, indeed, donned a helmet and appeared from the hatch. The text that accompanied the pictures attacked Dukakis on his position on national defense. One important note: The Bush message was false. Not just incorrect, blatantly false. An investigation by ABC News documented it. That caused Bush campaign operatives to call a meeting: Should they pull the ad since a major network had exposed their deception?

According to Bailey, the response was, "ABC is going to run that report once. We're going to run the ad 2,000 times. So let's keep it on the air." His theory: "If you run competent negative advertising, and your opponent does not answer it immediately with ads of his or her own, then your ads will be believed."

Political advertising people believe that premise. More ads are negative than positive. Key races at all levels of government are reduced to thirty-second shouting matches that perpetuate the bias against understanding. Given the downward spiral of voter participation, it creates a disconnect between the voters and the political process, too.

Big Increases Ahead

Watch television news and you'll hear stories of whopping profits for major corporations. Conversely, you'll hear stories of whopping losses. "Up 150 percent!" is typical of the statistics used, because superlatives make news. Because it's television, there's seldom time for an explanation.

In the blossoming economy of the turn of the millennium, superlatives were the norm. Companies grew at exponential rates, and profits escalated (that is, for those companies that actually had profits and not just mushrooming asset value). Hearing the words "Up 150 percent!" was not unusual.

Yet even in the 1970s, when government statistics showed that manufacturing profits in the previous twenty years had grown just over 4 percent on sales and just under 11 percent on stockholder equity, there were headlines shouting "Up 150 percent!" How could it happen in both situations? The headlines did not lie; they were just trying to get your attention.

The big percentages are not increases in profits, but the percentage change in profits from period to period, usually the change from the same quarter last year. The "same quarter, year ago comparison" is a technique widely used among stock brokers and in company reports on Wall Street.

When television takes even the most accurate percentage change from the *Wall Street Journal,* it easily confuses the magnitude of profits with the change of profits from year to year. TV's reporting on profits—and other matters of the economy—is often a gross exaggeration because big numbers are more newsworthy than little numbers.

The greater danger than the apparent inaccuracy of exaggeration is that people believe what they see on TV. Thus, good news makes people think corporations are doing better than they actually are. Bad news is even worse, because people get a negative view very quickly. The wired society is able to take shards of information and turn them into ringing cash registers or backlogs of unsold goods, virtually instantaneously.

The real trouble is that the economy—good or bad—is difficult to report accurately, because it requires two things the average reporter does not possess: time and context. Superlative comparison is much more quickly calculated than real profits (or losses) and how they fit into the overall picture.

During the oil crisis of the late 1970s and early 1980s, a Kuwait minister emerged from OPEC deliberations, stood before reporters, and said simply, "Arabian light at thirty-two."

"What's the current price?" shouted a confused American network correspondent, covering his first OPEC meeting. His colleagues answered him: "Thirty-four." The correspondent raced to the phone and told New York that OPEC was lowering oil prices. He didn't know that "Arabian light at thirty-two" meant that Saudi Arabia was raising its cheaper oil from $30 a barrel. It was an increase, not a decrease, and other OPEC nations would ultimately take the Saudi lead and raise their price by $2—from $34 to $36 per barrel.[26]

The stories in economic coverage are confusing at best. At worst, they are complex and abstract. Professional economists make them more baffling by talking in the jargon of Wall Street or of monetary management (as opposed to "money management," which we all deal with to one extent or another).

When credit card debt hit $400 billion in January 1996, that was a record level. That fact, coupled with credit card delinquencies at a ten-year high during the final quarter of 1995, caused news reports to predict a nasty recession. None came. The economy, in fact, got stronger and stronger.[27]

Conventional wisdom holds that high consumer debt means overextended consumers who may pull back their spending at any time. So when the Federal Reserve gathers information about credit card debt, it asks for the total amounts charged on cards in a given month. The total that January was much higher than previous reports.

However, the context of the increase offers insight and relieves anxiety: Credit card promotions offered consumers a variety of rewards to add additional cards: goodies including low interest rates, travel miles on a favorite airline, discounts on furniture, autos, or gasoline, and cash back at the end of the year. Higher delinquency rates resulted from these promotions, as lenders made cards available to less creditworthy households. The average U.S. household received two credit card offers *per month* during the years 1995 and 1996.

Only 44 percent of cardholders carried a balance at any given time. The others paid off the cards each month.

Television presents much of its news on the economy without context, and context is a great ally of understanding.

The Rich Are Getting . . . Attention

After some television news reports on the economy, a social activist is shown railing against the increased profits of large companies (even if the figures were actually same-quarter year-to-year comparisons). Somewhere in the sound bite you'll hear, "The rich are getting richer and the poor are getting poorer." It's been said often enough that people accept it as truth, just like the so-called rise in crime.

What's your reaction when you hear "the rich are getting richer"? What do you use as a comparison? Some of us think about wealth. Others think about their bosses or the presidents of their companies. Still others relate "riches" to their own personal income. These are all such different measurements that, unless context is given for the remark, we all make our own decisions on whether the statement is correct.

Wealth is the most difficult of the three to measure because it includes all assets—property, investments, insurance, and so forth. Given the complexity of the term, there's no way a sound bite on TV could explain or offer the depth of understanding needed.

Compensation for the heads of major companies makes terrific headlines and great promotion for *Fortune* and *Forbes* magazines. Any public company's annual report will give you some eye-popping numbers, especially during the recent boom fueled by the stock market. The compensation level for the average CEO is 200 times the average worker's salary. That's a difficult comparison, too, because this is a star system, with the CEO more akin to Michael Jordan and Ken Griffey Jr. than to the average worker.

Income is a fairer measure of the comparison between us, especially between rich and poor. According to a Rand Corporation report, between 1973 and 1993 the real income of the wealthiest 10 percent of the nation increased by 22 percent; the poorest 10 percent had a loss of 21 percent; and the 80 percent in the middle had an increase of 5.5 percent.

So the essence of the statement—"The rich are getting richer and the poor are getting poorer"—is true; however, everybody other than the poorest is in better circumstances.

There's an important point being missed: There will always be a bottom 10 percent, but the same people won't always be in the bottom 10 percent. We're a remarkably upwardly mobile society, and the composition of any cluster is constantly changing. To measure reality, we should follow the *same people* for twenty years, not statistics about where they were twenty years ago.[28]

The stories themselves create a bias against understanding, and the context in which they appear—television—allows the bias to proliferate. Television creates a unique context that strips its subjects of their contexts. Anything on TV is in the context of TV and only in the context of TV.

Similarities are as exaggerated as differences, and we lose our understanding of what each means. James Fallows says it well in *Breaking the News:*

> Half the news we read suggests that all "people of color" share an experience that is fundamentally similar, and also fundamentally different from

that of all whites. The other half of the news dwells on the deep differences that separate African Americans from Asian Americans from Arab Americans from Latino Americans, as well as the many caste and cultural splits within each group. Half the news out of Japan suggests that it is an unfathomably exotic culture, where the students kill themselves if they fail their entrance exams and people work frantically for the good of the state. The other half of the coverage suggests that Japan's government, business, and economies work by principles identical to those in America and therefore will respond to currency changes, election results, stock market trends, and so on, exactly as Western institutions would.[29]

The message of television is that the world outside our own is unfathomable and largely perilous, "a confusing and dangerous place filled with civil war and ethnic hatreds," says Tom Rosenstiel in the *Los Angeles Times*.[30] Most foreign flare-ups appear, then disappear from the newscasts so quickly that we develop a confidence that either they don't really exist, or, if they do, they'll go away just as quickly as they materialized. "We learn mainly to ignore them," says Fallows:

> Americans seeing the outside world on TV could be forgiven for believing that all countries fall into two categories: those that are so messed up we shouldn't waste time thinking about them, and those that are messed up in a way that threatens our security or moral sensibility, so we should invade them, withdraw quickly, and forget about them again.[31]

In the mid-1980s, international news made up nine minutes of the nightly news on TV. By the mid-1990s, the major networks spent an average of only six minutes of every evening newscast on news outside the United States. That's a significant reduction for news programs that run twenty-two to twenty-four minutes of total content. In the 1980s, "international news" meant social developments, political and diplomatic news, or economic trends. Today's "world news" involves natural disasters like typhoons and volcanic eruptions, shellings and other violence, or famine—especially if there are pictures of starving children. None of these stories offers insight or understanding as they flit through our media consciousness.

When Americans had the newspaper habit, there was time for understanding and room for learning. "Readers who cared could wallow in long gray columns about a worrisome war developing in Asia or reforms in the Soviet Empire," wrote Mort Rosenblum, the AP's chief special correspondent based in Paris. A *New York Times* editor told Rosenblum in 1975 that if only 2 percent of *Times* readers were interested in a story, the paper would run it.

"Television imposes a new imperative," Rosenblum admits:

> With broadcast news, a twinge of boredom can trigger the remote-control zapper. Ratings, i.e., survival, are at risk. Under television rules, the majority runs roughshod over any minority. Those citizens who want depth and subtleties about the world, however large a small slice they represent, are out of luck.[32]

Because Americans experience myriad choices in their media coverage, they've made a choice: They choose not to care about the outside world. Media don't offer the impression that the outside world relates to them. To some, "the outside world" is the international news that Peter Jennings, Mort Rosenblum, and their colleagues cover. To others, it's anything outside themselves—outside the personal world of their own creation. In any case, the consumer's position is, "If it doesn't relate directly to me, don't bother me with it."

The first victim of the profusion of information choices was the newspaper. Television became America's primary source for news in the 1960s as newspaper readership declined to 50 percent of the population. Then television itself fell victim. In a 1996 study, only 42 percent of the public said they watched a nightly network TV newscast, down from 48 percent in 1995 and 60 percent in 1993.

The report, from the Pew Research Center for the People & the Press, claimed that television news was in trouble with the American public and that "fewer adults are regularly watching it these days." The Pew Center proposed three reasons for the decline in viewership:

- Younger people turning away from TV
- Computer use preempting TV usage
- Lack of time

In a Knight Ridder/Tribune News Service story based on the Pew study, Jonathan Klein of CBS-TV said: "The pace of life is so hectic that people don't have the time to make an appointment to sit down every night to find out a lot of things they already know." Klein also said of television news: "We're not telling people the things they want to know or care to know."

Opinion of network news has also eroded. An independent nationwide survey conducted as part of the Pew Center study found that believability ratings for two of the four national news networks—ABC, CBS, CNN, and NBC—declined significantly from 1993 to 1996. (The Fox network was a relative newcomer and had no significant news operation in 1993, thus no comparison.)

The percentage saying they had watched TV news "yesterday" slipped to 59 percent in the 1996 survey. This percentage had been as high as 74 percent as recently as 1994. While the decline in television news viewing is most pronounced for the nightly network broadcasts, it was found for all TV news programming covered in the poll. Regular viewing of local TV news was still considerably higher (65 percent) than watching nightly network news, but lower than observed in 1995 (72 percent).

The dwindling television news audience was apparent in nearly all demographic groups and particularly evident among younger people. Network, local, and CNN audiences slipped the most among people under thirty years of age, followed by those thirty to forty-nine years of age.

The abundance of choices was a temptation for younger viewers. They turned from television to computers, according to an analysis of the Pew study:

> Declines in television viewing may be related to the increasing use of personal computers, which has grown markedly in the past year, particularly among younger people. The percentage watching TV news "yesterday" fell more among people who use computers and go online than among people who do not. Of note, reading a newspaper "yesterday" also declined to a greater extent among these groups, but was offset by increased readership among non-computer users. Listening to radio news, which often occurs while performing some other task, did not decline among computer users.[33]

Computer use allows these same consumers of news to be their own reporters and editors, choosing or avoiding the stories that don't relate to their personal construct of the world. The world as a flickering mosaic assembled from what's available from electronic media does not enhance understanding of what's going on around us.

Who Speaks for America?

When the Freedom Forum asked that question in 1998, it discovered that white men speak for America, at least in the context of television news. Conducted by ADT Research in conjunction with the Freedom Forum, the project analyzed six months of sound bites—everybody who was chosen to be quoted on weekday editions of the network TV nightly newscasts. Known as the tenth annual Women, Men and Media study, it showed that 87 percent of sound bites from "experts" on national newscasts were from men and 92 percent of those men were white.

However, those figures don't track with the real world. According to Census Bureau statistics, whites represented 72 percent of the population, but the study showed whites had 86 percent of all sound bites. Men and boys were 49 percent of the population, but had 76 percent of sound bites. Baby boomers, at 31 percent of the population, were represented in 52 percent of sound bites.

When the sound bites were divided into categories—Politicians, Experts, and Real People—further patterns emerged:

> Politicians, including government officials and newsmakers, had 18 percent of all sound bites and were mostly male—91 percent.
>
> Experts, including spokespeople, professional analysts and spin doctors, had 40 percent of all sound bites and were mostly white—92 percent.
>
> Real people had 39 percent of all sound bites and had a better overall mix, including women (41 percent), people of color (14 percent), children and teenagers (9 percent), young adults (10 percent), and the elderly (11 percent).[34]

Stereotypical TV

A report from a decade earlier said that America was very positive about what it said about women on television, but was considerably less positive about what it *showed* about women.

In a chronicle of television episodes over thirty-one seasons from 1955 through 1985, Robert Lichter and Linda Lichter of the Center for Media and Public Affairs and Stanley Rothman of Smith College tracked distribution, social background, and personal traits of 2,000 female characters.[35]

In general, women were a clear second to men. They were portrayed as the weaker sex, as less likely to be mature adults, and as holding lower status jobs.

The "good news" from the report seemed to be that women were only half as bad as men. Female characters committed only half as many crimes as males and were only half as likely to be portrayed as villains. Regardless of what women tried to accomplish in a given show, they were only half as likely as men to experience defeat.

Admittedly, the 1998 and the 1985 studies compare apples to oranges. One studies newscasts, the other programs. One was completed in 1986, the other in 1998. One chronicles television through three decades, the other focuses on one year's news output. Even so, they both show glaring biases in TV's portrayal of men and women. And they're just two of many sources of evidence.

Other studies yield the same result—that the dominant voice in American television is male. According to the Broadcast Education Association's (BEA) journal *Feedback:*

- A 1974 report in *Developmental Psychology* disclosed that female characters were underrepresented and most often stereotypically presented, a phenomenon described by Gaye Tuchman as "symbolic annihilation" in a 1978 essay.
- A 1989 study by Nancy Signorielli analyzed 20,000 TV characters and found they reflected an "aggregate image of conventionality, tradition, and status quo" through the decade of the eighties.
- A report by George Gerbner for the Screen Actors Guild and the American Federation of Radio and Television Artists in 1993 showed female impact lagging overall, as if there had never been a women's movement.

The fact doesn't escape the children, either, according to the same BEA study. The 1995 research showed that children aged nine to twelve perceived more boys than girls on television programs aimed at them. Further, while both genders recognized the inequity, boys were more aware at younger ages that most of the characters are males.[36]

The children in the study said that the gender-role characterizations they saw on television were not significantly different from those they encountered in the real world. That was attributed to "cultivation hypothesis," according to the Gerbner report: "The more time one spends 'living' in the world of television, the more likely one is to report perceptions of social reality which can be traced to (or are congruent with) television's most persistent representations of life and society."

The conclusions from yet another study corroborate and update the evidence. A 1997 study called "Reflections of Girls in the Media" had a simple synopsis: Men work and women date. Conducted for the Kaiser Family Foundation and Children Now, the study reviewed six media favored by teenage girls: TV shows, TV commercials, movies, music videos, teen magazines, and print advertising. Girls and women were frequently depicted as intelligent, honest, and capable of solving their own problems. At the same time, girls and women were more likely to be cast in roles where romance is more important than work and where beauty is the yardstick for measuring their value.[37]

Later that same year, Susan Douglas, author of *Where the Girls Are: Growing Up Female with the Mass Media*, reviewed the 1997–98 television season for *TV Guide* with an eye towards gender bias. She complained of "the endless parade of women no wider than a wheat stalk, the relentless emphasis on sex, and the sheer dearth of positive role models for girls." She quoted research by Dr. Jane Brown at the University of North Carolina showing a relationship between viewing programs full of sex and promiscuity and becoming sexually active at an early age.[38]

Parents were complaining, Douglas wrote, but parents weren't alone. Girls themselves, in a study done by the children's advocacy group Girls Inc., told interviewers "there is way too much sex" on TV and not enough shows in which girls have adventures. Douglas reminded readers that "just because teen girls are in a show doesn't automatically mean you would want your daughter to watch." She cited *Dawson's Creek* and *Beverly Hills 90210* as examples of shows "utterly awash in preposterous sexual titillation."

Television personality and author Steve Allen obviously agreed. He lent his name and support to an organization called The Parents Television Council. In full-page newspaper ads, he asked, "Are you as disgusted as I am at the filth, vulgarity, sex and violence TV is sending into our homes?"[39]

Poll Watching

Instant pictures, instant replay, instant analysis. Now, instant opinions and instant polls.

It seems there's a new poll every day giving some set of figures in an attempt to quantify our lives: 41 percent fear snakes; 26 percent fear public speaking; 61 percent are satisfied with their bank; 30 percent do their shopping on weekends; 79 percent support nuclear energy.

Survey research is a way of life, a means to intelligence about consumer behavior and attitudes. Business and media rely on research for planning and advertising. But, somehow, the word "poll" took on a negative connotation, the result of spin doctors using research data to manipulate our understanding of the underlying trends that surveys uncover.[40]

The results of polls can be distorted too easily. Twist a word in the question and the story changes, undermining understanding. Take one of the figures from a few paragraphs back: "79 percent support nuclear energy." It came from a 1994 Bruskin/Goldring survey of 1,000 U.S. adults. Critics of the nuclear energy industry say the figure is actually 13 percent. Both figures are right. It depends on your predisposition.

The poll asked a series of questions and elicited these responses:

- 79 percent said they favored keeping the option open to build more nuclear energy plants.
- 68 percent said nuclear energy should play an important part in the nation's electricity-generating mix.
- 52 percent said they favored the use of nuclear energy in the country's electricity-generating mix.
- 13 percent said they favored building more nuclear energy plants.

The same research was used by both proponents and opponents of nuclear energy to prove their points. Some media outlets used the same data in two conflicting stories, according to *Reputation Management* magazine.[41]

Here's another story of data in conflict. In 1992, 80 percent of Americans seemed to endorse spending on foreign aid. Was it true? The U.S. Agency for International Development (AID) said it was, and they had polling results to prove it. The agency, the federal bureaucracy that dispenses foreign aid, selectively reported favorable poll results and carefully ignored those that were not so favorable.

The question in question: Should the United States "share at least a small portion of its wealth with those in the world who are in great need?" Americans are by and large a charitable lot, so 80 percent of them said "yes," to no one's surprise. So the AID reported "Americans support spending on foreign aid." Newspaper after newspaper echoed the story.

But that question was not about foreign aid; it addressed helping the needy. Other data in the same study was conveniently ignored. For example, 75 percent said there's "too much" foreign aid; 64 percent suggested cutting foreign aid. Asked if they felt that aid never gets to the people who need it, 83 percent said "yes." Those figures weren't reported until the *Wall Street Journal* exposed them in an article titled "How to Rig a Poll." Clearly, the *Journal* took offense at AID's sleight of hand, and so it should.[42] AID might have made its case more effective by releasing *all* its poll results.

Legitimate polls are undermined by news like that and by advertising and political surveys that are blatantly biased. For example, these questions from what was described as a "National Public Safety Survey" were sent to homes nationwide:

> The latest FBI statistics reveal that 53 percent of murders are now committed by "strangers or unknown persons" and that a staggering 70 percent of all murders involve guns. How concerned are you about the escalating gun violence in this country?
> ____ I am extremely concerned and I want to do something about it.
> ____ I am concerned, but I feel I can't do anything about it.
> ____ I'm not concerned.

That "poll"—full of similar loaded questions—was distributed by Handgun Control, Inc., which ended the "questionnaire" with a solicitation for contributions.

Consider these questions from the "1995 Presidential Poll":

> Do you favor or oppose Republican plans to make huge cuts in entitlement spending, including $270 billion in reductions in Medicare which will force the average Social Security recipient to spend almost half of his or her

COLA just to cover resulting higher out-of-pocket Medicare costs?
( ) Favor ( ) Oppose ( ) Undecided
Do you favor or oppose Republican proposals to dismantle Head Start and programs that provide health care and nutrition to young mothers in poverty?
( ) Favor ( ) Oppose ( ) Undecided
President Clinton has proposed a balanced budget plan that doesn't place the burden on the backs of our nation's senior citizens. His plan protects Social Security, ensures the future of Medicare as a part of health care reform, and calls for real cuts in other areas of government—while opposing tax cuts for the wealthiest Americans. Do you favor this plan?
( ) Favor ( ) Oppose ( ) Undecided

That's a lot of highly charged deck-stacking. Phrases like "huge cuts," "dismantle," and "doesn't place the burden on the backs of our senior citizens" are downright pandering.

The "Presidential Poll" was no poll at all! It asked for contributions—to the Democratic National Committee. Are you surprised? It even had a check-off box for non-takers: "No, I can't become a DNC member right now, but I would like to make a special contribution of $10.00 to help defray the cost of processing the critical Presidential Poll." No wonder "polling" gets a bad name![43]

"I hate the word pollster," said one of America's leading pollsters, Daniel Yankelovich. "If you think about it," he said, "the word pollster goes with shyster or mobster or something. There's this idea that a pollster is a gun for hire by a politician, someone who then becomes part of a group helping to manipulate people."[44]

He's right. Polling is simply a matter of getting instant feedback from the marketplace, but the word "research" sounds better. Polling conjures some binary answer: Smith or Jones for governor. Yes or no to the council's proposal. More gun control laws or fewer.

Tactics like that reinforce bumper sticker mentality and strengthen the bias against understanding. They don't provide insight on an issue or understanding of people and their attitudes. While there's no reason to believe it's true, the word "polling" conjures "fad" and the word "research" indicates "trend." Fads get all the press. Fads are fashion. Fads are on MTV, in *People* magazine and on *Entertainment Tonight.* Fads are short-term.

Trends, on the other hand, take place over time. Months, even years go by before trends show themselves. The variation from measurement to measurement is often so insignificant that it's perceived as no variation at all. Trends are not the stuff that news is made of. For journalists, the worst possible news is a story that looks the same as yesterday's or last year's story. The news business craves change. It's news if it's startling. It's news if it stands out from the drone of the familiar. The cardinal sin of the news business, especially the television news business, is boredom.

As commentator Jeff Greenfield puts it, "We are all, put bluntly, 'trendaholics' looking for significance in every twitch of the national visage." The tendency ("tropism," declares Greenfield) has been magnified by the sheer number of writers attempting to be first to spot a new trend. If they can't identify it themselves, they want to be the first to take credit for it.

Greenfield says trendaholism explained the approach to the first few months of the Clinton presidency:

> Forty-eight hours after the inauguration, it's in 'disarray.' After the first speech to Congress, he's FDR. After 'hairgate' and 'travelgate,' he's on the verge of impeachment. After the healthcare speech, he's Thomas Jefferson.[45]

Any president now gets the same treatment as the press sniffs for the "big story," usually some triviality that obscures the reality of what's actually happening. The mass audience is so fragmented that any story construction that reconvenes it for even a moment is a victory.

Specific to the Clinton administration, Bill Kovach and Tom Rosenstiel believe that the stream of accurate and reliable information about Clinton's intern scandal was diluted with innuendo and pseudofacts. In *Warp Speed*, a book about what they call "the Mixed Media Culture," Kovach and Rosenstiel say, "It partly explains why the impeachment left so many Americans estranged, as if it were a TV show rather than a political crisis."

There are five main characteristics of the Mixed Media Culture that perpetuate the bias against understanding:

1. The never-ending news cycle. Kovach and Rosenstiel say the continuous news cycle makes the press choose allegations over truth. "Stories often come as piecemeal bits of evidence, accusation, or speculation—to be filled in and sorted out in public as the day progresses." The viewer becomes the interpreter of the news.
2. Sources are gaining power over journalists. They can shop stories from outlet to outlet to get the best play. Sources set the time frame and often demand anonymity. Say Kovach and Rosenstiel, "This shift in leverage toward those who would manipulate the press is partly a function of intensifying economic competition among a proliferating number of news outlets—a matter of rising demand for news product and a limited supply of news makers."

3. There are no more gatekeepers. While one news organization wrestles with corroboration, another runs with the story without corroboration. There's a much wider range of standards of what is publishable and what is not. "In practice," Kovach and Rosenstiel say, "the lowest standards tend to drive out the higher." The news consumer is left to wonder what is fact and what is speculation, even to assume it's all true. Or all false.

4. Argument overwhelms reporting. The reporting culture gathers and verifies information, but the "argument culture" makes a more interesting TV show. The rise of twenty-four-hour news outlets gives parallel rise to the need for content to fill the time. The pundit fills the time much more effectively and inexpensively than a staff of reporters and corroborating editors.

5. The "blockbuster" mentality. "As the audience for news fragments, outlets such as network television that depend on a mass audience are increasingly interested in stories that temporarily reassemble the mass audience," say Kovach and Rosenstiel. Celebrity, scandal, sex, and downfall are the keys to the big story. A combination of them all makes the story even bigger.[46]

During the investigation of the Watergate break-in and the resulting cover-up and scandal in the Nixon administration, the *Washington Post*'s Ben Bradlee established a rule for Bob Woodward and Carl Bernstein: Nothing could be used from an anonymous source unless it was confirmed by a second, independent anonymous source. It was not only good advice: it was the standard for reporting for more than two decades. It died when the twenty-four-hour news cycle was invented. The constant craving of the news machine consumes content at a rate never before experienced. Content is a more valuable commodity than accuracy.

By the time of the Clinton intern story, 83 percent of the stories relying on anonymous sources made no reference to the source's allegiances or biases, so the public had no way to know how the so-called source related to the story. More than 40 percent of stories about Clinton and Monica Lewinsky referred simply to "sources" with no other characterization. Kovach and Rosenstiel say that the press was not sufficiently skeptical:

> Journalists have acknowledged privately that at least some of the sources for some of these press accounts were not those directly involved in seeing the president and Lewinsky or even the investigators or prosecutors directly involved in the case. While a news organization may have two sources on a story, how much direct knowledge do those sources need to have before one can trust that a story has been verified?[47]

Careful corroboration takes time. And in today's media environment, speed is more valuable than accuracy. Lack of corroboration goes beyond the bias against understanding. It creates a bias against information itself.[48]

Proliferation of the Bias

With the rise of Internet distribution of what people call "news," the opportunities for misunderstanding are even greater. Self-interpretation is the rule for online distribution, and editing is done both by selection and exclusion.

So much of what is passed off as "news" online is little more than gossip, rumor, speculation, or opinion. Nothing wrong with any of those if they're appropriately labeled, but online, the labels fade, if they appear at all.

Any technology that makes good things easier will also make the bad things more convenient. The Internet is no different, and the Internet does not have a gatekeeper between the bad and the consumer, especially when it comes to the news.

News isn't gossip or uninformed speculation. Real news, the traditional definition, is the thorough investigation of a situation by professionals who aren't involved in the stories themselves and who maintain their objectivity as they investigate. Traditional news reports have the advantage of review by an editor, who can place the new development in a context that aids understanding.

Online, there's little reporting, little editing, and no context. That's how friendly missile fire got into the story about the crash of TWA 800. That's how President Clinton had an encounter with a "second intern." The stories were just wrong.

Even traditional news organizations get caught in the speedup of the news cycle by online transmission. The *Dallas Morning News* reported on its Web site that there was a third-party witness to Clinton and Lewinsky in the oval office. By the time the paper had corrected the story and pulled it from its online editions, MSNBC, CNN's *Larry King Live,* and ABC's *Nightline* had reported it.[49]

The Clinton saga generated a remarkable number of stories that appeared in cyberspace without facts being checked. For a complete analysis of the sequence, see Bill Kovach and Tom Rosenstiel's *Warp Speed.* It offers not only their take on the speedup of what passes for news in the age of mixed media but also analysis from the Committee of Concerned Journalists on how the Clinton-Lewinsky story was reported with little regard to fact.

It was during Monicagate that the balance of power for breaking news shifted from traditional media to online "publishers." The first news of the Clinton scandal was on the Drudge Report Internet site, regarded only as a Washington gossip site before the intern story and as gospel to some afterwards. *Newsweek* had the Clinton story ready, but decided not to release it until their editors checked additional facts. So *Newsweek* was scooped by "editor" Matt Drudge, who felt little need to corroborate his stories.[50]

Lack of corroboration leads to embarrassing situations. For example, comedian Bob Hope was very much alive on the day in 1998 when members of the U.S. House of Representatives eulogized him. The legislators were reacting to an obituary accidentally posted by the Associated Press, an organization whose news reports have been considered irrefutable for decades. The culprit? An errant keystroke.[51]

Later in 1998, investors received an early release of important data from the U.S. Bureau of Labor Statistics (BLS) because an alert market analyst found the information posted earlier than expected on the BLS Web site. The analyst first told the BLS, then he told his clients and the Bloomberg Business News service. That gave those with the information a half hour's head start—and fortunes can be made and lost in a half hour on Wall Street. It was a mistake, said the BLS, another errant keystroke.[52] But too late. Because of the Internet's ability to disburse information in nanoseconds, a story once released is difficult to retract. Mistakes travel with lightning speed.

The unsettling fact of life in the digital age: The Internet allows the general public to tap into sources once used only by journalists and government officials. That's democracy at its best when there are no mistakes. Yet misinformation and disinformation are aided and abetted by unsuspecting Web surfers who pass stories that interest them along to long lists of e-mail correspondents. Those recipients, in turn, send the messages to their friends and family.

"Everyday Americans starting down a trail blazed by traditional journalism," says *Wired* magazine, predicting that the line between professional journalists and the rest of us will be blurred, perhaps even erased.[53] On the Internet, everybody is a publisher, yet no one is held accountable. What begins as opinion is accepted as fact and ultimately becomes belief.

Futurist Alvin Toffler calls cyberspace "the technology of deception": "The dark side of anything delivered over the Web is that you cannot trust it. It is open to all kinds of manipulation, and it does not have the kind of filters" that newspapers and traditional media have. Toffler expects the situation to get worse as the Internet—specifically, the World Wide Web—mixes entertainment and news content with sophisticated special effects. "The more that technology makes deception possible, the more widespread is the adoption of a kind of post-modernist idea that there is no truth."[54]

We live in an era when it's easy to believe in anything because we've learned not to examine the beliefs closely. Guardian angels. Alien abduction. Friendly fire against a passenger aircraft. Truth is elusive enough when there's time to contemplate it. In our warp-speed environment of proliferating electronic media, truth is in deep trouble. Trust has been undermined, and the media consumer longs for something to believe, even if he has to create it himself.

Chapter 4

Seeds of Disconnect

Ivy is twenty-eight, six feet tall, and weighs 128 pounds. Her hair is platinum white and covers her ears and, sometimes, her pouting face. She's British, and her blood type is AB.

Her height is exaggerated by spike heels on boots that climb her long legs well above the knees. In one of her wardrobes, the boots are tied to a skimpy leather body suit that shows enough flesh to be titillating. In another, a tight-fitting red costume, she's ready for colder weather.

Ivy wears long leather gloves that stretch to the shoulder. In her right hand is a snake-like whip with metal arrowheads at the joints. The long glove on her left arm is covered by an additional glove of golden armor.

At the risk of dampening fervor, you need to know that Ivy doesn't exist. Sorry if you were enticed. She's a character in the computer-based combat game, Soul Calibur.

In Soul Calibur, your hero (e.g., Ivy, a foe of evil) roams the world, collecting points by winning battles you control. Working together, you and Ivy might face an arena overrun with poisonous rats. If she cannot meet the challenge, you enlist other heroes like Mitsurgi or Taki to take on lizard men or, possibly, an invisible opponent.

A reviewer in *Time Digital* was rhapsodic about Soul Calibur, calling it the "first fight game to realize fully our Homeric passion for epic one-on-one conflict." Obviously, Homer wasted his time passing *The Iliad* and *The Odyssey* through the generations if all we need to vent the passion is a computer, a joystick, and a little privacy.

Games enthusiasts call Mortal Kombat, Street Fighter, and the like "a great way to work off aggression." It's true that only bits and bytes are killed when you play a computer game, not people (or lizard men). In fact, Soul Calibur makes it a point to remind you that, if your character is defeated, he or she will live to fight again. ("Sophitia was seriously wounded, but the soul still burns," intones a booming voice.)[1]

Yet the same games also teach aggression and whet the appetite for blood and mayhem, don't they? J.C. Herz says no. "It's a kind of moving comic book which has lurid, over-the-top comic book violence," says the author of *Joystick Nation*. "There was not a spike in ritual decapitations when 'Mortal Kombat' came out," she explains. "I don't think when a kid is playing 'Mortal Kombat' it corresponds to any kind of real-world experience, because the characters have six arms and breathe fire. It's just so cartoonish."[2]

Soul Calibur changes that, because Ivy and her combative colleagues are not cartoons in the Saturday morning television sense. They're crafted so carefully that *Time Digital* says they are "rendered like a Greek god—not a pixel missing, hair fluttering realistically in the breeze. An epic symphonic score accompanies the battle; no redneck rock here." It goes on to describe the weapons as "wielded with such beautiful, dexterous precision that you'll think the Bolshoi Ballet has been motion-captured in close-arm combat."[3]

No wonder parents worry about their kids and games! But Herz defends kids, saying they're not attention-deficient or morally decayed just because they spend their time at arcades piloting virtual helicopters to hunt and destroy virtual terrorists in New York City (in the game Gunblade). "Besides," Herz says, "only 40 percent of the people in an arcade are actually playing the games at any one time. The others are watching or talking to each other."

Herz thinks parents who complain about kids and games are really complaining that the kids always win. "When your seven-year-old wipes the floors with you, there's a tendency to say, 'I don't know about these video games. There must be something nasty about them.' They're a threat to parental control."[4]

They're a threat to parental connection. They're a threat to time and attention. Take the case of "Phlendar," the online pseudonym of a fifteen-year-old computer game player profiled by the *Wall Street Journal* in a special Internet section.[5] Phlendar, "Phlen" to those he chats with online, spends hours of his high school career online playing Quake.

The *Journal*'s description captures the essence of the world of games, the reason parents are right to be wary:

> "I've got a double-barreled shotgun, a grenade launcher and a super nail gun," he boasts, his fingers twitching at the keys. "I can't be killed." He launches a grenade at an opponent—another Quake player linked via the Internet from halfway around the world—whose limbs break apart in a spray of blood as his head thuds onto the ground like a ripe tomato.

Phlendar, in real life Brian Wisotsky of Brooklyn, is described as "quiet and soft-spoken" until he grabs the joystick and encounters his unseen rivals in cyberspace. "I find it easier to trashtalk when I'm killing someone," he says. In a chat room on Mpath, he writes, "Feel like losing? I wanna see your insides all over the floor!" adding a sideways smiley face [:)] to soften the insult of bravado that springs from an imagination safely ensconced in a Brooklyn bedroom, not threatened with a challenge to its authenticity or its identity.

No parental dismay here. Phlendar is encouraged in his pursuit of guts and gore by his father, Mark Wisotsky, also a computer gamer, who claims about fifteen hours a week playing Quake and other games. "The violence is so unreal, it's funny," says dad. "Anyone with half a brain in their head can't take it seriously." Even if he doesn't take the violence seriously, given the nightly number of hours he spends, young Phlendar takes his gaming seriously.

Online gamers are connected to each other in ways no previous generation ever experienced. From opposite sides of the world, they slay the same monsters and splash the same caverns and passageways with the blood of the vanquished.

Wives of adult male gamers find themselves fighting for attention equal to the time their spouses spend online. The game Air Warrior spawned such intense passions and long sessions among its players that frustrated spouses formed an online support group, the Coalition of Air Warrior Widows.[6] One night a week, they kick their husbands off the keyboard and take over for an online chat session.

Are gaming and chatting real connectivity? Only in the most literal sense. In most cases, those "connected" don't know each other. Many take pains to keep it that way. Online communication often takes place behind alternate identities. Remember, he's "Phlendar," not "Brian." Chat rooms are rife with aliases (that is to say, "chat handles"): "Oblivious Child," "Agnostic w/o a Cause," and "Cyber23," to cite three of many millions.

They say that chat rooms are a great place to meet people, and the Air Warrior Widows are a good example. So are those online connections built around stroke survivors and other health matters, families scattered around the globe, or—as discussed before—communities as unique as embroiderers and nude skydivers. Many people in the Internet community socialize online with positive outcome and emotional attachment. The Web portal Geocities was an early manifestation of organizing online communities. America Online took the idea an exponential step further, allowing users to join existing content groups or to establish new communities via chat rooms that attracted like-minded surfers. By concentrating on specific subject matter, AOL aggregated millions of subscribers.

From Surfer to Stalker

Then there are chat rooms where meeting people is dangerous. Anonymity attracts the wrong kinds of people. How many stories have you read about chat room participants who discovered too late that a connection made in a chat room was a dangerous encounter? Typical is a thirty-year-old woman who began correspondence with a man in a chat room, then lost touch with him. After a few months, the woman found a flesh-and-blood boyfriend and began exchanging notes with him in another chat room. The first man reappeared and began threatening both the woman and her new boyfriend, finding her e-mail address and sending angry messages.[7]

She was lucky. She never met the man. She was able to contact his Internet service provider and interrupt the flow of vitriol. Others have arranged dates with chat room correspondents only to discover dangerous liaisons instead of the loving Adonis they had hoped to encounter.

Reams of personal information are available to a person who wants to use it for the wrong reasons. Offer too much information online and the casual cyberchatter may turn serious stalker. The problem reached such proportions that organizations like The Guardian Angels offer online courses in cybersafety, a kind of self-defense class. Another organization, SmartDate, offers women a registry for their dates, so if there's ever a missing persons report on a SmartDate member, the registry has information that could be helpful.

Michael J. Wolf expands upon this unfortunate commentary on society in *The Entertainment Economy*:

> Despite the fact that the Internet can connect us in ways that previous generations never experienced, one of the attendant costs of the autonomy that the digital revolution has brought is alienation. We spend more and more time one-on-one with technology (watching TV, working on the computer). This abets the process of social fragmentation that has broken down the multigenerational family and the communal workplace. We are, and have been for some time, what Harvard sociologist David Riesman first called "a lonely crowd."[8]

Separation and alienation. From 1998 to spring 2000, the time that the average Internet user spent online rose from 4.4 hours a week to 7.6 hours a week. Robert Wright jokes in a *Time* magazine essay that if that annual rate of growth continues, in 2025 the average Internet user will spend 590 hours a day online![9] Wright, the author of *Nonzero: The Logic of Human Destiny*, admits that extrapolation has its limits as a predictive tool, but there's no denying (and no joking) that cyberspace is absorbing more work time, playtime, and social time.

This expanding cyberculture simply does more of what it's done already: nourishing specific, self-indulgent, even narcissistic enthusiasms. In search of community and shared experience, the surfer of the future will find less to share and more to call uniquely his own, because the medium will be tailored exactly to specifications. The more sites that appear online, the easier it is to find your own special interest, no matter how special, no matter how narrow.

As bandwidth grows so that the online experience is virtually instant, narrow interests will become more attractive. As online use grows, obsessions will become online obsessions. This is the big downside of the future, says Wright:

> Obsessions are fine, but every minute you spend online—playing chess, talking politics, or just shopping—is a minute you're not spending off-line. And it is off-line, in the real world, where we find a precious social resource, people we have little in common with. The supermarket check-out lady, the librarian, the shoppers at the mall—all are handy reminders of the larger community we're part of—multi-cultural, socioeconomically diverse yet bound by a common nature.
>
> That's the trouble with cyberspace. It leaves nothing to chance. The Internet, with its antlike order, is in some ways becoming a Web of gated communities. It could deepen cultural and socioeconomic rifts even to the point of straining a nation's social fabric.[10]

The Internet, however, has no monopoly on obsession. Many bookstores assist the obsessed in finding the objects of their interests or fetishes. Magazines and catalogs proliferate with odd specificities that most of us cannot contemplate.

The least of the manifestations is the boom in erotica. Spending on sex-related items increased rapidly through the 1980s and 1990s. Because of fears of sexually transmitted diseases, people disconnected from their sex partners and bought paraphernalia instead. The range of substitutes runs from hard-core pornography and sex toys to reasonably tame romantic novels, which have grown to almost half of paperback book sales.

Instead of a Friday night date, consider this scenario for Sasha, a thirty-year-old single lawyer, described in the far-from-sexually-oriented *American Demographics* magazine.

> [She] takes off her business suit and satin underwear, massages herself with organic blue corn lotion, puts champagne into an ice bucket, slides

into a chiffon negligee, lights lavender-scented candles, and slips a new-age pornographic video into the VCR. In her night-table drawers are a vibrator ordered from a mail-order catalog, three romantic novels, and a box of condoms.[11]

Online Sasha could buy all the accoutrements needed for her Friday night's self-indulgence. She could even find a digitized substitute for Eric, her former lover of two years. Maybe the digitized version of Eric sounds like fantasy to you. Within a decade, cyberspace is expected to be rife with computer-generated simulations and animated characters that are indistinguishable from real people.

Martin Hash, the visionary behind Animation: Master, a software package for 3-D character animation programs, expects the Internet to yield a multibillion-dollar market for animation. "Only one person in 10,000 will purchase a $199 animation program," he told *Wired*, "but anyone will pay a nickel for five minutes of entertainment." The entertainment we get for our nickel will involve "a fantasyland for people with no life," to use Hash's words. "It will be for those of us who always wanted to be whisked into the land of the Hobbits, with all the trappings but less of the make-believe."

As interactive as the builders of Web sites want you to be, reality may be more like today's television. "Passive entertainment will still predominate because most people are basically lazy," says Hash. He believes some individuals will squelch their own personalities for those of their adopted personas. "Addictive behavior that prevents them from assuming real-world responsibilities must be expected and planned for." This provides one more opportunity for fantasy to take hold and to disconnect the fantasizer from the rest of the world. As Hash puts it, "People with an otherwise dull, mundane, unexceptional life could become whoever they want to be in the anonymity of Net culture. It's amazing how the brittle mantle of civility is shattered if even the thinnest veil of anonymity is provided."[12] And anonymity is the best friend of the disconnected.

Civic Disconnection

What's the distance between disconnectedness and alienation? Not far, says Harvard's Robert Putnam in "The Strange Disappearance of Civic America," his lecture on the decline of social capital.[13] Putnam asserts that the rise of television and the decline of cultural connectivity are in such parallel that there's cause and effect between the two.

Putnam is onto something: The fallout from America's immersion in instantaneous communication is much greater than television itself, although there's no denying that television is metaphor for news on demand, for cultural icons, and for images that myths are made of. Because consumers have access to such an enormous welter of information on demand at any time of day or night, they have an illusion of control over their collection of knowledge. Closer study shows that all that is being controlled is time and attention, which disconnects people who think they're connected.

In an academic paper titled "Bowling Alone," Putnam called disconnect–ivity a "puzzling fact." He based the paper on his observation of people at bowling alleys. "When you're in a bowling league," he told *Details* magazine,

> Most of the time you're sitting around waiting for other people to bowl, and you're talking. And more of the time you're talking about the latest "Seinfeld," but occasionally you're talking about community issues with people you know well. I know it's a little extreme to say that the fate of the republic hangs on whether we join bowling leagues, but that is the kind of point I'm making. Democracy has to be about conversations among people who really know each other.[14]

In his research, Putnam found a negative correlation between the number of hours spent watching television and the number of hours spent in community activities: "Television has the capacity to make us more passive spectators. There is some experimental evidence that suggests that actually sitting in a dark room watching television changes our mental processes. People who grew up without TV are more likely to be involved in their community."

Putnam describes us as frightened of each other and therefore so isolated that we look for "some group of true believers to hook up with. That's where the militias come in," he asserts. "The militias are in some sense a response to the breaking down of our communities."

Militias are, perhaps, an extreme example, but certainly a very visible one. More subtle signs of community breakdown are low voter turnout and neighbors who don't know each other. Putnam cites time studies conducted in 1965, 1975, and 1985 to demonstrate that the amount of time spent on informal socializing was down by a quarter; time devoted to clubs and organizations was down by half:

> Membership records of such diverse organizations as the PTA, the Elks club, the League of Women Voters, the Red Cross, labor unions, even bowling leagues show that participation in many conventional voluntary associations has declined by roughly 25 percent to 50 percent over the last two to three decades. Surveys show sharp declines in many measures of collec-

tive political participation, including attending a rally or speech (off 36 percent between 1973 and 1993), attending a meeting on town or school affairs (off 39 percent), or working for a political party (off 56 percent).

In his lecture, he goes on to cite trends from the General Social Survey that also show a drop of one-quarter in group membership since 1972 and a drop of one-third in social trust in the same period. Putnam reminds his audience that the rise of groups like AARP, and the Sierra Club (which he calls "mailing list organizations") are not associations where members necessarily meet each other. Rather, he says, "Their members' ties are to common symbols and ideologies, but not to each other."

What's causing the decline of social capital and the personal disconnect? Here's Putnam's list of possibilities:

- Busy-ness and time pressure
- Economic hard times (or [the opposite] material affluence)
- Residential mobility
- Suburbanization
- Women in the labor force and . . . the stresses of two-career families
- Disruption of marriage and family ties
- Changes in the structure of the American economy [chain stores and the service sector]
- Vietnam, Watergate, and disillusion with public life
- The cultural revolt against authority (sex, drugs, and so on)
- Growth of the welfare state
- The civil rights revolution
- Television, the electronic revolution, and other technological changes

Putnam leans hardest on television and technology as culprits, showing evidence that all the other "usual suspects" may appear culpable at first glance, but not after investigation. Of time pressure, for example, he says that while we all feel pressured, time studies show we actually have *more* free time on average, not less. Women in the workforce, the disruption of family ties, the welfare state, and all the other possibilities have no cause-and-effect relationship on the decline of social capital, Putnam asserts.

The one factor that correlates to civic engagement is age. "Older people belong to more organizations than young people, and they are less misanthropic," Putnam says. "Older Americans also vote more often and read newspapers more frequently, two other forms of civic engagement closely correlated with joining and trusting."

Moreover, civic involvement tends to rise steadily from early adulthood to a plateau in middle age. That is, until the Baby Boom. Putnam uses evidence from the General Social Survey to plot generational cohorts: "As various generations moved through the period between 1972 and 1994, their levels of trust and membership more often fell than rose, reflecting a more or less simultaneous decline in civic engagement among young and old alike, particularly during the second half of the 1980s."

What was happening at the time, as Putnam explains, was a "period effect," when all people who live through a certain era manifest the same effect, regardless of their age. Since Americans of all ages changed their minds about leaders' trustworthiness between 1965 and 1975, there was a period effect. Same for the 1980s, Putnam says.

He also feels that being raised after World War II imposed quite a different experience from being raised before the war. "It is as though the postwar generations were exposed to some mysterious X-ray that permanently and increasingly rendered them less likely to connect with the community."

The "mysterious X-ray" is television.

"First, the timing fits," he says. "The long civic generation was the last cohort of Americans to grow up without television." By the 1970s, viewing time was on the increase, fueled by Baby Boomers. "This massive change in the way Americans spend their days and nights occurred precisely during the years of generational civic disengagement," says Putnam:

> Evidence of a link between the arrival of television and the erosion of social connections is, however, not merely circumstantial. The links between civic engagement and television viewing can be instructively compared with the links between civic engagement and newspaper reading. The basic contrast is straightforward: Newspaper reading is associated with high social capital, TV viewing with low social capital.
>
> Controlling for education, income, age, race, place of residence, work status, and gender, TV viewing is strongly and negatively related to social trust and group membership, whereas the same correlations with newspaper reading are positive. Within every educational category, heavy readers are avid joiners, whereas heavy viewers are more likely to be loners. In fact, more detailed analysis suggests that heavy TV watching is one important reason why less educated people are less engaged in the life of their communities. Controlling for differential TV exposure significantly reduces the correlation between education and engagement.

So each hour spent watching TV is associated with less social trust and less group membership, while each hour reading a newspaper is associated with more trust and more membership. In Putnam's words, "An increase in television viewing of the magnitude that the U.S. has experienced in the last four decades might directly account for as much as one-quarter to one-half of the total drop in social capital."

Putnam reminds us that television is the only leisure activity that inhibits participation outside the home, especially social gatherings and informal conversations. He also reminds us that, in his original writings, he laid the blame on television, but he said that TV was not the sole culprit. In spite of the footnotes and the reminders, Putnam makes a key point: TV viewers are homebodies, and their leisure time is privatized.

The more private we become, the more insular and the less tolerant of those outside ourselves. If the privacy of our entertainments is easy to come by, so is anonymity. The city hides us. The online handle allows a character to be created in our stead. We're free with our opinions but less willing to listen to others, especially others whose opinions may not align with our own. We've become a nation of blabbermouths, but with no one listening. One-liners take the place of conversation.

Reducing social engagement creates a corresponding increase in social offense, from crude language to road rage. Cars that resonate with a thunderous BOOM, BOOM, BOOM as they wait at traffic lights; boomboxes carried through crowded streets by kids on skates who challenge anyone to resist their velocity; young girls shouting obscenities—these are the result of the reduction of social engagement.

Dirty Words

Comedian George Carlin had developed a pretty good name for himself before the government used his material in a landmark decision. Once a San Francisco radio station played a recording of Carlin's stage bit in which he repeated words not allowed on the radio, his became a household name. In 1978, the U.S. Supreme Court upheld the ban on using those "seven dirty words."

What a difference two decades made! The seven specific words of Carlin's stage act are still banned from broadcast, but who can tell, thanks to rulings softened by time-of-day restrictions. Nonetheless, they're easily available throughout nonbroadcast media. The bad little boys of *South Park* on the Comedy Network use words far worse than the dirty seven.[15] And they exchange obscenities with a character that's a piece of talking excrement. Even the networks stoop to sexual double entendres on the most family-oriented shows. Count the references to "boobs" and other body parts on the average sitcom.

Advance notice for *The Blair Witch Project* characterized the film as the "scariest movie ever made." The film received more notoriety after release, this time for excessive use of the words "fuck" and "shit." Defenders said that the kids in the movie simply talked like college students. That's a telling remark in itself. Clearly those words sell tickets.

Any taboo we held about language has been eroded. Words referring to body functions and body parts (especially those involved in sexual expression) were once used only by intimate friends. Senator Daniel Patrick Moynihan coined a memorable phrase, "defining deviancy down," to describe how we legitimize behavior that was antisocial or even criminal. While the senator was referring to more than language, his phrase surely applies to those who feel it's a sign of toughness and sophistication to utter a stream of obscenities.

Hundreds of comedians make their way from stage to stage displaying more talent for the quantity of obscenities in their performances than for the quality of their humor. Two very funny men—Richard Pryor and Eddie Murphy—showed their relatively tame sides on TV and in film, but took obscenity to the extreme (for their time) on the stage. In the film *Trading Places*, Murphy used his knack for street language to advantage when he played a foul-mouthed black punk who was cleaned up, *Pygmalion*-style, to trade places with the offspring of a wealthy white financier. In that setting, the language creates its own context. Most obscene language is used for its shock value and is obscenity for obscenity's sake.

Comedian Chris Rock picks up where Pryor and Murphy left off. You can count two or more "fucks" per sentence in Rock's stage performance. Occasionally, the word is used to refer to copulation, but most often it's an expletive, a verb in a two-word sentence ending with "that." Like Pryor and Murphy, Rock is a very funny man. His concepts are truly humorous. His ability to hold an audience compelled is a rare talent. But words get in his way and create a disconnect between him and a larger following.[16]

Language is part of "signaling," discussed in Chapter Two. Rock and his colleagues who string gratuitous obscenities throughout their performances are saying, "This is not for you if you can't handle it." Yet the result is the same as Senator Moynihan's "defining deviancy down."

Based on field studies of language use, women and children are swearing more in public. Timothy Jay, a psychologist and author of *Cursing in America*, cites a 1992 poll by Teenage Research Unlimited that shows 52 percent of teens questioned thought that cursing was cool. While it's hardly a dramatic revelation, Jay confirmed that school-age youngsters pick up language habits from their peers and claimed that exposure to profanity in movies, on television, and in music expands the use of swearing among kids. A 1998 study by the Los Angeles-based Parents Television Council found that vulgar language on national TV had increased 47 percent in two years.

Not too many years ago, there was cause for celebration when *All in the Family* pushed the envelope of attitude on national television. The sterile, make-believe days of *Father Knows Best* yielded to a television industry that was allowed to project a sense of reality. Archie Bunker was a redneck and his son-in-law Meathead was the perfect foil. Similarly, *Saturday Night Live* was applauded for stretching the bounds of language, again, approaching a reality that its audience could relate to.[17] Television, after all, was the medium that composed camera shots carefully so that the *Ed Sullivan Show* audience wouldn't see Elvis Presley's gyrating hips. The tenuous steps taken by Archie Bunker's producers were tantamount to enlightenment. We've come a long way since Lucy and Ricky Ricardo slept in separate beds. For that matter, Rob and Laura Petrie slept in separate beds even more recently.

Now television does much more than push the envelope. The new boundaries move constantly, reconstructing TV's stories as way too real. The result is dysfunctional families venting their frustrations. That's the sitcom genre, not the TV talk show genre. The talk shows are beyond dysfunction. They're just national shouting matches.

The Age of "Whatever"

The envelope being pushed now is the envelope of good taste. And the envelope cannot stand up to the pressures of a culture losing its civility. A coarse society jeopardizes all respect, including self-respect. Columnist George Will calls it "Dennis Rodman's America," writing that "America has liberated itself from...what is now considered the tyranny of taste." Basketball bad boy Rodman could certainly qualify as the antitaste poster child, given his outrageous hair colorings, cross-dressing as a bride to promote his book, and carefully placed blows to a photographer working courtside at a basketball game.

Citing essays in the *Wilson Quarterly*, Will traces some of the history of American civility. Using uniformed ushers in theaters, for example, sprang from the need to get along in public after urban density took over from frontier society. Sometimes the ushers distributed printed rules—"No talking," for example. The rules of civility smoothed the surfaces.

Will reminds us that we no longer live on the newly refined frontier. Today's rude disconnect "occurs in a land where plenitude inflames the sense of entitlement to more of almost everything, but less of manners and taste, with their irritating imitations of authority and hierarchy."

We know Will as the conservative pundit of TV's weekend news shows. He's right on track for conservative and liberal alike when he calls the eclipse of civility "a fact fraught with depressing significance." Will quotes James Morris of the Woodrow Wilson International Center for Scholars:

In this age of "whatever," Americans are becoming slaves to the new tyranny of nonchalance. "Whatever." The word draws you in like a plumped pillow and folds round your brain: the progress of its syllables is a movement toward…a universal shrug. It's all capitulation. No one wants to make a judgment, to impose a standard, to act from authority and call conduct unacceptable.[18]

Here's what "whatever" means: rude and insensitive. The evidence is everywhere. Scott Donaton of *Advertising Age* called it "the *Maxim*-ization of American society," referring to the male-targeted magazine, *Maxim,* a sophomoric collection of locker-room humor for frat boys whom the magazine addresses as "real men." *Maxim* topped one million in circulation with "articles" like a party prank that involves covering a toilet seat in plastic wrap. The text talks about getting soaked and "if he has to take a dump, even better."

For Christmas 1998, Abercrombie & Fitch won a place in controversy's spotlight by filling its catalog with drinking games and mailing the catalog to college dorms. For 1999, the retailer moved from the bar to the bedroom by featuring sex tips from a porn star, a profile of a perverted shopping mall Santa Claus, and an interview with an actor who described how oral sex replaced alcohol in his life. So much for A&F's "preppy" image.[19]

Shock jock Howard Stern broke ground on the radio by comparing all of life to the size of his penis and reminding us that life hardly measured up. By taking such a bold lead in the battle against good taste, Stern inspired a decade of copy-cat disc jockeys who substituted for talent words their mothers would never let them use at the dinner table. Maybe they hope mother will never hear the show.

Radio has no monopoly on rude or crude. TV advertisers create their own disconnect from good taste. In commercials for Web retailer Outpost.com, gerbils are shot from a cannon, and a high school marching band is attacked by ravenous wolves. A young girl in another commercial hops into the front seat of her date's car and, while he's crossing around to the driver's side, she lets rip with thunderous expulsions of gas loud enough to embarrass a fraternity house. That commercial is designed to sell SmartBeep, a paging service. In yet another commercial, a guy sitting on a bus manages to take his jockey shorts off by pulling them down a pants leg. The viewer is left to wonder what that has to do with Excite, the Internet portal.

"It's the age-old question of breaking through the clutter," says Eric Silver, creative director at Cliff Freeman & Partners, New York, the ad agency responsible for commercials for both Outpost.com and SmartBeep. As it turns out, nothing's off limits and nothing's too nasty to exploit. In today's marketing, you use "anything you can to get noticed," says Silver.[20]

"Pop culture is always going to be a mixture of the uplifting and the re-volting," says Gary Edgerton, co-editor of the *Journal of Popular Film and Television*. "Stupid humor, physical humor, has always been part of pop cul-ture, but now it's all tied in with the bathroom and a 12–year-old's view of sexuality. We're really overdosing on that perspective now."[21]

He's right. We're getting more than our share of the revolting. Crude is in, and crass has gone middle class. Taste takes a back seat to popularity, espe-cially popularity as measured by ratings. Content quality no longer matters if there's an audience to aggregate. Marketers chase the audience, support the garbage, and then emulate it. There are some clear reasons:

1. Money. The networks' dominance is fragmented by ever multiply-ing cable channels, which have none of the same rules about ob-scenity or vulgarity. The result is a general lowering of standards to keep audiences from eroding further.
2. The young male. Two-thirds of all moviegoers are between twelve and twenty-nine years of age. Among teens, boys pick the movies. Girls tend to be tolerant of movies aimed at guys, but guys don't reciprocate. Adolescent males like bathroom humor, and movie ex-ecutives know that.
3. Teenagers. There are a lot of them—close to 24 million twelve-to-seventeen-year-olds. They have a lot of money. And it's all dispos-able income. They spend more than $100 billion annually, almost $4,000 each.
4. A puritan heritage. America has long been obsessed with and re-pelled by the body. We love to giggle, to point, and to be horrified. Polite society was based on the assumption that there were two sepa-rate and distinct worlds: the public and the private. TV tends to erase that difference.
5. The clutter of advertising. In today's media environment, the only way to get noticed is to scream louder. Obscenity cuts through the fastest.
6. Television and movie producers. They are terrified, worried so much about the bottom line and the successful formulas that they keep cranking out the same stuff over and over.
7. Connectivity. In the electronic environment, the rude and crude is amplified and dispersed instantaneously, so it's suburban and main-stream in a flash.

People have blamed the teenagers for going astray since the days of Socrates, yet teenagers are not alone in producing today's reduced civility, increasing rudeness, or deteriorating taste. According to Gary Edgerton, the new vulgarity gives us "permission" to tap into a twelve-year-old male that he says lurks in all of us, eager to get out and snicker at a rude or cruel joke. "We just went through a year of scandal in the White House, when it was hard to separate the talk shows from the real news," Edgerton says. "We're in a very down, very cynical period, and I think our entertainments reflect that."[22]

The ancient Romans, the raunchy Elizabethans, and the Americans of the Wild West notwithstanding, there have been periods in history—even our own history—when manners existed, people were polite in public, and sex was behind closed doors. The height of print culture was a time of "secrets," which fascinated the Victorians as well as Joshua Meyrowitz at the University of New Hampshire:

> The Victorians were fascinated with the multiple layers and depths of life: secret passageways, skeletons in the closet, masks upon masks upon masks. But the awareness of these layers did not push the Victorians to destroy secrecy, but rather to maintain and enhance it as an enriching aspect of the social order.

There might have been an occasional eye at the keyhole, but the rare glimpse was just a hint of the secrets that lay behind the titillation. Our age, in contrast, is fascinated by exposure. Skeletons that previously stayed in the closet are paraded via national television—daily if the skeleton's owner is famous. But once is enough, as Meyrowitz explains:

> The act of exposure now seems to excite us more than the content of the secrets exposed. The steady stripping away of layers of social behavior has made the "major scandal" and the exposure of the "deep dark secret" everyday affairs. Ironically, what is pulled from the closets that supposedly contain extraordinary secrets is, ultimately, the potential banality of everyone. The unusual becomes commonplace.[23]

Are manners possible today? There's a strong objection to manners by those who put individual self-expression above society's overall interests. Manners, some say, are artificial and hypocritical; it's wrong to be polite to people you don't know and have no affection for. Others say that manners are restricting, that they prevent us from being ourselves, making us subservient to a role from an etiquette book. A third view is that manners institutionalize inequality, for it was manners that kept the lower classes and women in their subjugated roles.

"Of course manners are artificial," writes Digby Anderson under the headline "Civility Under Siege" in the *Wall Street Journal:*

Of course they are hypocritical. And a good thing, too. Imagine a society where people were civil only when they had warm feelings for each other. It would be no society. Moreover, manners indeed restrict self-indulgence and assertion. This is not repression, however, but self-control. . . . And certainly manners restrict self-expression. But so does the learning of language restrict the babbling of a baby. It does so only to give him a common language the better to express himself with others who share it.[24]

Manners and laws keep a society in order. Senator Moynihan's "defining deviancy down" deserves repetition here. We now legitimize behavior previously regarded as unmannered. Fewer and fewer behaviors are considered antisocial or criminal. As James Twitchell points out in *For Shame,* "As deviancy is normalized, so the normal becomes deviant. When dysfunctional becomes the norm, the functional turns abnormal." Twitchell feels that, like deviancy, the same "defining down" has occurred with shame. As deep-seated as we may think shame is, he warns us, it can evaporate overnight:

Western culture, led by American popular culture, is rapidly removing central shaming events that developed over generations and replacing them with often trivial and short-lived concerns. Instead of viewing shame as a powerful socializing device, we see it as a hindrance to individual fulfillment. Of course shame inhibits behavior—that's the point. It retards action, it increases reticence, it invokes self-censorship. Of course it makes the individual feel bad. But it does so in the name of a higher social good. Shame is the basis of individual responsibility and the beginnings of social conscience. It is where decency comes from.[25]

Twitchell agrees with Putnam that there's a reduction in the shared sense of community. "Certainly this effacement of shame norms started with the industrial revolution," Twitchell says, "but it really picked up momentum in the 1960s with the advent of television."

In the days when manners and laws imbued us with a sense of shame, the novel carried the message. As Twitchell points out, you cannot read most nineteenth-century novels without a keen awareness of the social convention of shame. Consider Jane Austen, the Brontës, Thackeray, Poe, and the Russians, too, especially Tolstoy and Dostoyevsky. Dickens's prolific works are the best examples, "the *vade mecum* of shame in the novel," says Twitchell. The reading public of Dickens's time lined up ten deep to buy the latest installments of the shaming experiences he described.

Fast forward from the novel to the photograph, when "the life of any stranger became personal in a moment," to use Twitchell's words again. With the photo, we could stop human action, see it up close, examine it, and interpret it ourselves. "If not for the close-up, we might live today in a world where the only famous people are those who deserve to be on the basis of deeds," Twitchell says. The photo brought us pictures of shame and shamelessness side by side in newspapers that took advantage of the new technology.

Move forward again from the photograph to the motion picture, that world of "affronted senses and collapsed time" described by Matt Matsuda in Chapter One. The subject and its image became one, the "truth of illusions," Matsuda calls it.[26] Early motion pictures extended the Victorian-era message of shame. Ultimately, the movies undermined the message.

That brings us to today, where electronic media accelerate the deterioration of shame and manners. As already noted, we're certainly not ashamed of what we say. Nor are we ashamed of our attitudes toward shame. Some examples from New York City in the 1980s:

- Claus von Bulow was considered very fashionable after his first trial when he was convicted of trying to murder his wife. His fashionable image was tarnished by a second trial, in which he was acquitted.
- There was a junkie in a lower Manhattan park who kept many a yuppie alive by testing heroin and cocaine for drug dealers.
- When Borough President Donald Manes of Queens slashed his wrist in a suicide attempt, it inspired a work of art at a trendy gallery. (Manes tried again and died.)

Stories like these could come from any city. New York accumulates them by having more people to generate them.[27]

Another disconnect from shame: Asking "What mother wants an ugly child?" a fashion photographer set up a Web site to auction the eggs of beautiful models. Ron Harris, whose photos had appeared in *Playboy*, announced the site in 1999: "Choosing eggs from beautiful women will profoundly increase the success of your children and your children's children for centuries to come." He claimed a "serious bid" of $42,000 for one model's ovum. If the deal was consummated, Harris would get 20 percent as a finder's fee and his "angels," as he calls them, would get the bulk of the money.

For some time, geneticists have been working on and hoping to offer the world gene enhancement, the ability to add selective traits to an embryo. A few years ago, a California entrepreneur opened a sperm bank of Nobel Prize winners. Dozens of women responded, longing for the opportunity to deliver a genius. *Boston Globe* columnist Ellen Goodman reported an ad in a college newspaper offering $50,000 for the sperm of a five-foot-ten Ivy Leaguer with a combined SAT score of 1400.[28]

Greet any mother and her newborn, and you're likely to say, "The baby looks just like you!" New technologies and new ethics may disconnect us from annoying family traits like acne, baldness, or freckle-faced beauty. In a Harris poll, 43 percent of parents said they would use genetic enhancement to make their children more attractive. Impregnation with the sperm of a Nobel Prize winner may yield one result; the sperm of an NFL running back may yield something else entirely. And does the egg of Miss American insure beauty? What if the DNA doesn't reflect collagen injections, a nose job, and silicon enhancements? You could be stuck with a baby as ugly as your own.

There's more for sale online. Auction site eBay offered autographs of convicted killers, artwork from death row inmates, and personal items from other known criminals. The items for sale on eBay included wall calendars, clocks, T-shirts, and address labels with either names or pictures of infamous killers. More troubling to the families of crime victims were personal collectibles from the killers, such as handprints, letters, and autographs. A killer responsible for the deaths of at least eleven New York women offered a lock of hair for sale. Dirt from the crawl space under the home of John Wayne Gacy—where Gacy buried twenty-seven of the young men and boys he killed—sold for $22. A hand-drawn sketch of the crawl space had an opening bid of $75. Copies of victims' death certificates were part of one collection.

The most "famous" of the collections offered by eBay was from the murder of actress Sharon Tate. A set of photographs displayed stab wounds of Charles Manson's victims. One showed Tate with a rope around her neck. Opening bid: $28 for twenty-eight photos.[29]

Beyond poor taste, these items disconnect us from the seriousness of the crimes and allow the killers celebrity they don't deserve.

The Enemy Is Us

Every day the headlines bring additional evidence of disconnected America.

"Sixteen minutes, 13 dead, 21 wounded" was the stark lead of *USA Today*'s account of the report issued by the Jefferson County, Colorado, sheriff on the April 1999 massacre at Columbine High School near Denver.[30] The sheriff's grisly scrapbook followed the minute-by-minute detail of two boys' assault on their classmates, their school, and the sensibilities of a nation.

The offensive included enough explosives in two propane tank bombs to kill all 488 students in the cafeteria at the time of the attack. The devices malfunctioned, leaving the killers to perform individual executions. The day before the attack, one of the two, Dylan Klebold, wrote a detailed itinerary for the day: "Walk in, set bombs at 11:09, for 11:17. Leave, drive . . . & park.

Gear up. Get back by 11:15 park cars. Set car bombs for 11:18 get out. Go to outside hill. Wait. When first bombs go off, attack. *Have fun!*" ("Have fun" was underlined in the diary.)[31]

When the bombs didn't detonate, Klebold and his accomplice, Eric Harris, threw small bombs, hoping to ignite the larger ones. From 11:19 until 11:35 A.M., the two boys did what their failed bombs were supposed to do for them: kill students and then themselves. The events inside the school were completed in 16 minutes.

The official inquiry offered no conclusion about motives, but extensive writings from the two boys showed alienation and disconnection. As early as two years before the killings, the boys were writing about hating life, about not fitting in, and about suicide. Klebold wrote in Harris's yearbook about "killing enemies, blowing up stuff, killing cops!!" Harris had posted death threats on his own Web site.

Harris anticipated the analysis that would follow the murders and wrote his own story: "It's my fault! Not my parents, not my brothers, not my friends, not my favorite bands, not computer games, not the media, it's mine. I'm full of hate, and I love it."

A rash of school shootings seized the headlines before and after the massacre at Columbine High, although Columbine's was the most dramatic. The evidence of the plot by Klebold and Harris against their schoolmates was a chilling aspect of the crime. Days after Columbine, kids across the nation copied the process, posting threatening messages on Web sites and interrupting classes. None of the threats was as elaborate as the Columbine attack, and few actually yielded weapons.

Violence in the nation's schools shifted the attention parents paid to their dangerous and unruly offspring. Before kids began shooting kids, parents lived in fear that the uprising would be against adults. For decades, the worst-case scenario for our children was the image of Anthony Burgess's punks in *A Clockwork Orange,* the frightening narrative of a *bezoomny* gang of louts who spend their days attacking their elders, instilling fear (or *strack,* as it's called in Nadsat, the language Burgess designed for the book).[32]

The new wave of teenage violence in America's schools shifts the image in the minds of adults from Burgess's gang to William Golding's tale of original sin in *Lord of the Flies.* Absent any adult supervision, Piggy, Simon, Jack, Ralph, and the rest of the boys of the island fall from grace and turn upon themselves.

Burgess's punks had to roam the streets and underpasses to wreak their havoc. They lived in a world of someone else's making. Golding's boys had their own island, a community they developed themselves. At the end of *Lord of the Flies*, Ralph weeps for his "true, wise friend called Piggy." Golding said that Ralph wept for the end of innocence and the darkness of man's heart.[33]

Today's teenage terrorists are not moved to tears. "It's my fault" is admirable as confession, but self-serving and narcissistic. Left to their own devices, the Columbine killers concocted stories that they acted out in meticulous fashion. Products of the electronic age, they produced videos to exhibit the hate they proclaimed and cataloged their plans for attack online.

ABC-TV reported that teachers in other cities felt threatened by Web sites hosted by their students, their fears heightened by the specter of Columbine. Some were justified, because the postings were truly threats.[34] One woman called authorities when one of her students suggested that others "shun" her, which seems tame compared to the intricate plans for bombs and bloodshed developed by Klebold and Harris.

Gone are the influences of family, school, church, or culture to buoy sinking souls. Christopher Lasch writes that the modern family "is the product of egalitarian theology, consumer capitalism, and therapeutic intervention." In *The Minimal Self,* he claims that the replacement of family by "other socializing agencies" exposes children to new forms of manipulation:

> The school system, the child-care professions, and the entertainment industry have now taken over many of the custodial, disciplinary, and educative activities formerly carried out by the family. Their attentions to the child manage to combine the worst features of earlier systems of child-rearing. On the one hand, they reinforce the social segregation of the young that has always been so characteristic of bourgeois society, thereby depriving children of exposure to adult conversation, of practical experience of the world, and of participation in the community's work life.[35]

Lasch adds advertising to his list of substitutes for the family, claiming that advertising "further weakened parental authority by glorifying youth. Advertising, like the service professions, insisted that parents owed their children the best of everything while insisting that they had only a rudimentary understanding of children's needs." Lasch associates the neglect of children to the broader pattern of reckless use of natural resources and the pollution of air and water.

Writing in the seventies and early eighties, Lasch could not have known the full ramifications of the electronic media age. But his statements about "children paying a heavy burden for the new freedom enjoyed by adults" show that he knew what was coming:

> They eat junk food, listen to junk music, read junk comics, and spend endless hours playing video games, because their parents are too busy or too harried to offer them proper nourishment for their minds and bodies.[36]

Trusting Only So Far

So concerned are parents that they take up spying. In Altamonte Springs, Florida, just outside Orlando, a middle-aged working man spent his afternoon in the U-Spy Store looking over surveillance devices. The store typically provides equipment to restauranteurs who keep an eye on the cashiers or to business owners who want to watch the loading dock with video cameras.

On this particular day, however, the U-Spy Store had sold a recording hookup to a man who wanted to listen to his wife's telephone conversations. Another sale was to a family who wanted to use video cameras to watch the person hired to spray-paint their house. So the man in the blue shirt was not out of place at the surveillance counter. Stores like U-Spy attract more individuals these days, now that we've disconnected our trust from our fellow man, and that disconnect runs to husbands, wives, and children.

He stood in a room that was watching him while he studied the merchandise. The clock on the wall next to the door had a camera inside. The clock radio on the counter had a camera inside. The gooseneck lamp, too. He was lucky there was no fire: that was a camera, not a smoke detector, in the ceiling.

And the teddy bear the man was squeezing? That, too. The cute little stuffed animal decked out in western gear just happened to have a one-inch camera hidden inside its cowboy hat. The box that carried the bear bore the words "Hi, I'm watching you."

Next, the bear would be watching the man's children. So would one of the other hidden cameras. His children spent too little time at home. He questioned their choices of friends. His teenager was reticent to talk to him or his wife. "I'm not trying to invade their privacy, but I want to get into their lives a little bit," the man told an *Orlando Sentinel* reporter. He exposed his disconnect by adding: "I trust my children, but only so far."[37]

Were the man's purchase and his attitudes about his children in response to the coverage of the Columbine massacre, which happened just a few months before? No doubt he watched the reports on TV about how Dylan Klebold and Eric Harris seemed like "normal" teenagers to their families and friends. The darker sides of the two killers were shared only with each other. Would the Klebold and Harris families have benefited from a gooseneck lamp with a spy camera inside? Should parents spy on their children rather than ensuring a trusting, communicative relationship?

Affluence as Effluent

Bored teenagers with nothing to do but plot against their peers. Affluent adults who measure their time against planners and Palm Pilots but squander the time they should spend nurturing their children. They assign themselves time for time management but no time for life management. Absorbed in the stock market, absorbed in extreme sports, absorbed in "amusing themselves to death," parents create a disconnect.

Was the Florida working man so self-absorbed that he couldn't ask a question of his own children? Was he better off distancing himself with electronic spy gear? Wouldn't dialogue have yielded more than distrust? In his own family he became an eavesdropper and a Peeping Tom.

Affluence is key here. We are able to spy on our kids with sophisticated equipment because we can afford it. We can afford it because some company has poured enormous sums of money into development and manufacture so that prices, once prohibitive, are now within easy reach of the working man.

The peacetime epilogue to World War II was affluence for virtually all Americans. Despite complaints about the economic hardships of some Americans—and they're true—the majority of us do very well. The standards of living of our poorest citizens are well above the poor of previous American generations and certainly ahead of the poor in other parts of the world.

The wealthy are doing very well, indeed. Thanks to the rise of dot-com Internet companies, the number of millionaires in the United States reached 4.6 million. A Merrill Lynch study reported that 30 percent of the world's millionaires (seven million in all) live in the United States.[38]

Those in the middle are doing well, too. The so-called American dreams are realities for many. Home ownership is accelerating. Half of Americans have investment programs through company 401(k) plans or stock purchases. Automobile registration constantly increases. Luxury items seem more like necessities. The booming economy of the late 1990s gave rise to "lifestyle consultants" like Martha Stewart, who advise us on how to deal with disposable income.

Consider this real-world scenario: An executive whose salary runs well into six figures tells a colleague about how unhappy his wife is. They have a comfortable southern California home, perks from the company and from vendors who vie for the executive's attention with free travel, generous gifts, and lavish nights on the town. He's about forty-five and talks of retirement within ten years because the stock options from the public company he works for are already worth millions. Even without the options, his 401(k) plan assures a comfortable retirement under ordinary circumstances.

His wife does not work. She doesn't have to. That's a situation they strove for. The kids are in good schools, something else they strove for and saved for. Together, they achieved the American dream through hard work, planning, and effective investments.

So why is the man's wife so miserable? The couple has no worries, no struggles to encounter. They, like so many Americans, have pursued the dream only to wake up and find it reality. No more wishing for riches or hoping for happiness. They have it, but cannot appreciate it.

The crises of American life are now reduced to the slow download, the VCR that flashes "12:00" constantly, and the cell phone that crackles and spits when used indoors. This is a nation of enormous wealth and resources with precious little training on how to use them effectively. We take "the pursuit of happiness" literally, as if happiness is the mandate and not the law. We look for anything from *South Park* crudeness to public lewdness, to take our minds off the things that are on our minds.

This leads us from "do your own thing" to "whatever," from brusque behavior to road rage. The headlines tell about the shootings on the Los Angeles or Houston freeways. But there are many other stories that don't get media attention: At the traffic light on Santa Monica Boulevard at Century Plaza East, a man jumps out of his car, runs to the vehicle ahead, and punches the driver through an open window. Drivers in lanes on either side wonder what offense caused the fist to fly and whether they're next.

When the light changes to green, the driver who threw the punch turns onto Century Plaza East while the recipient of the blow drives straight ahead. The surrounding drivers learn who's to blame when they see the lead driver U-turn across Santa Monica to circumvent a left-turn lane and cross a line of oncoming traffic to enter a parking lot. Each driver is the center of his own universe; his context is self.

We've taken what used to be a nurturing mass culture and subdivided it until it's the culture of me, the culture of self. Focusing on self allows us to take incivility to a new high, as if it's an art form. We are Narcissus at the pool, looking longingly into our own eyes. What is it we see?

Sudden wealth in the context of the disconnect created by electronic media breeds a new emptiness. In a nation that can have whatever it wants when it wants it, why is the emptiness filled only by hostility and incivility?

"Affluence brings with it boredom," said Robert Bork in *Slouching Towards Gomorrah:*

> Of itself, it offers little but the ability to consume, and a life centered on consumption will appear, and be, devoid of meaning. Persons so afflicted will seek sensation as a palliative, and that today's culture offers in abundance.
>
> This brings us to the multiple roles rapidly improving technology plays in our culture. America was a nation of farmers, but the advance of technology required fewer and fewer farmers and more and more industrial workers. The continuing advance required fewer industrial workers and more white collar workers, and eventually still more sophisticated workers

of a kind that made the term "white collar" seem denigrating. Hard physical work is inconsistent with hedonism; the new work is not. With the time and energy of so many individuals freed from the harder demands of work, the culture turned to consumerism and entertainment. Technology and its entrepreneurs supplied the demand with motion pictures, radio, television and videocassettes, all increasingly featuring sex and violence. Sensations must be steadily intensified if boredom is to be kept away.[39]

Affluence, especially with technology assisting, makes us value personal convenience, primarily because it's available to us. Home shopping, personal shoppers, video-on-demand, instant meals in the microwave oven—they're all the products of convenience.

With everything done for us, boredom increases. What's the next amusement to help us steer clear of boredom?

Our own stories and ourselves.

Chapter 5

The Community of Me

Her name was Echo and she was beautiful. Fond of the woods and the hills, she devoted herself to activities that would keep her outdoors. She was a particular favorite of Diana (the goddess, not the princess). Echo's job description was "nymph," and she served at the pleasure of the gods and goddesses of ancient Greece in the age of the fable.

Pretty Echo had but one failing: she talked too much. Whether a pleasant conversation or a contretemps, Echo wanted—and got—the last word. That trait was a benefit to the others in the nymph corps on a day when the goddess Juno thought her husband was amusing himself with the nymphs. Echo talked her way out of the situation, and while she talked, the other nymphs escaped.

Peeved at the outcome, Juno pulled rank and punished the nymph: Echo could never start a conversation again, only end one. Echo was sentenced to reply and repeat. She would forever get the last word.

Having to wait for someone else to start the conversation is especially awkward when the cursed falls in love, as Echo did when she saw Narcissus in the woods with his friends. She wanted to get his attention, but she couldn't speak first.

When he was finally alone, Echo made enough noise to be noticed, and Narcissus shouted, "Who's here?" "Here," echoed Echo. "Come," said Narcissus, and Echo repeated, "Come." Yet no one came, and Narcissus gave up on a conversation he felt was going nowhere.

That left poor Echo to pine away, to lose both strength and body mass, and ultimately turn to rock on a mountainside (where she echoes yet). Since Narcissus's rebuff of her affection was considered cruel in mythical times, Echo hoped that the goddess Aphrodite would think so, too, and would retaliate on Echo's behalf. It took a few more arrogant rejections by Narcissus of other nymphs before Aphrodite, indeed, acted.

Aphrodite's action makes Narcissus the focal point of this tale. One day, after a hot and sweaty chase through the woods, Narcissus came upon a pool of water, described as so clear it was like silver. As he looked into the still pool, Narcissus saw a face so beautiful that he immediately lost his heart. He thought it was a water nymph staring up at him from the pebbles on the bottom of the pool.

With sudden passion, he reached for the apparition, but as he touched the water, the nymph vanished. As he stepped back in astonishment, the waters regained their smooth surface and once again the image appeared. Now Narcissus was intrigued and he looked more closely, only to find the image returning a gaze as intense as his own. Could this elusive creature be as much a victim of love and despair as he was? Convinced that was the case, Narcissus repeated his glances and his attempts to touch. Time and again, day and night, he repeated the same pantomime, attempting to communicate with and to reach the nymph.

Narcissus was so enamored that he stopped eating and eventually died, little suspecting that the nymph he so fancied was his own image reflected in the clear, still waters.

In a dramatic change of heart, the nymphs prepared a funeral pyre for Narcissus, but couldn't find his body. In its place were purple flowers surrounded with white leaves that bear the name and preserve the memory of the young man who fell in love with his own image and became so enamored of it that he caused his own death.[1]

Like Narcissus, we look into the pool every day to catch our reflections. The pool is media. Television, especially, allows our reflection to appear either real or in disguise, as if we're the lead players in a show about ourselves. A Jerry Springer talk show reflects the people we hope we're not. The local news shows the criminals we hope won't choose our house next. A public station displays our hopes for higher thinking. The WWF presents the gladiator we all know we can be. Television is our electric mirror. It lets us know our stories are valuable and our individualism has worth.

Individualism was unknown in the Middle Ages and would have been considered psychotic in the ancient Greece that propagated the Narcissus story. That's why Narcissus existed in mythical lore, to guide man against such self-conceit. Echo's story, too, was a learning device to teach control of the tongue. [2]

Most of our early stories were handed down from above and delivered through the church or other worldly representative of an Almighty, whether pope or king. From the heavens the stories flowed through the priest-interpreters to the people, first in song, later in verse, then via paint and sculpture.

"There is no nation, no community, without its stories," writes Idries Shah in an essay on the teaching story:

> Children are brought up on fairy tales, cults and religions depend on them for moral instruction: they are used for entertainment and for training. They are usually catalogued as myths, as humorous tales, as semi-historical fact, and so on, in accordance with what people believe to be their origin and function.[3]

The tradition of teaching stories is a long one. Aristotle, Confucius, and Jesus all relied on the parable to get their points across. Shah continues the tradition, creating teaching stories of his own, usually featuring the Mulla Nasrudin, a Sufi holy man and judge. ("'What is fate?' Nasrudin was asked by a scholar . . .")

From the Bottom Up

Gutenberg's press changed the direction of our stories, allowing them to move sideways, from writer to editor to publisher to reader. The electronic world provides the individual control, moving the story from the bottom up. Americans tend to create their own stories and cling to them. For that matter, Americans tend to cling to individualism itself, as if it were a universal attribute.

Alexis de Tocqueville was the first to remark that the quest for individualism yielded what he perceived as uniformity in the 1830s United States.[4] Little could he have known what was to follow, as rampant individualism not only conquered the wide open spaces of the West, but also populated and altered the enclosed spaces of the psyche.

Mass media—newspapers, radio, and television—homogenized America in a way de Tocqueville could only hint at 160 years earlier. Today's new media—personal, one-on-one digital connections—allow us to see ourselves more closely, more clearly, and more separately. "Welcome back," says MediaPost.com with a specific greeting by name to a user its system recognizes. Connect to Amazon.com's site and a list of books is awaiting, based on your previous buying habits and what Amazon interprets as "your taste." In each situation, there's an appeal to the sense of self, to the person you perceive yourself to be.

The sense of self has roots in eighteenth-century Europe, when the upper classes dressed like actors and performed like actors. There was an unstated assumption, says Neal Gabler, that public life was a performance in which you projected to others how you wanted to be perceived.[4] Everyone understood that the role had little to do with anything other than role-playing. All the world's a stage, after all.

Americans took to the idea of performance as life, but with a twist: The raw frontier encouraged theatricality. The truth of most of the stories told or acted on the American frontier could not be verified. It was a combination of creating a story for oneself and of releasing the restraints inherent in the European cultures most of the newly arrived Americans had escaped.

One thing the performance culture of 1800s America disavowed, however, was affectation, which was identified with what Americans perceived as the decadence of Europe. With interesting irony, the same Americans who eschewed affectation enthusiastically embraced the trappings of success. Success came from hard work and determination, highly individualistic traits.

The result was a rash of personal stories and public performances that revolved around being rich without being aristocratic. All walks of life externalized themselves with clothing they didn't need and signs of success that were often only symbols, not the real thing. An 1896 textbook taught students how certain gestures corresponded to specific emotions. Today we'd call it "body language," an important ingredient in the evaluation of personal performance.

Narcissus as warning is warning unheeded by those of us who live on "socially constructed realities," as Walter Truett Anderson describes our stories. Anderson claims that there are six "givens" of life in the postmodern era:

1. The society itself is a social construction of reality. All the things that identify and define a "people"—such as its boundaries, its culture, its political institutions—are the (usually refined) products of earlier inventions.
2. Individual identity is also a social construction of reality, and the concept of a "self" is different in different societies and at different stages of history.
3. We regard the collective beliefs of individuals (rather than the mind of God or the laws of history) as the ultimate repository of social reality (what is true is defined by what we all believe), and we know that beliefs can be modified.
4. Consequently, all sectors of society are deeply interested in finding out what people believe (public opinion) and modifying those beliefs (advertising, propaganda, brainwashing, public relations, and so forth).
5. In a postmodern society we perceive life as drama, and our major issues involve the definition of personal roles and the fabrication of stories that give purpose and shape to social existence.
6. Public happenings have the quality of scenes created or stage-managed for public consumption. They are what David Boorstin called "pseudo-events" in his landmark book, *The Image,* in 1961.[5]

"The human mind is a prodigious maker and consumer of stories," Anderson says. And today's human mind has all the tools needed to be quite prolific. It's too easy to construct a story, especially when some media channel provides the perfect reflection of the self we want to see. Commercials targeted at "the cult of me" with copy and imagery honed to sound like your personal story are described in Chapter Two.

Even before we make up our story, there's a story that is already written—ancestry, DNA, environment, metabolism, evolution, and so forth. The cumulative outcome of all those "stories" is a predictive model of the future. In addition to those pre-written stories, there are the stories we tell ourselves and those around us. From them we model our behavior and strive for an outcome, which may or may not materialize.

If we get an acceptable outcome, the story's "true." If not, we choose another story, and the truth is in the telling. Since most stories are told once and then repeated, repetition adds to belief. Stories most widely told are those most believed, thus, the "truest." Like Narcissus's tale, stories tend to outlive those who tell them. Even lies take their essence from the "truth" of repetition and widespread belief.

Television adds another dimension to life as movie: a fanciful, personal, and self-interpreted incarnation of reality. With television as the base reality, we use the Internet to add on to our own stories by forming "communities"—some large, some with only a handful of others—that reflect our psyches most clearly. Think of Narcissus at a terminal connected to the World Wide Web. With little effort, he could have found the woman or man of his dreams. He would not have been able to touch any better than he could in the pool. However, the image would have been better crafted to his hopes and needs. With an "advanced search," he could define his story and reflect even more of himself to no one but himself.

We used to watch other people's performances as our entertainment; now we are consumed with our own. And we don't have to wait for a novelist, a movie producer, or a television producer to write and direct.

Most personal stories never get to be bigger than life. Consider these, for example:

Meet Our Cover Girl

Gretchen Stockdale is an attractive enough young woman with large brown eyes and a large smile framing a pinched nose. Call her "cute," but not "beautiful." She's a full-time model and actress who graduated cum laude from the University of Missouri, where she majored in speech communication. She enjoys golf, kickboxing, ice skating, and swimming.

Do you care? Maybe if you're Gretchen's parents, her friend, or a talent scout. Otherwise, probably not. To most of the world, Gretchen is just a model holding a sign for postal automation software on the cover of a business catalog from Mailer's Software of Rancho Santa Margarita, California. It's the fourth catalog with Gretchen's picture, so the company decided to tell you a bit of Gretchen's story.

There's more if you really want her story: "If you would like to follow her career, visit her Web site." Why would someone want to? Nothing against Gretchen, but she didn't invent mailing software. She's not an expert in the direct mail business. She's simply a hired hand, enlisted to dress up an otherwise mundane catalog.

Beer Cans to Cocktails

When writer Rob Walker and his girlfriend, "E," moved from New York to New Orleans, they decided to do what any right-thinking newcomers would: They attempted to deceive people in New Orleans.

As Walker explained it, "Where I come from, nothing says 'class' quite like lavish, over-the-top expenditures." So he and his mate spent over a thousand dollars on caterers to host a party for people neither of them knew in New Orleans, mostly friends of friends in New York. The goal was to "hoodwink new acquaintances into thinking we're players." Did it work? People arrived at the appointed time and apparently loved the oyster turnovers and the skewered scallops.

Why the story found a place in *Forbes Small Business* magazine is as much a puzzle as Rob and his girlfriend were to their guests. But Rob Walker literally and figuratively wrote his own story.[6]

For Immediate Release

This news release is a perfect example of writing a personal story. It was mailed to a Houston radio station:

> John Lee Hudson, President for [sic] the American Business Consultants Corporation, a Houston-based firm, announced today that he will wed Shana J. Hickey.
>
> Miss Hickey is the daughter of the prominent Edward Hickey family of Dallas. The wedding will be held at the famous Adredge House in Dallas on Friday, December 16, 1983, at 8:00 p.m., by permission of the "Medical Wives Society." The Adredge House was chosen to shoot the pilot film for the television series, "DALLAS."
>
> President Ronald Reagan, Governor Mark White and Nelson Bunker Hunt are just a few of those on the invitation list to attend.
>
> Sonny Bono has been invited to sing at the wedding.

Hudson's release was clearly designed for the gossip and celebrity columns. But does including high-profile names as "on the invitation list" insure their arrival at the happy event? Hudson may have known the celebrities intimately—for that matter, they may have been there to drain the last magnum of champagne—but the invitation was pure puffery, an attempt at constructing a personal story.

Design for Living

A woman named Cindy Jackson is reported by the *New York Times Magazine* to have undergone twenty plastic surgeries so she would look like a Barbie doll.

The same article describes a series of public surgeries by a French performance artist named Orlan. The so-called work in progress was titled "The Ultimate Masterpiece: The Reincarnation of St. Orlan." After the offending parts were tucked or removed, Orlan sold pieces of skin as souvenirs.[7]

Essentially Immortalized

Faye Resnick claimed that taking her clothes off for *Playboy* magazine was a "liberating experience." For those who *don't* read the articles, Resnick was the O.J. Simpson trial hanger-on who asserted in *Playboy* that Simpson repeatedly threatened to kill his wife Nicole. "Because of what I've been through in the past two and a half years I had lost my sense of joy." She called the nude photos her "first taste of freedom." They also provided her a personal story beyond the Simpson trial. A psychologist quoted in newspaper accounts of the Resnick exposure said that being a *Playboy* model means "You're essentially immortalized."[8]

Reinventing God

In October 1987, Tessie Jayme had a dream or a vision—she's not clear which—in which a passage from the Bible was written in the sky. She says that as she watched, an invisible hand erased many of the words. That was her sign that she was to reinterpret the Bible so that it would "more closely reflect the original energy of the experiences narrated by the storytellers."

The result was a book available online that contained the words the hand left behind. It also suffered a few from Jayme's own hand. For $4.95 you could learn, among other things: "The Biblical world, around 1200–700 B.C., was a primitive one, intensely focused on the primal need to survive.

There were no 7-Eleven stores in those days to provide quick sandwiches if you didn't feel like cooking, or a cash machine if you ran out of money."[9]

God is more tolerant than we deserve with the stories we invent.

The Paid Announcement

Newspapers are the historical venues that feed the personal story. In the smallest towns and the largest, papers carry birthday greetings, wedding announcements, and obituaries. The liberties taken with the language and the truth are often amusing and telling:

> Andrew P. Shea, formerly of Lima, Peru, and Great Neck, New York, graduated from St. Aloysius Grammar School (fourth in his class), Cranwell Preparatory (lettered in hockey and football), Georgetown University (swim team).

The parentheticals in Shea's announcement appeared just that way. His fiftieth birthday prompted his announcement, which went on to list country clubs where he was a member and additional clubs where he "had access."

> The BURNS-STANDLINSLOWKI FAMILY of HALIFAX, NOVA SCOTIA, CANADA would like to formally announce an engagement of their heir, and her intended to the family, and to the world at this time.

What parentheses are to the Sheas, capitalization is to the Burns-Standlinslowkis. News of their happy event consumed several pages, as they assured themselves that the world knew their story. In addition to the hyphenated surname, the bride-to-be had ten given names, all written in capitals.

"All the world is a stage and men and women are merely players" was the opening to an announcement "In Memoriam" to a young woman. The family referred to the "front row seats" they occupied in the life of their daughter. It ended with an assertion: "Those who love you so dearly have faith that when you took your final curtain call and stepped inside that glowing curtain of light know you will be waiting in the wings to greet us." There's more sentiment than sense in the sentence. It reinforces a personal story about a personal "performance."

Love Me Tender

When Ellen Kay Umbach and Donald Herrick Jr. were married in 1995, there was a double ring ceremony and an appearance by "Elvis, the King of Rock and Roll," according to the couple's announcement in the *Houston*

Chronicle. The wedding took place at the Graceland Wedding Chapel in Las Vegas, so, naturally, Elvis was there. The King serenaded the couple and pronounced them "a hunk, a hunk of burning love." The wedding party ended the day with a seven-course Roman wedding feast at Caesar's Palace. If their stories aren't complete, add the fact that the bride designed her own "short dress of white crepe."[10]

Stories for Sale

If you're uncomfortable writing your own story, you need Dan Hurley's help.

Hurley works in a yellow sport coat and yellow fedora just in front of the Liberty Bell in Philadelphia. He asks you a few questions and then his fingers begin to jab at a 1937 Remington portable typewriter. In a minute or so, Hurley has written a story based on your answers to his questions. Once the story is completed, he reads it aloud, usually to the applause of onlookers. He hopes for a few dollars from the subject of the story.

After 20,000 "60 Second Novels," Hurley knows he's found a niche for himself. In addition to the money he makes on the streets, he's hired as an entertainer at parties and conventions and writes his novels for customers at department stores during special promotions. Of course, by doing so, he has constructed a story of his own.[11]

A cottage industry has grown up around the personal story. "Personal historians" record and write the stories of families and—especially—of elderly family members whose reminiscences will be lost when they are gone. Some personal historians work on paper and deliver a bound book for family members. Others work in video, presenting a finished "documentary" about a family or an ancestor. Most who recount their life story don't expect to become best-selling authors. Their aim is to leave a family history as insight for future generations.[12]

Something to Believe

"The trouble with Americans is they believe so many things that just ain't so," said Charles Farrar Browne. It sounds like a lament of the electronic age and a cry for myth, but it's not. Browne wrote and lectured in the mid-nineteenth century using the name "Artemus Ward."

What would Ward do today if confronted, as Baltimore police were, with frantic calls from citizens about a gang of kids who were said to be going from school to school spraying the heads of other children with purple paint? In the worst of the complaints, the gang was said to have shaved the heads of younger children.[13]

Ward was a good reporter (for the Cleveland *Plain Dealer*), so he would certainly investigate. However, he'd discover, as Baltimore police did, that there were no such instances. There was no evidence other than the hundreds of calls to area police and a few references on local radio talk shows.

Nonetheless, Ward would say again that folks believe things that ain't so.

How would Ward approach the following story, which happened in 1983? A little old lady at shopping malls would tell patrons that she was sick and needed transportation home. Once in the car of a sympathetic shopper, the little old "lady" turned out to be a man in disguise ready to strike with a concealed ax.[14]

One more: In Houston, those loving little blue characters from TV cartoons were causing panic. "The Smurf Gang" was said to be terrorizing junior high students in the city's school district. There was talk of rape and murder. "Everybody was really on edge," said a seventh grader. "I've heard all these rumors that they killed a bus driver and two students." One principal reported that a little boy with tears in his eyes had seen fifty Smurfs getting off a school bus.[15]

In Houston, as in Baltimore, police were baffled. There was no basis for either story. No evidence of decapitated shoppers. No trace of an ax-wielding man in little old lady's clothing.

Only in Houston was there even a kernel of truth. Five students had been arrested near a junior high school for "creating some mischief," to use a school official's words. A policeman apparently labeled the group "The Smurfs" for his own amusement, and the story took on a life of its own.

There *are* many things that just ain't so and Americans are anxious to believe them. These beliefs are reinforced by electronic dissemination, which appears to the untrained eye to be the ultimate documentation. If the media say so, it must be true.

For example, a flood that kept business away from the London Bridge. It was the summer of 1983, and the bridge had been purchased by an Arizona businessman who took it apart stone by stone and moved it to the Colorado River on the California-Arizona border. The town that sprang up around the bridge is called Lake Havasu City, and it was plagued by what city fathers called "the phantom flood."

There was a flood on the Colorado that year. The U.S. Bureau of Reclamation raised the gates of Hoover, Davis, and Parker dams to let the melting snows of the Rocky Mountains go downstream. But Lake Havasu City is located upstream, and both the town and the London Bridge were high and dry.

Being high and dry should have brought in about $173 million in tourist revenues in 1983. In fact, the Chamber of Commerce expected even more, because the areas south of Parker Dam were flooded. But media reports said the bridge area was devastated. Lake Havasu City suffered, as revenues dropped 43 percent.[16]

The rumors that plagued the Baltimore and Houston police departments and the reports that bred Arizona's "phantom flood" are not the same. Yet they spring from the same sources: sketchy information delivered by media channels that half tell the story to a public that half hears yet believes deeply in whatever it chooses to believe.

Remember when word spread nationally that the Federal Communication Commission might curtail religious broadcasting? There was no truth to the rumors, but people believed because they wanted to. For more than seven years, the FCC received more than 20 million cards and letters protesting something that did not exist—a petition by atheist leader Madelyn Murray O'Hair to take religious programming off U.S. airwaves.

Members of the FCC staff tried to get the word out that there was no such petition and that there never had been. O'Hair even went on talk shows and news interviews to say that there had been no such petition. Part of the problem was the backlash of public opinion against the controversial O'Hair. No sooner had the allegations been denied than the cards and letters started again to the FCC's Washington offices.[17]

The response was fed by churches who ran their mimeograph machines overtime to spread the word, never pausing to ascertain whether the word had any basis in truth. If all 20 million of those who sent cards and photocopies to the FCC actually listened to religious broadcasts, those programs would not be relegated to the wee hours of weekend mornings or to low-power broadcast outlets.

Look to the Skies

The decade-long hysteria about the O'Hair "petition" is reminiscent of the overnight hysteria created by radio during the Mercury Theatre broadcast of *The War of the Worlds* in 1938. The radio medium was younger then, and so was the ability of the listener to make sense of what was heard. The newspaper accounts the next morning told the story: In Pittsburgh, a man returned home to find his wife with a bottle of poison in her hands; in Oakland, an excited man called police to ask where he could volunteer to fight the Martians; in Birmingham, people gathered in groups and prayed.

The same magic that had given Jack Benny a moat filled with alligators to protect his fortune—radio—had created a "real" invasion by Martians! The aliens landed in Grover's Mills, New Jersey, October 30, 1938, an unlikely venue on a quite likely evening—the night before Halloween. The program was by no means an attempt to upset the public. CBS broadcast the clear disclaimer, "This is a dramatization."

Very few got the message. The listener who heard the entire hour's drama realized that time passed quickly. Minutes on the clock were hours of dramatic time. Before radio's hour had ended, morning had broken in Grover's Mills. All that was lost on the casual listener. Edward Tatnall Canby revisited the events for *Audio* magazine:

> In times of emotional stress, in broadcasts that offer stressful material, the fact-absorbing ability of the listener goes down virtually to zero. It is an awesome phenomenon. Most of Orson Welles's 1938 audience heard only a few moments of the show, not too many listened the full hour. But a predictably tiny portion of all listeners got the essential message—This is dramatization. In that time of profound unrest, right after the Munich settlement that settled nothing, most listeners grasped just one horrible idea—CATASTROPHE—right here at home. It was a living nightmare coming true, right on the radio, and without a second thought, thousands of them turned and ran for their lives.[18]

It was easy to recognize H.G. Wells's story in the Mercury Theatre update—that is, if you were familiar with Wells's original. When Wells was told of the national panic after the U.S. broadcast, he said with British understatement, "How odd!" He knew the appeal of fiction. He had been writing it longer than many of the Mercury Theatre actors had been alive.

The combination of the highly believable scenario set in modern New Jersey with a medium as powerful as radio gave Wells's story an all-new impact. Canby's point about an unsettled world further set the stage for believing something that just wasn't true.

Crimebusters

A woman in Shreveport, Louisiana, was a victim of her own belief and then a private panic. That city, like many others across the nation, has an anti-crime program that reenacts crimes on TV in hopes of getting leads for the local police department. On July 31, 1981, there was a gas station robbery in Shreveport, and city and county police hit nothing but dead ends as they tried to solve the case. On August 9, the crime was re-created by police officers on the "Crime of the Week" feature with an announcement that residents with information about the crime could call in confidence. Wanda Faye Dennis presented herself to police and asked if they had a warrant for her. "No," said the police, not knowing what she was talking about. When she was taken to detectives, they realized that the twenty-year-old woman had seen the reenactment and thought that police cameras had caught her in the act.

Sometimes, television provides too much help. A police officer in Houston received anonymous tips on crimes that had not been committed. "The body's in the trunk behind the barn at the chicken coop," said one long-distance caller to Detective John Donovan. At first he thought the frantic woman was referring to a Houston bar called the Chicken Coop, but could find no reports or evidence of foul play. A fellow detective alerted Donovan to an NBC-TV soap opera set in Houston. On the program, a fictitious detective named John Donovan investigated bizarre murders. He appeared on the series only a few times, played by actor Geoffrey Pierson. When the real Detective Donovan received calls with the "tips," the fictional Donovan had not appeared in five months.

Work of the Devil

There are probably people who still believe the Procter & Gamble rumor. It surfaced on the West Coast in the early 1980s and spread eastward. According to the rumor, the thirteen stars in the company's trademark were linked to satanic religion and devil worship. In addition, it was said, a P&G executive appeared on the *Phil Donahue Show* and discussed Satanism and how it related to the trademark.[19]

The logo art in question is a crescent moon that resembles a bearded man's profile facing a cluster of thirteen stars, a symbol Procter & Gamble began using in 1851. By January 1982, the company had completed a mailing to every newspaper, every television station, and every radio station in California, Oregon, and Washington, explaining the background of the trademark. The mailing included a letter from the *Donahue* show saying that no P&G official had ever appeared on the program discussing Satanism.

By that summer, however, the rumor had swept eastward. *Management Review* magazine reported that P&G received as many as 15,000 telephone calls per month during the height of the rumor. An Atlanta television weatherman used the story in a speech to a group of retirees. He told the group that the firm's trademark was a symbol of devil worship and urged a boycott of Procter & Gamble products. This time public relations was not enough. P&G filed suit against the weatherman, Guy Sharpe. Finally, the suit was dropped when Sharpe made a public apology: "I deeply regret that I took the word of someone else, and it proved to be wrong. I know nothing derogatory about P&G and I have no reason to believe that P&G or its trademark have any connection with Satanism."[20] A Procter & Gamble representative said that the sole purpose in filing the lawsuit was to stop the spread of the rumor and that the apology was enough.

From time to time on radio talk shows, the issue arises again and a caller will calmly inform the host that he knows "for certain" that Procter & Gamble practices Satanism. "Have you ever seen their trademark?" the caller will ask.

McDonald's faced a similar problem in 1978 and launched its own, less visible campaign against charges of Satanism. The rumor was that Ray Kroc, the founder of the chain of golden arches, was contributing money to a California cult that engaged in devil worship.

The company decided against an open public relations campaign, because the rumor had been confined only to church bulletins. Going "public" might have fueled the rumor, as it probably did for Procter & Gamble. Instead, McDonald's traced the church bulletins to the source and insisted the source issue another statement saying that the story was wrong. As the revised bulletins appeared, they squelched the rumor.[21]

McDonald's encountered another problem, this time in the Southwest. This rumor had it that the company added worms to its hamburger. The immediate effect was a 20 percent drop in sales in the area. Church bulletins were not enough for this one. A new advertising campaign was launched, emphasizing the use of "100 percent pure beef."[22]

In New England, Entenmann's bakery had to launch an antirumor campaign to deny a widely circulated story that the company was owned by Reverend Sun Myung Moon's Unification Church. It was not. And is not.

Frederick Koenig, a sociology professor at Tulane University feels that the best way to stop a rumor is to go public with the denial and announce it frequently. Making the rumor "news" changes its character, Koenig says, and most people won't pass on a story they know isn't true. Many public relations people disagree, thinking that denying the rumor simply turns an ember into a blaze.[23]

In the book, *Rumor and Gossip*, Ralph Rosnow claims that uncertainty and anxiety fuel rumor. Even if the person telling the rumor is scared by it, "it gives them psychological solace."[24] Read "solace" as "something to believe." Repetition of the stories—whether they equate Procter & Gamble with Satanism or describe ax-wielding men in little old lady's clothing—provides a mantra of belief in evil. It asks, too, for an assertion of "good" or "right." The person telling the story or passing the rumor probably believes that he's doing the right thing by warning neighbors and, especially, fellow church-goers. Denying a rumor often spreads it further.

This is the stuff of "urban legend," those stories that crop up at cocktail parties and over dinners with friends. You know, the story about the dead boy whose image is seen in the movie *Three Men and a Baby*. Or the story about the dead mouse found in the bottom of a soda can. Or the story about the break dancer who died filming a Pepsi commercial with singer Michael Jackson. All false. All rumors. All urban legends.[25]

"The truth never stands in the way of a good story," said Jan Harold Brunvand, a folklorist and newspaper columnist. "It's not just a joke or a fairy tale. The story is told as if it's true and there is this truth element—there is a video of *Three Men and a Baby*, and there is something there that looks like a boy." Even when the stories are pure fiction, they're given credence by someone saying they heard it on a news program or a talk show. "They'll say they heard it on 'Paul Harvey,' that's a favorite one," says Brunvand, who feels the legends are an attempt to "satisfy the hope or wish that there's still some mystery left in the world."[26]

Signs and Wonders

Paralleling the growth of rumor in stressful times is the emergence of pseudo-Messiahs who openly claim to be God or an emissary from God. Sometimes it's a matter of shoring up self-esteem, sometimes a ploy to get attention. "In times of social stress," says Laurence H. Stookey at Wesley Seminary in Washington, D.C., "we want to latch on to someone who gives easy answers, someone who can give certainty and security about the future." Clinton McLemore of Fuller Theological Seminary says that self-proclaimed Messiahs have difficulty distinguishing between inner religious experiences and reality, between healthy expressions of faith and pathological responses.

The expectation of a Messiah or a returned religious figure is essential to so many of the world's religions, and easy answers are essential to belief.[27]

Some who don't claim to be the Messiah claim instead to have regular communication with him. Like a woman in Bayside, New York: Jesus told her that Russia was going to invade the United States and that a warhead was planted in an abandoned Manhattan subway tunnel. Veronica Leuken also received news from Jesus about plagues and disasters. The woman claimed to have received "heavenly visitations" from Mary, the mother of Jesus, and from the Lord himself. An assortment of angels and saints also made the pilgrimage to Bayside to visit Leuken, a Roman Catholic housewife and mother of five.

Near Stockton, California, they called it a "miracle" when the wife of a church volunteer saw a statue of Mary cry a sticky sort of tears. In the small Mater Ecclesia Church, attendance at Sunday Mass tripled when the word spread about the tears. The statue was also said to have moved from its pedestal to a point twenty feet away. It only moved on the thirteenth of the month, the date the Virgin is said to have appeared to three children in Portugal in 1917. When each of the people who had a key to the church began to suspect each other of perpetrating a hoax, they decided to lock the church with the statue bolted to its stand. A few days later, it's said, the statue had moved toward the altar.

Another California story: The image of a crucified Christ was said to be cast on a garage door in Santa Fe Springs. People from miles around came to see and worship at the site.

UPI reported that 4,000 pilgrims crowded the small French village of Saint Etienne hoping to catch a glimpse of a fourteen-year-old girl who claimed to have seen the Virgin Mary in the sun. Neither the girl nor the Virgin appeared the day the crowds arrived. The father of young Blandine Peigay said that his daughter was staying inside her house. "The virgin will not appear either Saturday or Sunday to punish the journalists," he stated.

The girl claimed that she had seen the vision thirty-one times. According to reports, she gazed into the sun, which would then commence to spin in the sky. The mayor of the village of Talaudière, near Saint Etienne, told crowds, "If you look at the sun until you have the impression that it is spinning, it is not any miracle. It is that your retina is completely burned."

On the occupied West Bank of Jerusalem, as many as 10,000 Christian Palestinians per week make pilgrimages to a spot called Beit Sahor, where the faithful claim that several white chalky lines on the wall of a grotto are the proof that the Virgin and her husband Joseph appeared there. The grotto is already a local landmark, for it is said to have been a stopping point for the Holy Family during their flight into Egypt. In 1979 A Greek Orthodox woman claimed to have seen an image of Mary. Then others affirmed seeing lights, or mists, or the Virgin herself, about three feet tall. Two days after the first "visions," a second image appeared, more chalky marks on the grotto wall. The lines resembled a man in long robes with his arms outstretched. The new image was about eighteen inches tall and is said to be Joseph, the carpenter.

In an unusual case that sounds ridiculous in description, the likeness of Jesus as it appears on the famed Shroud of Turin was formed by skillet marks on the edge of a flour tortilla fried by a farm woman in a small New Mexico village. The image was only wafer-sized, but it was preserved in a glass case and put on display.

Signs and wonders were a vital and visible part of the early Christian church, were mentioned approvingly by church patriarchs and historians. Succeeding stalwarts of faith such as Martin Luther, John Wesley, and Dwight L. Moody also made effective use of signs and wonders.

"Miracles" come and go. There have been long periods of relative dormancy or decline in the reported occurrence of visions and apparitions in the history of the Judeo-Christian religion. Now there's a renewal of these phenomena in both Protestant and Roman Catholic circles that parallels the renewal of spirituality that transcends specific religion. It's a search for something to believe.

The Cry for Myth

"There are very few people nowadays who are able to make the necessary use of stories," says Idries Shah. To Shah, "the necessary use" is teaching with stories and parables: "an ancient yet still irreplaceable method of arranging and transmitting a knowledge which can not be put in any other way." Some stories, he says, are valid representations of fact, a mathematical formula, for example. "Like any scientific textbook or mathematical formula, however, stories depend for their higher power upon someone to understand them at the higher level."

As an example of a higher-level story, Shah uses the example of a stream, paraphrased here:

> Beginning at its source in a far-away mountain, a stream passes through every type of countryside until it arrives at a desert. As it runs into the sand, its waters disappear. The stream feels its destiny is to cross the desert, and the desert feels the same, saying to the stream, "The wind crosses the desert, so can you."
>
> "But the wind can fly," the stream replies, to which the desert responds, "Allow the wind to carry you to your destination." The desert suggests that the stream could be absorbed into the wind for the trip.
>
> The stream does not like the idea, for it has never been absorbed before. It does not want to surrender its individuality. Once having lost individuality, how could the stream be sure it could be regained?
>
> "You cannot remain the same stream you are today whether you spill into the sands and become a quagmire or join the wind as vapor," asserts the desert. "You are called what you are today because you do not know which part of you is the essential one."[28]

Shah and the other teachers who use such allegories use them to remind us that we are more than individuals; we are a part of something beyond what we see. Individuals who focus on their own stories see nothing more than reflections of themselves, as Narcissus saw what he thought was a beautiful creature at the bottom of the pool. Our cultural speedup at the hands of electronic media shows us reflections rather than the essential parts of ourselves.

Just as Shah's disciples learn from his teaching stories, so do we learn from the electric myths of our lives and ourselves presented nonstop via media and advertising. Then we construct our own reality to fit the personal myth we've chosen, whether that choice was conscious or not.

In Shah's definition, personal stories would be confined to the lowest level, because there's no higher truth to yield. There's no need for understanding outside the person who creates the story. There's no understanding at a higher level.

Christopher Lasch views personal stories as part of "the fantastic world of commodities." He describes "a new kind of self-consciousness that has little in common with introspection or vanity." Identity as written in the personal story is like a commodity, because commodities are produced for immediate consumption. As Lasch puts it, their value is not in their use or permanence, but, rather, in their marketability:

> Both as a worker and as a consumer, the individual learns not merely to measure himself against others but to see himself through others' eyes. He learns that the self-image he projects counts for more than accumulated skills and experience. Since he will be judged, both by his colleagues and superiors at work and by the strangers he encounters on the street, according to his possessions, his clothes, and his "personality"—not, as in the nineteenth century, by his "character"—he adopts a theatrical view of his own "performance" on and off the job.[29]

Private fantasies and public life merge when personality becomes commodity.

Thomas Heywood left us "The world's a theatre, the earth a stage, which God and Nature do with actors fill." Heywood may have been the inspiration for Shakespeare, whose character Jaques in *As You Like It*, says, "All the world's a stage, and all the men and women merely players," followed by an account of the seven "acts" of life.

Neal Gabler calls life a movie. "While the general public is an audience for the life movie, it is also an active participant in it," he writes. To Gabler, postmodern life has no stars, only celebrities, and celebrity is the modern state of grace:

> An ever-growing segment of the American economy is now devoted to designing, building and then dressing the sets in which we live, work, shop and play; to creating our costumes; to making our hair shine and our faces glow; to slenderizing our bodies; to supplying our props—all so that we can appropriate the trappings of celebrity, if not the actuality of it, for the life movie.[30]

Gabler refers to "the celebrity with a thousand faces" as ongoing entertainments about the foibles of actors or athletes or musicians that coalesce into social myths "that gave them an importance out of all proportion to their seemingly inconsequential origins."[31]

Begin with the personal stories of the celebrities—Gabler cites Tom Cruise's professionalism, Julia Roberts's search for love and independence, and Oprah Winfrey's triumph over crisis. Through repetition on television and in popular magazines like *People* and *Us*, these stories become myths we all believe. They buoy the culture with shared stories at a time when stories are fragmenting. Celebrity myths provide instruction about how to deal with our own lives.

Rollo May calls myth "a way of making sense in a senseless world . . . our way of finding meaning and significance." Like beams of a house, myths are not exposed to outside view, but they hold the house together. That is, until they are undermined as our myths have been by the speedup of our lives through electronic media. May looks at it this way:

> Our myths no longer serve their function of making sense of existence, the citizens of our day are left without direction or purpose in life, and people are at a loss to control their anxiety and excessive guilt feeling. People then flock to psychotherapists or their substitutes, or drugs or cults, to get help in holding themselves together.[32]

May calls the condition a "lonely search for internal identity." In the absence of belief, a million substitutes emerge. Whether cult, subcult, or personal construction of reality, *something* will fill the vacuum left by eroding myth. Walter Truett Anderson says we live in "an unregulated marketplace of realities in which all manner of belief systems are offered for public consumption."[33] There's a division between those who believe and those who have beliefs. The former group withers while the latter group mushrooms.

Ironically, myth is one of the mushrooming belief systems of a demythologized world. The man who knew so much about the power of the myth, Joseph Campbell, said before his death that students were crowding lecture halls to hear him speak because "myths bring them messages . . . stories about the wisdom of life." And he knew better than anyone that schools don't teach the wisdom of life. Greek, Latin, and biblical literature were once the basis for any education. When they were dropped, the entire tradition of mythological information was lost. As Campbell described it:

> One of our problems today is that we are not well acquainted with the literature of the spirit. We're interested in the news of the day and the problems of the hour. It used to be that the university campus was a kind of hermetically sealed-off area where the news of the day did not impinge upon your attention to the inner life and to the magnificent human heritage we have in our great tradition—Plato, Confucius, the Buddha, Goethe, and

others who speak of the eternal values that have to do with the centering of our lives.[34]

Is there any wonder that television and electronic images find a welcome home? Is there any question about how we have become the centers of our own myths, by allowing the stories that come into our homes to create reflections of ourselves? The only life models are the myths of movies, television, and electronic interconnection. And, as Campbell said:

> On this immediate level of life and structure, myths offer life models. But the models have to be appropriate to the time in which you are living, and our time has changed so fast that what was proper fifty years ago is not proper today. The virtues of the past are the vices of today. And many of what were thought to be the vices of the past are the necessities of today. The moral order has to catch up with the moral necessities of actual life in time, here and now. And that is what we are not doing. The old-time religion belongs to another age, another people, another set of human values, another universe. By going back you throw yourself out of sync with history. Our kids lose their faith in the religions that were taught to them, and they go inside.[35]

In some cases, "inside" means a drug experience. The fashionable drug is "e" or Ecstasy. A colorful pill with a Nike "swoosh" logo or the three diamonds of Mitsubishi Motors is enough to make the skin tingle and the personality become loving as never before. It's called the "hug drug," because of the effusive expressions of empathy it releases in its users. They become so loving that they collapse into what one student described as "cuddle puddles"—group embraces and massages on the dance floor.[36]

Once the province of the elite club set, Ecstasy reached the mass market quickly. The users, usually teenagers and young twenty-somethings, score the pills at clubs, raves, fraternity houses, and school. The corporate logos help the users identify the pills that have an extra kick, and they ask for them by brand name, much to the dismay of the companies whose logos have been co-opted.

Ecstasy is a substance called MDMA, pharmacologically related to amphetamines and mescaline, but without the jangling, wired feeling typically associated with them. It also has the advantage that it doesn't create the addictive cravings of speed or the hallucinations of LSD. In fact, its popularity is based on the relatively few downsides found in "e." Even police agree that the drug isn't as dangerous as heroin or crack cocaine in the short term, unless it's cut with other drugs. The most common physical problem related to Ecstasy is dehydration, especially among first-time users who aren't told to drink water.

The biggest danger with the drug is that it gets confused with another club drug, GHB, also known as "Liquid X," which can cause coma or death. GHB is not related to Ecstasy at all, except by virtue of the environment in which it's used. At one time, Ecstasy was legal, used for psychotherapy. There are therapists who lobby today for reestablishing its legality, and they are champions of young "e" users.

In the absence of the religious or mythological experience of ecstasy, a chemical Ecstasy fills the gap.

The Mythologization of Me

Not every kid turns to drugs. Some are hooked on the pharmacological nature of electronic media, the manufactured myth. Christopher Lasch addresses that issue in *The Culture of Narcissism*:

> Overexposure to manufactured illusions soon destroys their representational power. The illusion of reality dissolves, not in a hightened sense of reality as we might expect, but in a remarkable indifference to reality. . . . This indifference betrays the erosion of the capacity to take any interest in anything outside the self.

Lasch calls the condition "transcendental self-attention," saying, "To live for the moment is the prevailing passion—to live for yourself, not for your predecessors or posterity. We are fast losing the sense of historical continuity, the sense of belonging to a succession of generations originating in the past and stretching into the future."[37]

The result is the "Mythologization of Me."

Television and the baby boom grew up together, so boomers—those born in the period from just after World War II to roughly 1964—are the first to have television as the basis for their mythology and their personal stories. As boomers age, the culture of television does not age with them. Television seeks the new, the young, and the fresh. So the parade of thin, beautiful women that filled the boomer's screen from the medium's flickering beginnings stays young and stays thin.

Because they compare their own images to what television has shown them and sold them for better than forty years, baby boomers fuel the market for products that flatten the stomach, smooth the eyelids, and hold the breasts at attention. When they confront the flab of middle age, female boomers buy body-shaping undergarments—please, don't call them girdles!

Looking good gets more difficult in a society that idealizes slender youth. Yet the vainest baby boomers are reluctant to give up fatty foods that challenge the waistline. So the compromise is buying products and services that help them look younger and thinner than they are. What the fashion people call "the natural look" is the popular beauty image, and women aged thirty-five to fifty-nine increasingly rush to the aid of nature in achieving it. As *American Demographics* puts it, "Baby-boom women are not purists about how they achieve the 'natural' look, and the Wonderbra's success is graphic proof." A spokesman for the company that makes the Wonderbra says, "The Wonderbra corresponds to a mindset, not an age."[38]

The use of cosmetics increased from the mid-1980s to the mid-1990s, with hair spray, mascara, eyeliner, hair gel, and lip liner showing the largest percentage increases. While women are the primary cosmetics buyers, a trend began with cosmetics for men who wanted to keep their youthful good looks.

When covering it is not enough, reshaping is also an option. Elective cosmetic surgery is also popular, especially among baby boomers. Again, women dominate the market, but men are likely to yield to the knife for facial improvements like cheek implants, chin augmentation, and eyelid surgery. The more popular reconstructive surgery becomes, the more advertising there is in mass media. "Sometimes becoming your best requires changes—even changes in your physical appearance," says an ad headlined "Life looks better when you do."

Boomers have no hold on the market, even though their fretting about advancing age makes them prime candidates for reconfiguration. Responding to the culture of perfection portrayed by film, TV, and magazines, young women are having themselves rebuilt in record numbers. "I was considered attractive before," said twenty-one-year-old Mandy Whitt. "Now, I'm considered very attractive," she said after breast enlargements, a chin implant, nose surgery, and liposuction on her legs, abdomen, and buttocks. Another twenty-one-year-old used photos of movie stars, a model, and a pop singer to "order" the individual features she wanted in her new "look."[39]

It's called "cosmetic surgery" for a reason. It's a surface fix only. Psychotherapist Christine Wagener, who sees young women after their reconstruction, says that, for women who want an extra boost, the surgery is fine. "For people who do it to find something magical internally through external means, they will become depressed," she says. They expect their lives to change and only their nose or their thighs change. "Some people think if only they look perfect they will feel perfect and have the perfect life."

Wagener tells the story of a young woman who became depressed and angry after her surgery. The patient, once a homely girl, had multiple plastic surgeries. The result was that men became very interested in her for the first time. She realized that the men were responding to the way she looked and not who she was.

One estimate says that 75 to 80 percent of American women felt badly about their bodies. They also felt that it was their option to engage a reconstructive surgeon. When asked, "Under what conditions would you approve of cosmetic surgery such as a facelift or nose job?" 62 percent said, "Whenever a person chooses to improve his or her appearance." A quarter said, "Only to correct really unattractive features," and only 9 percent said "Under no conditions."[40]

When it comes to the job market, beauty is more than skin-deep, it's a deep economic advantage. The better looking a worker, the more likely he or she is to be paid more. Attractive people average 5 percent more per hour than those with average looks. Homely workers earn about 7 percent less than average. Men with below-average looks suffer a 9 percent earnings penalty, compared with 5 percent for women.

The study, conducted in the 1970s and 1980s and released in the early 1990s by economists Daniel Hamermesh of the University of Texas and Jeff Biddle of Michigan State, indicated that the beauty factor was not limited to specific occupations. For example, in a job where appearance presumably plays no role—bricklaying is the example the authors used—looks were as important to higher earnings as they were in retail and service jobs.[41]

A woman is being interviewed for a job. "Please describe yourself in a way that gives me a sense of who you are." The candidate replies, "Do you mean physically?" And the interviewer tells her she is free to choose. The woman begins, "I'm short, blond, a bit overweight," and continues with a catalog of physical attributes. In dozens of similar interviews, women began their answers by describing their bodies, not their jobs, not their relationships to their careers, not their potential value to the company interviewing them.

When psychologist Marcia Hutchinson selected more than 100 subjects for a study of body image, she carefully chose women of normal weight with no history of eating disorders or mental illness. She discovered that only one out of the hundred was *not* trying to lose weight. All the rest were dieting and suffering from poor body image.

"Body image is in constant flux, influenced in part by how closely the real body conforms to the prevailing norm," said Rita Freeman in a *Vogue* magazine article adapted from her book, *Beauty Bound*. "If there is a great discrepancy between the ideal and the real (for instance, if a cult of thinness defines most women as overweight), then the majority of women feel pressured to remodel themselves to fit the popular mold."[42]

With few exceptions, the images on TV and mass media feed the obsession. It's all about glamour and thinness. And it's more than the individual buying in to the idea. We've accepted it as a culture.

Heal Thyself

Who could stand up to the comparison? Only the supermodels and the superstars.

Men and women a few pounds overweight fail against the culture of thinness. A child with a facial birthmark fails against the culture of beauty. The teenager with a disability fails against the culture of perfection. ("Didn't your mother teach you not to stare?") That's why we tend to develop our own stories.

Instead of comparing ourselves to the culture of perfection projected by mass media, we compare the outside world to ourselves. Our stories change us from "the different" to "the standard." Others have to measure up to us. If they don't, no matter. A personal permanence stretches our fifteen minutes of fame into a lifetime of identity.

Often that identity involves a personal malady—especially one that has been overcome, like drug addiction or criminal activity. Thousands of Americans revel in their emotional instabilities, parading their most intimate details on TV talk shows, in books, in magazine articles, and in casual conversations with perfect strangers. Untold others bare their souls with less public attention in congratulatory support groups.

The most self-indulgent of the self-introducers are the guests on TV talk shows who are encouraged to tell their stories, usually unremarkable stories about insubordinate children or a spat with a spouse. They tell their stories with a sense of pride in the disconnect they have encountered, and the audience feels a sense of obligation to listen and empathize.

In the decades since Alcoholics Anonymous introduced America to the concept of peer support and the twelve-step program, public acceptance of support groups has grown. The "I'm OK, you're OK" feel-good attitudes that accompany the recovery movement spawned an entire field of pop psychology and the self-help industry. With them grew the obsession with self as product and projection.

The natural outgrowth of that growth is the tendency to extend victim status to anyone who has felt hurt or neglected. As Robert Hughes complains in *Culture of Complaint*:

> The range of victims available ten years ago—blacks, chicanos, Indians, women, homosexuals—has now been expanded to include every permutation of the halt, the blind, the lame and the short, or, to put it correctly, the differently abled, the other-visioned and the vertically challenged. Never before in human history were so many acronyms pursuing identity.[43]

All part of the mythologization of me. Now it becomes an individual celebration of the dysfunctional human condition. Author and lecturer John Bradshaw, a one-man cottage industry of self-help, says that 96 percent of the nation's population comes from dysfunctional families. That leaves very few to be considered normal. But just because you've ever felt unhappy or unwanted doesn't mean you're dysfunctional; it means you're human.

As Hughes says, "If the Inner Child doesn't let you off the hook, the embrace of redemption will." Media are full of redeemed souls who ask for forgiveness: a president who falls from grace with an intern; an actor caught with a prostitute; the drug-dependent rock band taking to the stage again. The less famous are included too: the parent who cannot control her child; the child who runs away from home; the husband obsessed with his wife's sister.

Everybody has a support group, even the man who confessed online that he murdered his five-year-old daughter by setting his house on fire with the girl inside. Then, the confession continued, he climbed out the window and "set about putting on a show of shock, surprise and grief to remove culpability from myself." His reason? He killed the child to "rid me of her mother's interferences." He wrote and directed his own story, then joined the parade of victims by complaining about the girl's mother. Several members of the murderer's online support group didn't want to report the incident to authorities. One urged the man "to seriously think about contacting a therapist and working things through with yourself in a safe manner."[44]

Victims ask for forgiveness and seem to express innocence. What they're claiming for themselves, however, is blamelessness. And the national support group accommodates them. "It is an instructive paradox that the culture that so prized rugged individualism should now be the culture that so willingly countenances victimology," says James Twitchell. "Okay, they seem to say, I did wrong, but you should have seen what was done to *me*. If you think what I did was bad, well, what about how I was treated?" As Twitchell says, people like this are part of our popular culture not because they are unique, but because they are exaggerations of recognized types—they remind us of ourselves.[45]

Ordinary folks create their stories and hear the cheers of their contracted circle of influence. As Jerzy Kosinski says, "When the 'show' is 'brought to you by' yourself, its consequences can't be changed like a channel."[46]

Chapter 6

Context Free

China's ancient city of Xian holds a most amazing sight. Buried underground centuries ago were tens of thousands of life-size terra cotta statues representing an army ready to keep Emperor Qin Shihuangui safe in his afterlife journey. It is difficult to imagine the work necessary to mold each statue from clay and to form enough different heads and helmets to hide the repetition of expression and style.

Once the statues were crafted between 221 and 210 B.C., they were assembled in long lines like an army of the time; then they were buried. Acres of the earthen statues lay sheathed in mud until a road crew began digging in the area in 1974 and found the first fragments of statuary. Digging opened the eyes of the locals in Xian, and later the archaeologists of the world, to the magnitude of the find.

It was in that city that President Clinton arrived in China for a 1998 trip designed to diffuse the strained relationship between the United States and the People's Republic. At home, the newspapers wondered whether Clinton scheduled the visit to take the national eye off his indiscretions with a White House intern. Those supporting the president hoped he'd take the opportunity to set those Chinese straight about running down protesters in Tiananmen Square just nine years before.

The date of his appearance was an unfortunate choice: June 25, 1998. Without a mention, without an acknowledgment, the head of the free world landed in Xian on the anniversary of the beginning of the only war the United States ever fought against China. "The Chinese Intervention," it was called, in the euphemism of the "peaceful" 1950s.

On June 25, 1950, North Korea invaded South Korea and drew the United States into a fight against Chinese troops in the Taktong Mountains of North Korea. Ultimately, the conflict would kill 54,000 Americans soldiers, end

143

the career of General Douglas MacArthur, and open the door to Dwight Eisenhower's presidency.

Bill Clinton had not reached his fourth birthday at the time, so we can't blame his memory. But couldn't someone in the Clinton White House have recommended a change of schedule even by a day? Or add a mention by the president during a speech in China?

James Brady caught the significance of the date. Writing in *Advertising Age,* he said that by the time he had his second cup of coffee that morning, he was steaming mad, talking to himself as he read the news:

> What the hell was going on here? Does no one in the Clinton bunch have any sense of historical perspective? A thousand people in his entourage and all those brainy presidential assistants and Cabinet members and archivists and gofers? Sandy Berger? [Richard] Holbrooke? Bill Richardson? What of Madame Albright? The secretary of state signed off on a Clinton arrival on the anniversary of the start of our one and only war with China? What was she thinking about? Are any of these people even marginally competent?
>
> We were young then and fought great China in a terrible war in appalling weather in their own back yard, six American divisions against 40 divisions of Chinese regulars and we beat the bastards back and ground them to a halt, saving as we did a small country far away.

Brady, a Korea veteran, was right to be angry. He wondered whether Korea had become "a forgotten war." And it had.[1]

Clinton is America's first president to grow up in the electronic media age. He and his staff and advisors weren't consciously ignoring the anniversary of the Korean War. It just slipped away into the haze of an amnesia-like state that has lost so many other significant events. The electronic media president was responding the way electronic media respond. All history is presented at once, leaving us no sense of continuum, no context for judgment.

Perhaps to a television viewer, the Korean War didn't begin on June 25, 1950, but on the date of whatever PBS show brought the historical recap. Who knows? It might have begun on last night's *Biography* on the Arts and Entertainment channel.

Or the television viewer may think it didn't happen at all. In the case of the Korean War, little of the conflict was recorded on film for television. The collective memory of television has little space for what it cannot show.

The images of the television age blind us to all the ages that precede it, even if that age was closely aligned. As Bill McKibben discovered as he reviewed all the output of all the channels on his local cable system: "To the list of neighborhood and region and continent and planet we must now add television as a place where we live. And the problem is not that it exists—the problem is that it supplants."[2]

Just as television supplants history, it also supplants context. While the specific complaint by James Brady was that President Clinton did not remember the date of the Korean War, the greater complaint is that Clinton missed the context of his message against the message of the "Chinese Intervention."

Barry Levinson's film *Avalon* contains another powerful demonstration of a disconnect in context. In the film, an immigrant grandfather tells and retells the stories of the family's American origins at the turn of the 1900s. The old man is a household shaman, a contact with a world long gone. When television arrives in the household, the old man's position as storyteller is gradually supplanted.

The final scene takes place in a nursing home, the grandfather's new home. The old man's grown son brings his own little boy to visit Grampa on Thanksgiving Day. For decades, the family Thanksgiving custom had been listening to Grampa as he wove the magic and the mystery of coming to America. The feeble old man begins the tale, but cannot capture the young boy's attention. The television is on, as is so often the case in nursing homes, and the boy watches the Macy's Thanksgiving Day Parade. The words of an old man can't compete with the marching bands and cartoon character balloons.

One Thanksgiving tradition is laid waste by another. The former is an immigrant family's unique context. The latter is a commercial venture in no way connected to the family, the boy, or—for that matter—to the origins of Thanksgiving. Yet the parade is context for the little boy.[3]

Television led us from a word culture to an image culture. That does not imply that images are bad, for we've lived with images for centuries. Books, architecture, stained glass windows, and tapestries all carried images with no particular negative effect. But the speedup of perception caused by the images created in electronic media is a negative result. It fosters images with no context except themselves and whatever image went just before.

Mediamnesia

Umberto Eco reports seeing Stanley Kubrick's groundbreaking film, *2001*, some years after he had seen it the first time. It was "a classic we remembered with admiration, affection, and respect," says Eco. After revisiting the film, he feels disappointment and so do his friends.

> That film, which had stunned us only a few years ago with its extraordinary technical and figurative invention, its metaphysical breadth, now seemed to

repeat wearily things we had seen a thousand times before. The drama of the paranoid computer still maintains its tension, though it no longer seems amazing; the beginning with the monkeys is still a fine piece of cinema, but those non-aerodynamic spaceships have long lain in the toybox of our now-grown children, reproduced in plastic . . . the final images are kitsch (a lot of pseudophilosophical vagueness in which anyone can put the allegory he wants), and the rest is discographic, music and sleeves.

Eco continues, and it's easy to agree with him: Kubrick was an innovator and a genius. His vision astounded us from the first notes of *Also Sprach Zarathrustra* through the last fading image. When we first saw *2001*, we saw it in a different context—a context of time and space much different from that even a few years after the film was released.

Eco calls mass media "genealogical" and, at the same time, he says, media have no memory. Those attributes should be incompatible, but they're not:

> The mass media are genealogical because, in them, every new invention sets off a chain reaction of inventions, produces a sort of common language. They have no memory because, when the chain of imitations has been produced, no one can remember who started it, and the head of the clan is confused with the latest great grandson. Furthermore, the media learn; and thus the spaceships of *Star Wars*, shamelessly descended from Kubrick's, are more complex and plausible than their ancestor, and now the ancestor seems to be their imitator.[4]

The "genealogy" of media suggests that the original images are stored for retrieval long after the succeeding images have been viewed. With electronic media, especially television, the child is often father to the man.

That's why television has no sense of history. That's why Americans suffer a national amnesia. The fifty-plus years of television's hold on America has compacted all of history into one brief period. It's a distortion of our sense of time, and we seem all too willing to accept it. As Bill McKibben writes in *The Age of Missing Information*, the one thing television remembers clearly is television:

> We know the period because we watch it constantly, over and over. The history—social, cultural, musical, economic, political—of the last forty years appears every day a thousand times on our screens, more and more frequently all the time. There are now a hundred channels airing TV shows—most of them produce at best a few hours a week of their own programming. So they must turn to the shows produced by just three networks for forty years, and show them again and again. You could spend an entire day

hopping from channel to channel, never leaving sixties sitcoms. And this is not mere filler. Cable channels like Nickelodeon have discovered large numbers will watch the past head-on against network fare—in a row they run *Dobie Gillis*, *Bewitched*, *Green Acres*, *Saturday Night Live*, *Rowan and Martin's Laugh-In*, *My Three Sons*, *Patty Duke*, *Make Room for Daddy*, then back to *Dobie Gillis*.

McKibben calls us "happily trapped in a familiar museum," condemned to know in minutest detail the attitudes and styles of one period—the era of television. TV can't go back before 1900 because there were no pictures before 1900. The fuzziest stills and the shakiest black and white films feed TV's images of the time, but TV is hesitant to use even those.[5]

The image orthicon, or video camera, made things appear more real, more believable. Digital advances enhanced the view if not the reality. Yet there's a disconnect. The beginning of the twenty-first century is a period chained to imagery, primarily the imagery of television. If the cameras aren't there, is the event real?

- The Korean War allowed only a few glimpses of the action because of the difficulty of getting equipment into the mountains.
- The bloodiest war since 1945 raged between Iran and Iraq during 1985, but few TV cameras were allowed to record it.
- There was no famine in Africa until a BBC camera crew stumbled across it.
- Before South Africa's liberation from apartheid, the government banned cameras, an easy way to avoid the world's wrath.

If there's no record, there's no reporting, and we're further disconnected from events and their context. George W.S. Trow says television is *Within the Context of No Context*, the title of a thin volume of diary entries and essays presented like television itself, blip by blip, one shard at a time. Trow originally published "Within the Context of No Context" as an article in the *New Yorker* in 1980 and later added commentary (and, some would say, context).

The form of the little book is as important as its subject matter. Here and there a linear-sequential stream of paragraphs. Here and there fragmented ideas that repeat and expand. If Trow wasn't trying to duplicate television's nonlinear patterns, he achieved it anyway. Anticipating the words of McKibben, Eco, and others, Trow calls television

> . . . the force of no-history, and it holds the archives of no-history. Television is a mystery. Certain of its properties are known, though. It has a *scale*. The scale *does not vary*. The trivial is raised up to the place where

this scale has its home; the powerful is lowered there. In the place where this scale has its home, childish agreements can be arrived at and enforced effectively—childish agreements, and agreements wearing the mask of childhood.[6]

"Childish" is a good word for television.

"Childlike" is best for the way we consume television. We approach the floods of images with innocent acceptance. As they all wash over us, our perceptions begin to blur. The ambiguous border between perception and reality is the enemy of context. As images carom from comedy to drama to breaking news to commercials to sports events, they create "oxymoronic schemes," in the words of Curt McCray, who describes one from the middle years of television:

> The heaviest demands on credibility and the most jarring juxtaposition between reality and unreality, however, occur within the shows themselves and their commercials. While some ads, like those for Gulf Oil Co. during the Apollo 14 flight, attempt to meld their spiel with the show, the majority do not. On the late show one evening *Death of a Salesman* was interrupted by an undertaker's ad just after Uncle Ben told Willie [sic] that he went into the jungle and "by God I came out rich," and Willie's [sic] automobile suicide was followed by a used car salesman.[7]

Using a description from TV's earlier days shows that the juxtapositions have been going on for some time. They are the product not of MTV or ESPN, but of the essence of television—compression of images into easily assimilated units of time.

Just Like Us

George Trow claims that television shifted the power of context when Dwight Eisenhower ran for the presidency, when the candidate's slogan was "I Like Ike":

> It shifted from General Eisenhower to someone called Ike, who embodied certain aspects of General Eisenhower and certain aspects of affection for General Eisenhower. Then it shifted again. From "Ike," you could see certain aspects of General Eisenhower. From "like," all you could see was other Americans engaged in a process resembling the process of intimacy.[8]

As a nation, we reduced NATO's Supreme Allied Commander, the man who led the Allied forces to a victorious end to World War II, to a cozy nickname and the role of a kindly uncle smiling at us from the television set. Eisenhower was clearly uneasy with television. He bumbled through news conferences and talked in circles when he ad-libbed.

His successor, John Kennedy, showed a real affinity for the medium. Kennedy proved his understanding of television so many times, none better than during his debate with challenger Richard Nixon. It was the first instance in which what a politician said was less important than his ability to look like he meant it.

In his television presidency, Kennedy was the aristocrat who became one of us. His smile, his natural wit, and his choice of bride made him welcome in every American living room. Like an entertainer, he engaged his audience with humor and a hometown style of "aw-shucks" self-deprecation. After a state dinner in France, the president stopped to talk with reporters, grinned, and said, "I am the man who accompanied Jacqueline Kennedy to Paris."

Political life changed because Kennedy understood the power of television. He knew the relatively new medium would be his connection to his constituency. Kennedy's assassination set the politics of television back a few years, but his funeral fed one of the first mythic events of the television era. Joseph Campbell called the solemn state funeral for the slain Kennedy "an illustration of the high service of ritual to a society." It evoked mythological themes rooted in human need.[9]

John Kennedy's charm and mastery of the intimate medium of television made him one of us. In death, however, he became bigger than us, larger than life, the stuff of myth, like the gods of the ancients.

Many of the world's myths address the lure of immortality, life after death, or resurrection. Hindu and the Sufi myths are excellent examples. Greek myths, however, introduce us to the opposite: the lure of mortality among the gods.

Zeus, for example, falls in love with Alcmene, the wife of Amphitryon, a general in the Greek army. For the entire affair, Zeus exhibits exceptionally human traits for a god: he can't resist looking down from Mount Olympus at the shadow the general's wife casts upon her window. Mercury suggests that Zeus arrange a convenient military maneuver so that the general would be called away. Zeus could then disguise himself as Amphitryon and fulfill his yearning.[10]

He does, but he finds something disturbing. Alcmene talks to Zeus about being young and about being old. Most worrisome to Zeus is her saying something about when she dies. As Zeus tells Mercury of his reactions, he says, "This stabs me, Mercury. We miss something. We miss the poignancy of the transient—the sweet sadness of grasping for something we know we cannot hold." As Rollo May puts it, Zeus misses "the charm of mortality."

What the Greeks introduced, we have perfected. Zeus took a lover. Thor visited the land of the giants. Jesus worked at carpentry. The gods, indeed, join the earthlings in most major religions of the west.

Today, we bring our newly ordained gods to earth as well. Julia Roberts uses the Laundromat, or so she says in a television interview. Does anyone watching wonder why someone making $20 million per film would go to the Laundromat? Roberts also claims she can slip out of the house and go to the grocery store without being recognized. She wants her fans to think she's just like them.[11]

Madonna transformed herself from the tough-talking, taboo-challenging pop icon to the ideal of motherhood. At one point, the singer challenged propriety by naming one of her companies "Slutco" and shocking David Letterman with a stream of four-letter words on his late night TV show. Then her star cooled. *Esquire* called Madonna "The Most Boring Woman Who Used to Be Interesting," and *Entertainment Weekly* declared her "cold."

Today, Madonna's just like us. She appears on the cover of *Redbook* with "the surprising plans she has for her daughter." The woman who lived life beyond the margin of taste is transformed by a celebration of motherhood.[12]

Diana, "the fairy tale princess," wore sports logo jackets by day (Philadelphia Eagles fans rejoiced!) while glittering with high fashion at night. She was seen on television in exercise clothes and driving her own car, hardly the stuff of royalty.

Absent context, the line between day-to-day life and fame diminishes. Gone are the divisions between public and private lives, politics and show business, notoriety and fame.

Television moved us from a word culture to an image culture, but "contrary to the popular saying, a picture is not worth a thousand words," says Joshua Meyrowitz:

> Television encourages us to apply private criteria of evaluation to public issues and people. We do not generally marry someone on the basis of a resume and a writing sample, and before the TV-fostered image culture we rarely considered voting for a presidential candidate because of the sparkle in his eye.
>
> Polls now show that many people will vote for a candidate with whom they disagree on the issues because they "personally like" him or her. . . . Such a reaction makes sense only when we feel we have met and "know" our leaders personally. And television gives us that feeling.[13]

We are more likely to think we "personally like" a candidate or a movie star when that person seems like us. Andy Warhol's "fifteen minutes of fame" now moves both ways. Just as the common man seeks his fifteen minutes, the extraordinary talents attempt to project the image of being more real, down-to-earth.

Just like us, only more so.

We enjoy the humbling of the famous, especially when we discover that they're in drug rehab or confessing some criminal activity. It gives us the chance to feel superior to them if we feel our lives are more in order; they're just not as good as us. If we feel insecure, there's comfort in knowing that the mighty also have their flaws. We disconnect the famous from what gave them fame in the first place—their ability to seem bigger than life.

Rewriting History

The stuff that cartoons are made of: the brutal murder of an entire family, including a disabled eight-year-old boy, a group of caregivers, and the family's pet spaniel.

In order to make that plot work as family entertainment, we'll have to make some adjustments. First, we won't show the murders; we'll set the scene later; and we'll add a few sprightly songs. Design a train crash scene. Create a character who's part ghoul. The story needs a beautiful heroine. Now, use a charming animation style. Finally, there's a story the whole family can enjoy!

But what of the brutal murders? Who was the family whose tale was so ignored by the animated feature? It's the Romanov family of prerevolution Russia. Incurable romantics know the legend of how the youngest daughter of Czar Nicholas II survived the massacre of her family in 1918 only to end up a mad, lonely, beautiful waif in Paris. She was the genesis, but not the story, of the animated movie *Anastasia*.

The ghoul in the story was elaborated from Rasputin, in real life the power-mad, destructive advisor to Anastasia's mother. The girl wasn't quite the durable survivor that the cartoon portrayed. Even though the death squad that wiped out her family missed her, evidence from a grave in Siberia suggests she was clubbed to death by yet another group. There was no song and dance about that in the film.

Columnist Jacquelyn Mitchard asked if *Anastasia*'s "perky spin on such horrific real-life events" sends children the wrong message. "Doesn't it lead to the idea that cute pictures and musical aromatherapy can pretty up the ugliest stains on humanity?" she wondered.[14] Of course it does. It creates a disconnect with the truth and adds to the context-free zones our children live in.

Consider another story, this one a love story, about a tall, blond, smooth-shaven captain and a copper-skinned Native American beauty with full lips and a fuller figure ("and her Pert Plus hairdo," adds Mitchard). If you saw

Disney's *Pocahontas,* you recognize those characters. If you know the story of the Jamestown settlement, you don't recognize them at all.

Captain John Smith and Pocahontas existed, of course. But Smith was dark-haired, bearded, and short. Pocahontas was eleven years old at the time, hardly a full-figured bombshell wearing deerskins from Victoria's Secret. Pocahontas did marry an Englishman, but it was years later and it wasn't Smith.

Hearing criticism about the historical accuracy of the 1995 animated feature, a Disney executive told the *Washington Post* that "nobody knows the truth of her legend," so the studio set out to make "a beautiful movie about the Native American experience." Plenty of historical documents exist, including the records of the Jamestown colony. Details about the way Pocahontas saved the American colony appear in multiple English sources.[15]

We know, for example, that the Powhatan tribe was an expansionist group that taxed their conquered people to the tune of 80 percent of all they grew, caught, or created. The collected loot went directly to Chief Powhatan, who traded regularly with the English. Smith was a scholar of the Powhatans; he studied their language and culture. The film, however, portrayed Smith as out to kill the natives and the Powhatans as antimaterialistic.

Hollywood often takes liberties with history to weave a good yarn. The context of *Pocahontas*, the Disney cartoon, was not the context of colonial Jamestown, but the context of the prevailing values of the time in which it was shown: political correctness and box-office power. Mix a threat of genocide and a strong environmental message and you've got a line of ticket-buyers.

Disney has a tendency to sentimentalize reality, which creates a disconnect with the context of history. There was an outcry when Disney proposed a theme park in northern Virginia, just miles from colonial Williamsburg and from Civil War battlefields. Plans were abandoned amid fears of Civil War pony rides and virtual reality arcades. Among those who fought the theme park was historian Shelby Foote, who charged that Disney would do to history "what they have already done to the animal kingdom—sentimentalize it out of recognition."[16]

That's Entertainment

Disney is not alone in constructing themed environments. The Disney name has simply become synonymous with the idea. The Mall of America, near Minneapolis, attracts more visitors than Disneyland, Walt Disney World, and the Grand Canyon combined. It's important to note here that the Grand Canyon is not a Disney property, nor has it succumbed to the "entertainment-for-entertainment's sake" attitude that often overtakes the shopping experience in our malls.[17]

Any major-league baseball park is as much a theme park as a Disney establishment. So far, however, major-league baseball still allows a game to be played on the field without enhancement by "imagineers." The carnival atmosphere around the game changes the context from the days when baseball was the reason fans attended, not swimming parties, carnival rides, and live bands.

The penchant for entertainment attracts us to theme parks in spite of the disconnect from history or reality, or, maybe, because of it. The "Virtual Elvis" tour in the summer of 1998 was a traveling theme park. The tour used big-screen video to show footage of Elvis Presley while a band played live on stage. Concertgoers are so used to watching performers on giant screens during concerts that they get caught in the illusion. After a few songs, it doesn't matter that Elvis is not there.[18]

The theme park called Las Vegas contains theme parks within the larger park. Patrons can explore Paris, Venice, and New York, among other cities reconstructed as themed environments. Want something not so earthbound? Step onto the deck of the starship *Voyager* or into a restaurant modeled after the canteen on *Star Trek,* complete with blue beer called Romulan Ale.

People get lost in the Vegas theme park. That's the intention: Get lost, stay longer. Vegas creates its own context.

Take, for example, a woman aged at least sixty-five, maybe seventy. She was at the edge of her chair, leaning slightly forward, her body secured against the leatherette armrest. Her eyes, not quite glazed, aimed at the near distance but never seemed to focus. At the other end of the armrest was a plastic cup that could hold twenty to twenty-four ounces of liquid. No liquid today. The cup was half full of quarters and weighed close to four pounds. Weight was no object. She selected the quarters one at a time and thrust them into the slot machine in front of her.

From her machine and from uncountable numbers of others around her came bells, sirens, whistles, and synthesized electronic music, taunting the solitary players, most of them about her age. It was early by Las Vegas standards, just before 9:00 A.M. on a spring-like Saturday morning.

Ten feet or so to her rear was another bank of slot machines that sporadically erupted with a recording of the TV studio audience chanting "Wheel of Fortune!" just as they do at the beginning of the television game show. There was something otherworldly about the sound effects and music overlaid with the familiar phrase:

"Wheel (pause) of (pause) Fortune!"
"Wheel (pause) of (pause) Fortune!"
"Wheel (pause) of (pause) Fortune!"
"Wheel (pause) of (pause) Fortune!"
The cacophony did not attract the woman's attention. None of the casino's

sounds did. She was disconnected from the noise, from the people around her, and from her own actions. The quarters went into the slot. The bars and symbols spun before her eyes. The music erupted. She began anew.

Vegas attracted her attention, or she wouldn't be there. But once there, she disconnected from everything but the chance of winning. Not the *hope* of winning, only the chance. There was no acknowledgment of passersby, no awareness of other players along the same line of slot machines.

Las Vegas gives the visitor a strange sense of timelessness. Except for the blazing desert sun by day, there's no indication of time. When the lights on the strip begin to glow at night, there's a perpetual "daytime" that lulls the visitor into ignoring the clock. It's a city that never sleeps, part of its charm to those who want to get away from schedules and calendars. Las Vegas attempts to create context where there is none.

Context Busters

Imagine a time when context was easy to identify. It was home, hearth, community, or, as McLuhan described it, the village and the campfire. The so-called campfire cultures knew the power of repetition, because a story had to be passed from parent to child and from village to village in order to stay alive in the culture. Oral cultures told the stories again and again, like the old man in Levinson's film *Avalon,* keeping the family history alive for another generation.

The community stories created a sense of order in the village. There were rules in the stories, whom to respect, whom to reject. There was knowledge of hunting, how much to kill and where to find the beasts. There was news of the season of gathering, how the planting should be handled, and what shaman would invoke the spirit of the growing gods. Not a hundred channels, but one, where a single program repeated year after year with variations from the teller, but the same story nonetheless. Thus our mythology and our holy scriptures survived.

As McLuhan realized, there's a lot of tribal villager in us, because we thrive on repetition. Bill McKibben put it this way:

> Where English teachers once identified the six conflicts in literature (man against man, man against nature, and so on) they could now list for their students the six sitcom plots: man struck on head gets amnesia, woman has half a winning lottery ticket, man dislikes his daughter's boyfriend, man finds himself in an unconventional living arrangement (for instance, his roommates are three busty cheerleaders). . . . The most powerful repeating element is obviously the commercial. Advertisers, the most diligent students of human nature, know that it is useless to advertise just once or twice—the ad must be repeated a hundred times, a thousand times, till it "penetrates" the "clutter."
> Against this tide, the exceptional drowns.[19]

And so does context. The more we use television as our idea of the order of the world, the more we're likely to encounter contextual disconnect.

When President Clinton produced a comedy video for the Washington Press Club "roast" dinner, he enlisted comedy writers and Hollywood actors. The short skits portrayed how lonely Mr. Clinton would be at the White House once Mrs. Clinton mounted her campaign for the Senate from New York. The networks played segments of the tape for several days. And ABC had Regis Philbin from *Who Wants to Be a Millionaire* as a reviewer during the Sunday morning *This Week* news show. Philbin commented on the president's timing and the fun factor in his jokes.

Also on ABC: Newscaster Elizabeth Vargas told the story of a Brinks truck that overturned in Miami and spilled its cargo of money. People on the street picked up approximately $400,000. Vargas ad-libbed, "It was a bad neighborhood." To which weatherman Spencer Christian replied, "Maybe it was homeless people. I hope they put it to good use." The two sounded as if they condoned stealing the money. Did the people who stole the money not understand that it came from their neighborhood grocery stores, their banks, and their own payrolls? Clearly there was no context.

The Braves faced the Mets in a Saturday game of the week during an Independence Day weekend on Fox TV. To celebrate the occasion, commentator Tim McCarver decided to read the Gettysburg Address. "It's shorter than an at bat," McCarver said, and set about to read Lincoln's words quickly enough to prove that fact. Even though he sped through it, the batter struck out before he finished. Lincoln delivered his speech at the bloodiest battlefield of the Civil War, and McCarver trivialized it in three strikes.

When Channel 3 television in Memphis interrupted a football game to announce a tornado warning for nearby Jackson, Tennessee, people called the station to complain. Eight people died in the storms.[20]

CNN interviewed a scientist who once worked to split the atom. The same scientist had gone on to develop the pat of butter and later a squeeze tube to replace the little envelopes for ketchup at fast-food restaurants. In the interview, the atom-splitting scientist wrote "Hi, CNN" in cream cheese.[21]

Each of those stories created a context-free zone.

Unreal Cult

Consider this online message: "We kill. It's OK. It's not our fault any more than breathing or urinating." The posting was at Heat.Net, the Web site of the CyberDiversion movement. The movement's founder, Dr. Bartha, was quoted as saying the proper way to deal with the urge to kill was to play video games in cyberspace.

When Dr. Bartha's Web site downloaded, the first thing seen was a banner for "Fast, Free, Guiltless Killing." Next was a circle with the words "Sign me up" inside and the word "Killing" on either side of the circle. Deeper into the site was this message:

> We are a nonprofit fellowship of Christian men and women who have found Dr. Bartha's teachings of CyberDiversion to be valuable in helping us lead a more complete Christian life.
>   What does CyberDiversion Theory have in common with Christianity? How can we grow Spiritually from diverting the primal self into Cyberspace and away from our Brothers and Sisters in Organic Reality? Well, as is always the case, the Answers lie where all Answers lie—in Scripture, where hope, love, and peace are still alive and well and waiting for us to become entrapped by them.

Headquarters for the CyberDiversion Movement was a converted warehouse in Santa Monica called the CyberDiversion Institute. Dismantled wings of old fighter planes served as partitions in the offices, and CyberDiversionists sat on B-52 ejection seats. An old school bus was painted with the CyberDiversion name and a slogan: "A life killed in cyberspace is a life saved on Earth."

The CyberDiversionists staged a rally at the Santa Monica courthouse during the second O.J. Simpson trial. Their activities were covered by Los Angeles television.

The CyberDiversionists are no more real than Ivy, the hero of *Soul Calibur.* Dr. Bartha is neither a militia-style killer nor a cult leader. He's a fabrication rendered by an advertising agency (in Santa Monica, which shouldn't surprise you). The company developed the Heat.Net Web sites as a promotional tool for SegaSoft online games in 1997. All the sites (13 in all, including an anti-Bartha site called Mothers Against the Movement) had a homemade look that made them seem non-commercial.[22]

The timing of the Web presence was unfortunate, since it was launched for testing just a month after thirty-nine members of the Heaven's Gate cult committed mass suicide waiting for a spaceship to emerge from behind the comet Hale-Bopp and return their souls to the heavens.

Even if the launch of the CyberDiversionist sites had not been so close on the heels of Heaven's Gate's purple-shrouded suicide, the idea was questionable. Would teenagers, for whom the sites were targeted, discern the difference between the "Fast, Free, Guiltless" prokilling messages and the prosafety, antikilling message buried deep in the CyberDiversionist text? Only a teenager can answer. Was the idea prudent? No. Parents are concerned as it is.

How much more concerned are they when they know their kids may not be able to sort the real from the fanciful, their own fantasies from some ad agency's concoction?

Context by the Numbers

Until the twelfth century, the concept of time was governed by the rise of the sun and the cycles of the moon. That was interrupted by the invention of the mechanical clock. A group of Benedictine monks in Europe developed the clock to give order to their monastic lives. Among their religious obligations were seven prayer periods during the day, so what better than an automatic signal that it was time to pray? The bells of the monastery rang to signal canonical hours, and the devotions were ritualized.

The clock moved from a strictly religious timekeeper into the public sphere in the year 1370, when King Charles V ordered all citizens of Paris to schedule their lives around the bells of the royal palace clock, which struck every sixty minutes. The churches, too, were to regulate their clocks according to the king's time, and canonical hours were abandoned.

Following the clock made regular working hours possible. That resulted in greater control of the labor force and, therefore, greater production. As Neil Postman wrote in *Technopoly*, "Without the clock, capitalism would have been quite impossible."[23]

The clock is a contextual reminder. The slow sweep of the hands mirrors the rising and setting of the sun, even the coming and going of the seasons. The face of the clock is said to represent different parts of the day or the circularity of life.

Today the clock augments our desperate attempt to control time. Fortunes are spent on elaborate calendar management systems to anticipate and record the most minute time increments.

Only in our age of speeded-up time would we attempt to slow it down by dividing it into smaller and smaller increments. The monks divided the day into seven segments, King Charles V into twenty-four. We sliced it further by creating clock faces that show the time minute by minute. Then we added another hand to tick off the seconds. Our video players divide time into ever smaller units, frame counts of a hundredth of a second. High speed computation is done in nanoseconds, one-billionth of a second. The result is not a slowing down, but a speeding up of time and ourselves.

Enter the digital watch with nothing but numbers, and we've completely abstracted time. Time without context. Time without the movement of the sun or the phases of the moon. Time without planets or without seasons. Time as numbers.[24]

Your day may start with the first song of the mockingbird. Your city-dweller sister's may begin with the first blast of an auto horn. Neither abstracts the day; each defines it. If your day starts at 6:15, however, that's abstracted from both the bird and the blast.

Abstract numbers, like abstract words, create distance and serve as an emotional shield. They disconnect us from the thing counted. We reduce the homeless population to abstract numbers. We reduce our politics to polling numbers. We reduce our lives to daily schedules and hours billed.

From top 10 lists to 10k races, we've become fixated with numbers, as if reducing everything to a numerical abstract will give it context. The Dow Jones Industrial Average broke through the 10,000 level and Wall Street cheered, even though the average represents only thirty stocks, not the hundreds of thousands on the world's exchanges.[25]

Of course using a popular index makes it easy to keep up. A quick look at the Dow makes us think we know whether the market is healthy or not. The reaction of traders on Wall Street to any hiccup in the Dow should tell us otherwise. None of us tracks the U.S. population, but it's easy to say "about 265 million." We won't be impugned for our imprecision.

The dizzying pace of change and the rapid erosion of context overwhelmed people in the twentieth century, so they took matters into their own hands, breaking time and experience into bite-sized numbers. It was only in the twentieth century that the decades were named, the Roaring Twenties or the Greedy Eighties, for example. Before that, periods of time were usually related to historical events, Reconstruction, for example, or the Victorian era. The spans of those "ages" went beyond specific increments of time.

The numbers game provides comfort, control, and a sense of context.

Chapter 7

The End of Mass Media

Don't tell the networks, but mass media ended in 1983. You probably don't remember a formal announcement. There were no headlines, no news bulletins.

The only evidence at the time was an essay by Italian philosopher and semiotician Umberto Eco. He suggested that the 1960s and 1970s model of the mass media was already passé in 1983. The old model—a centralized transmitter with precise political and pedagogical plans, controlled by an "Authority," with signals sent through recognizable channels to what he called "victims of ideological indoctrination"—needed new interpretation.[1]

Eco's remarks were prescient since they were written far earlier than the true fragmentation of media. The backdrop in America was just a few years of HBO and the fledgling CNN on cable. U.S. television was dominated by the same networks that held our attention from the beginning.

Media's origins were innocent enough. This book began with Plato's warning that writing induced forgetfulness. Plato would be shocked to see how many ideas mankind has off-loaded and forgotten, including some of his.

Every new technology yields unforeseen results. As described in the previous chapter, the clock made us first timekeepers, then time-savers, and now timeservers, to paraphrase Lewis Mumford. We traded our world of reverence for the sun and the moon for one measured in minutes and seconds. With the clock, eternity ceased to serve as the measure and focus of human events. "Moment to moment is not God's conception, or nature's," says Neil Postman. "It is man conversing with himself about and through a piece of machinery he created."[2]

The legacy of the recent millennium is the democratization of information. We take for granted that most people—at least those in developed countries—have access to a great deal of information. We seldom pause to consider that this is a recent phenomenon and that we're still trying to understand all the ramifications.

The printing press extended Authority by promulgating ideas and simultaneously undermined Authority by putting interpretation in the hands of the consumer, who became Authority. Gutenberg, a devout Catholic, would be horrified at the fact that his invention allowed each member of his congregation to become a theologian.

The telescope further undermined Authority by showing man the vastness of where God lived. Earth lost its place as the center of the universe, and man began to wonder if God had enough time to tend to man's needs and the needs of the universe at the same time. Man could not only marvel at the heavens, but speculate about them as well.

Electric media had their own unforeseen results. The early motion pictures startled audiences, making them run for cover when a train pulled into the on-screen station. Many a theater manager told stories of patrons who pulled back the screen, wondering where the actors were hidden.

The most famous men in electronic media could get it wrong, too. Thomas Edison, for example, expected the telephone to transmit music and news. Until recently, when telephone companies began to align themselves with cable operators, Edison seemed mighty wrong. He also viewed the cylinder recorder as an answering machine for people with no telephones: A central telephone office would capture messages so customers could pick them up at their convenience.

Early documents about radio predicted that the medium would be used for personal communication, not mass broadcasting. Radio was seen as akin to today's cellular phones. David Sarnoff thought otherwise. He envisioned radio as a mass medium, but predicted six super-powered radio stations would blanket the United States so everyone could hear the programming. That's a far cry from the 11,000 or so stations that serve America today. (That's one radio station for every 22,000 Americans, a figure that astonishes visitors from outside the United States.)

Early uses of both radio and telephone were reversed, based on what we know today. AT&T developed "Toll Broadcasting" on its New York City lines in 1922 and attempted to sell advertising on the new service. At about the same time, the city of Budapest was wired for sound in an experiment to bring music into each home.[3]

Media Squared

You'll remember E.B. White's anxiety about television when he first saw it demonstrated in 1938. As you read in Chapter One, he expected "either a new and unbearable disturbance of the general peace or a saving radiance from the sky." Now that we have more than fifty years of television fare to judge, we know White was right to fret.

Television established itself as Authority by riveting our attention. The medium's first big star, Milton Berle, dressed in women's clothing while cracking jokes that other comedians accused him of stealing from them. The medium that previously trained its eye on a theater's stage or a radio performer's interview came into its own with a celebrity who used the visual expanse of the medium on its own terms.

Television was political Authority in its early incarnation, bringing together whole neighborhoods whose residents stood in front of store windows to watch election results counted on the tiny screen.

In the first wave of consumer-controlled media, the individual made up his own media complement with the remote control and the dashboard pushbutton. Umberto Eco attempted to make sense of those changes, too:

> The consumer's freedom may not have increased, but surely the way to teach him to be free and controlled has changed. And, for the rest, two new phenomena have slowly progressed: the multiplication of the media and the media squared.[4]

"Squared" seems too small an exponent now that electronic media multiply channels upon themselves and give us the options of individual connectivity. Every consumer can create a culture, a personal story, and a connection with as few as one or as many others as desired.

Online, a thousand new publishers a day undermine Authority as none of the new technologies ever could in the past. When new media finally dominate, "authority" will be written in lower case from that day forward.

A new use for technology emerges virtually every day. However, when the new idea catches hold, it takes two, sometimes three years to get a product to the marketplace. That's why the predictions we hear about market saturation of new media are often far wrong.

Media consumption seems like a zero-sum game, since there are just so many hours in the day and so much attention to go around. The expectation is that new media will push old media out. That hasn't happened to date. We still watch cable and over-the-air television. We surf the Internet and listen to radio. We keep finding new ways to cram more media experience into the limited time we have available to us. Since it takes no particular skill to use media, we tend to use them a lot.[5] Worse, we don't seem to know how to turn them off. The trash as well as the treasures sweep over us with equal velocity, and we take it all in.

Still, it's difficult to overlook the early evidence that new media may be just as unenlightened as old media. Junk e-mail, violent games, and XXX porn sites are all too present and accounted for on the Web. The *New York Times* warns of "networks of people lurking out there with alien values, and . . . anyone, any age, might stumble upon them with a mouseclick." Superficially, that's just not true. It's difficult to "stumble" onto anything in cyberspace, because you have to request it first, then link to something else, another request.

Any technology that makes good things happen makes bad things more convenient. As *Wired* suggests, the local call girls were first on the block to buy a telephone answering machine, and drug dealers were the first to use pagers. Interactive multimedia catch their share of criticism, usually with large headlines in traditional media. The *New York Times*, for example, used these headlines:

- A Seductive Drug Culture Flourishes on the Internet.
- Go Ahead, Be Paranoid. Hackers *Are* Out to Get You.
- Old View of Internet: Nerds. New View: Nuts.

To which *Wired* responded, "And now *The New York Times* has discovered, potheads are trading information on the Internet." The same article said that articles about computer hackers often follow a predictable formula: "three parts fearmongering to two parts salacious lip-smacking . . . railing against unseen dangers is a sure-fire way to pull in the crowds."[6]

Until the "I Love You" virus attacked European and North American e-mail and Web sites, hackers were viewed in the Internet community as lovable nerds who attempted to show just how vulnerable the system is. They were often considered "legends," "heroes," and "geniuses," according to the *Wall Street Journal*.[7] America has always been a sucker for a clever crook, whether it was Jesse James in the Old West or Bonnie and Clyde during the Great Depression. Hollywood dresses up legends that word-of-mouth mythology doesn't embroider.

Democracy to Chaos

Both the good news and the bad news about the Internet is that it's very democratic, but also very chaotic. That's why it troubles those who feel vulnerable. We live in an "interactive interim," poised between technologies, awaiting the completion of merging and converging that the technical people have been predicting since the early 1990s.[8] Traditional media hold fast to their hopes for a mass audience while thousands of new ideas strip away your time to watch or listen.

The result is confusion for those who want to manage their media exposure and protect their children from unwanted and unwarranted influences.
The teenager who thinks she's chatting online with a friend discovers that
the reality behind the letters on her screen is an adult male stalker. The stories are real. Insults and hate are as free in cyberspace as the people who
have keyboards. The difference on the Internet is the ease of anonymity.

The online connection creates the global village Marshall McLuhan anticipated. The early word about the Internet was that it would be a place
where people from all backgrounds came together to form one community.
Now it's emerging as the one-to-one connection where people of all backgrounds come together with people of their own background or interests.
Instead of one big village, there are as many villages as there are villagers
interested. Democracy reigns. But it's democracy on the verge of anarchy.

Perceived dangers prompt Internet users to order blocking software to
prevent their children from finding anything unsavory. Others move to "gated
communities" online, where they pay a price to be with their own. The registration and the password are the Internet equivalents of the secret handshake.[9]

The response of the Net community to the idea of blocking software is
negative. Some blocking systems, for example, would prevent access to
literature's greatest contributors because of the interpretation of a word or
phrase. On the other hand, the Net community embraces the private Web
sites that effect the "gated community" because of friendly environment and
a sense of security.

Teenagers talk to teenagers on sites that require a parent's permission.
The idea makes it difficult to cheat, because mom or dad has to submit a
personal e-mail address or contact site administrators by phone. Parents love
these sites. Kids don't. Sites that cater to the gay and lesbian communities
monitor membership closely to keep out gay-bashers. Their users do appreciate the security. America Online established its brand based on development of communities and was among the first to offer African-Americans an
online community.

Gated communities are symptomatic of the threat of open connectivity.
When groups want to protect themselves in this way, it's a clear indication
there's something to be protected from. It's easy to understand the desire to
escape the threat of stalking, gay-bashing, and racial hatred. In their book
about the radical right and radio, *Waves of Rancor*, Robert Hilliard and Michael
Keith create a long list of "resource Web pages for radicalists and freedom
fighters" to show the extent of distribution of material in cyberspace by groups
affiliated with the Ku Klux Klan, the neo-Nazi movement, skinheads, Christian identity groups, and the like.[10] While Hilliard and Keith focus on radio
talk shows and short wave transmissions, it's instructive to see how militias,

patriot groups, survivalists, and grassy-knoll conspiracy theorists use the Internet to distribute their ideologies. Their postings are opinion accepted as fact by the faithful.

Anything Goes

Groups on the political fringe have no monopoly on the Internet. The greatest threat of easy access to the Internet is the Wild West attitude of "anything goes." At any moment, the reality of cyberspace yields amusement, horror, or deception. Any word, phrase, or idea can be posted, forwarded, and re-forwarded until it appears as "fact" by repetition.

Take the "Sunscreen" speech for example. Some heard it first as a hit song on the radio by Baz Luhrmann. The so-called intelligentsia heard about it as a commencement address delivered by novelist Kurt Vonnegut at MIT. It was pure Vonnegut: "Ladies and gentlemen of the class of 1997: Wear sunscreen. . . . Keep your old love letters. Throw away your old bank statements. Stretch." It was a wonderful example of satire and irony, and it had some good advice to boot. Who couldn't appreciate it?

Mary Schmich didn't appreciate it. After all, she wrote it. The "Sunscreen" speech wasn't a speech at all. It wasn't written or delivered by Kurt Vonnegut. None of the words were said at MIT (until Luhrmann's record was released). Schmich, a columnist for the *Chicago Tribune,* wrote the advice to the Class of 1997 as her article for a spring day near graduation time.[11]

Then someone posted the column on the Internet. Then it was identified as a commencement address by Kurt Vonnegut. Those who read it liked it. The speech was forwarded through cyberspace, friend to friend, multiplied a million or more times by address books and listserve distribution. As these things happen, one of the recipients of the virtual chain letter was Kurt Vonnegut, who said he would have been pleased to have written it, but he did not.

The essential democracy of the Internet leads to untruths like the Vonnegut "speech." Every day, a similar abuse of ideas and intellectual property occurs. An article is forwarded and a key piece of information is left off, say the author's name. In the next forward, the sender becomes the author. A long e-mail about how our culture has become more entertainment than reality rang a bell with a reader who discovered that it was a chapter lifted verbatim from Michael Wolf's *The Entertainment Economy*. Those who distributed the article took at face value that the author was one of their colleagues who wanted to share his "insights" on the state of affairs.

There's a slippery road here. Even the most basic facts online can quickly become fiction with a few keystrokes, altering biography and fueling hoaxes, rumors, and urban myths that take on lives of their own. Repetition sells.

Advertisers have known that for years. Now everyone repeats and we get suckered into "things that just ain't so," to reprise Artemus Ward.

These instantaneous distributions of spurious information cannot be recalled like a faulty toaster, nor can they be corrected the way a news organization prints a retraction or clarification. The Internet is capable of turning floods of fantasy and error into what large numbers of people take as truth, because they're looking for something to believe. As the *Wall Street Journal* said in an editorial after the Vonnegut incident:

> In a country like ours, in which much of organized religion has given up promoting its belief systems in favor of saving welfare bureaucracies, it's hardly surprising that people would start believing in whatever strikes their fancy—a neat Kurt Vonnegut non-speech, the greenhouse effect, bottled water, the sudden but professedly innocent appearance of subpoenaed papers on a White House table, the beatification of Gianni Versace.[12]

The public mind can believe in anything, but trust in nothing. The TV show *The X-Files* captures the spirit of that feeling with its contradictory slogans: "I Want to Believe" and "Trust No One."[13]

On the surface, we've set ourselves up for what could be disaster. What we need is an all-new discipline that teaches young media users how to cope with the information that will overwhelm them, confuse them, or stultify them. The Internet will not ruin us, but the people using it could. The Internet is not a medium; it's a bunch of wires and packets of information working in the service of other media. Because it allows many systems to converge, it appears to be an entity of its own.

"The medium is the message," said McLuhan. Umberto Eco hears it in a slightly different accent (Italian, of course): "The mass media do not transmit ideologies; they are themselves an ideology." Neil Postman chimes in to reinforce: "[Television] is not neutral."

Postman takes the thought a step further in an interview with *Spin* magazine:

> Each technology has its own agenda, its own bias expressed through its very structure. . . . We have to understand the idea implicit in every new machine and find out if it's good for us or not. And if it's not so good, modify it to suit our needs. Once a technology is admitted to the culture, it does what it's designed to do, it plays out its full hand.[14]

McLuhan gives us these questions as a litmus test to examine the "grammar and syntax of each artifact" of technology. There are only four questions, he says, and they are in analogical proportion to each other:

1. What does it enhance?
2. What does it obsolesce?
3. What does it retrieve that had been obsolesced before?
4. What does it flip into when pushed to the limits of its potential?[15]

A fifth question might be, "Are we too late to ask these questions about merging and converging electronic media?"

If the medium is not only message but metaphor, then constantly accelerating electronic media are in metamorphosis, creating yet a new ideology. The alphabet changed our culture's cognitive habits over millennia; the printing press over several centuries. The telegraph changed our sense of distance over several decades. The automobile altered our social and sexual lives, to say nothing of our forests and our cities, within a generation.

But electronic media, with instant transmission of images without context, creates a cultural revolution almost daily.

Is There a Remedy?

It's easy to blame the Internet or the World Wide Web for the ills of society, just as it's easy to blame television. Let's take a look at where blame has been laid, beyond some of the finger-pointing already done in this book. Blame is the easy way out. Diagnosis without prescription is not useful. So it's time for perspective and some suggestions about remedy.

Just as Plato warned us about writing, Neal Gabler warns us about remedies:

> To pretend that one can provide a remedy would not only be naïve but duplicitous, since it would necessarily indulge the same sort of fantasy that got us here in the first place: that problems, like crises in movies, are susceptible to simple narrative solutions. You simply present a monster in the first reel and then have the hero vanquish it in the last.[16]

If our situation is crisis, then we're waiting for a hero. Until the hero arrives, there are remedies we can consider, some too vague to help us, some too radical to be of any use, some worth pursuit.

Neil Postman sees a bright side in the darkness of technology that prompted him to write *Technopoly*. His remedy is taking on the role of the "loving resistance fighter." Here is the loving resistance fighter's doctrine:

> By "loving," I mean that, in spite of the confusion, errors, and stupidities you see around you, you must always keep close to your heart the narratives and symbols that once made the United States the hope of the world

and that may yet have enough vitality to do so again. You may find it help-ful to remember that, when the Chinese students at Tiananmen Square gave expression to their impulse to democracy, they fashioned a papier-mâché model, for the whole world to see, of the Statue of Liberty. Not a statue of Karl Marx, not the Eiffel Tower, not Buckingham Palace. The Statue of Liberty. It is impossible to say how moved Americans were by this event.[17]

Postman reminds his readers that immigrants still come to America in hopes of finding relief from one deprivation or another in their homelands. "Americans forget, but others do not," he says of the images of freedom in the United States, "a series of experiments that the world watches with wonder."

Postman develops additional tenets of the loving resistance fighter: pay-ing no attention to polls unless you know what questions were asked and why; refusing to accept efficiency as the preeminent goal of human rela-tions; taking seriously the meaning of family loyalty; knowing the difference between the sacred and the profane; admiring technological ingenuity with-out thinking it represents the highest form of human achievement.

James Twitchell's remedy is to feel bad. He's not suggesting illness, but that red-faced feeling that used to be so prevalent in American intercourse—shame. "We had better learn how to invoke shame, because so many of our current problems can't be solved by clicking the remote control," Twitchell writes:

> Since the relatively recent replacement of a hierarchical culture, controlled from above, with a carnival culture, controlled from below, our temptation has been to think that feeling bad is just not 'right.' Bad feelings, we think, must be a sign of some disturbance, some churning of otherwise still wa-ters, some flaw in the personality or in a relationship. Losing face hurts and it is often not fair. In our typically adolescent response to painful anxiety, we say to the shamer, 'Don't be a downer. Quit laying this trip on me. Leave me alone. Don't pass judgment.' This is the language of child to parent, and it has become the baby boomer's lingua franca.[18]

Historically, the church was the arbiter of shame. More recently, we al-lowed the schools to join the arbitration. Both institutions changed because their constituencies changed. They discovered that several generations raised by television had expectations that neither church nor school could meet. So church and school alike abandoned shame as a core tool and tried to enter-tain. "Entertain or be turned off is the modern correlative," says Twitchell:

> I'm okay, you're okay, we're okay. We rarely consider that feeling bad,

feeling the blush of shame, may indeed be culture's way, the family's way, and even the individual's way of maintaining social balance and purpose. Sometimes you are not okay. Me too.[19]

Twitchell preaches intolerance, but only of behaviors that ultimately injure us all.

Symptom or Disease?

Robert Bork measures the distance between the 1930s hit "The Way You Look Tonight" and Snoop Doggy Dogg's 1990s recording "Horny" and finds a gulf. "The collapse of popular culture," Bork calls it in *Slouching Towards Gomorrah*.[20] He's right but for the wrong reason. Bork presents Snoop Doggy Dogg's song as if it was as big a hit as the 1930s classic, but it wasn't.

There's no question that it's symptomatic of a significant change from the days of "moon, spoon, and June" as popular lyrics. So is "Big Man with a Gun" by Nine Inch Nails, which Bork also cites.

"The obscenity of thought and word is staggering," Bork says, again correctly. Yet he combines anything not related to Bach or Gershwin into a collection that includes the worst of the music of recent generations and also its best. Bork's culprit isn't music, although he says, "The fixation on self first became obvious with rock 'n' roll, which evolved into hard rock. . . . Now we have moved on to rap, which is less constrained." There's no arguing with Bork when he accuses rappers of singing about criminals and, in some cases, being criminals themselves.

Television is not as bad as rap, Bork says, but it "displays the same traits as the movies and music" because it has come "under the influence of the Sixties generation." There's the root of Bork's evil—the Sixties, with a capital "S." That's the source of "modern liberals [who] seek to cure the disease of politicized culture with more politics." He cites the rise of intellectual and artistic classes and their subsequent size and prestige. Bork insists he's not talking about "true intellectuals," people involved with serious mental work. Rather, his complaint is against those "people whose mindset is very like that of the student radicals of the Sixties: hostility to this culture and society coupled with millenarian dreams."

Quick translation: The ills of society are caused by the Left—with a capital "L." In Bork's world, the Left has infiltrated media, government, and the Supreme Court. He also notes that technology and affluence are factors in softening religion, law, and morality. "A culture obsessed with technology will come to value personal convenience above all else, and ours does," he says, adding what is his most profound contribution to this canon: "A person whose main difficulty is not crop failure but video break-down has less need of the consolations and promises of religion."[21]

Bork, onetime U.S. solicitor general, acting U.S. attorney general, and appeals court judge, suggests a dramatic remedy: censorship. "The very fact that we have gone from Elvis to Snoop Doggy Dogg is the heart of the case for censorship." Not even Robert Dole and William Bennett, stalwarts of the conservative right, mounted a case for censorship. If anything, they were quick to separate themselves from the idea.

Bork shows no such reticence. Given his judicial background, he appears to have the law on his side. He says that, until recently, no one raised the question of the First Amendment in cases against pornographers, and "it was not thought relevant even by the pornographers." He cites a unanimous 1942 Supreme Court decision: "It has been well observed that such utterances are no essential part of any exposition of ideas." First Amendment jurisprudence, Bork says, has shifted from the protection of ideas to the protection of self-expression—"however lewd, obscene or profane."

At least Bork sees censorship only as a last resort. He makes two alternate suggestions that he suggests we try before committing to censorship: One is the boycott of other products sold by the offending company; the other is simply refusing to buy the offending product. He admits that the ideas may not be effective. "What happens if the company does not market other products that can be boycotted?" he asks. "So long as there exists a lucrative market for obscenity, somebody will supply it." To those who say, "If it offends you, don't buy it," Bork predicts that someone around you will buy it and "the aesthetic and moral environment in which you and your family live will be coarsened and degraded."

Bork's case for censorship is an unsettling solution. Even he feels he's outnumbered on the censorship issue, so he wondered with a group of friends about some event "that could produce a moral and spiritual regeneration." The group settled on four scenarios: "A religious revival; the revival of public discourse about morality; a cataclysmic war; or a deep economic depression." Bork holds some hope for the first two. The latter two, he says, are "social policies lacking broad public support."

What a relief!

Coping with the Future

In *The Image of the Future*, Fred Polak systematically examines the visions of the future held by the ancient Greeks, the Persians, the Hebrews, and the church of the Middle Ages, in addition to scores of other philosophers and writers of the past. His conclusion is that what a culture *thinks* its future will be has an enormous impact on the actual future.[22]

The idea should be useful to us in linking the past to the future, but that's a discipline that seems lost, especially within those institutions best organized to make use of it—the schools. Commenting on the concept, Nell Eurich says she finds it strange that the typical presentation of the humanities by teachers is dull when the subject matter—the creative works of the human race—is exploratory and bold.

> The most outstanding contributors actually shaped the future, giving us new theories, creating new art forms, joining common elements in new combinations that went beyond what had been known before. Dante dared to fabricate a whole system for the universe and created an immense structure for religious thought that sweepingly embraced purposive principles and prescribed behavioral responses for man.
>
> Creative imagination formed images of things no human had ever seen before, expressing visions in poetry, epics, paintings and music, in dance movement and in ritual form. Imagination transcended inherited models, transformed them into expression that lived and became the base from which other creative minds could take off in the future.[23]

Eurich admits that we cannot foretell the future: that's not a skill given to mere mortals, however often we try. We can analyze the present; we can apply our analysis to the lessons of the past and create scenarios for the future. The best to hope for is the ability to anticipate future effects of events that have already occurred. This restriction should not render our imaginations powerless.

Our universities have set themselves into binary units: "thinking" units and "doing" units. The doing units follow the processes that allow success in life. The thinking units shrivel by ignoring the new language of imagination. Humanities departments are valued as reliquaries, while more technical (and profitable) departments get the attention and the budgets. David Marc calls humanities "more . . . an antiquarian ornament than a dynamic epistemology—sort of like a charmingly nostalgic if somewhat dysfunctional old building that the campus just wouldn't be the same without."[24]

The humanities take the brunt of budget cuts and command the lowest salaries for teachers. Humanities professors are alarmed and rightfully so. At some schools, a college graduate's only brush with the English department may be some course in academic protocol to help write better papers in other courses. Foreign language requirements can be satisfied with study of computer "languages."

The result is a choice of "either one or the other," and the end product is niche specialization, not the rounded understanding of the generalist. Computer literacy is vital to our ability to cope with daily life in the digital age. However, it should not be a replacement for courses in classical understanding.

There's no surprise that the average American has allowed reading to be elbowed out of daily life by television and electronic entertainments. Reading takes a long time, and time is precious. Books are hard work, too. The reader has to buy in to the imaginative constructions offered by the novelist or the opinions proffered by the nonfiction author. Either work at it or be shut out. With television, you can relax. Voice, sight, sound, and character development are delivered together. And you can do something else at the same time—eat, drink, smoke, talk, even read a book. Why do we choose television? The path of least resistance, says David Marc.

Can the Schools Do It?

At the risk of seeming pedantic, a key tenet of communication must be stated here: There are three key elements in the communications chain—the source, the channel, and the receiver. Because of the proliferation of media choices and personal electronics, the battle for media survival will be at the receiving end, not the source.

There is a difference in how each is viewed at the university, according to Marc:

> While the humanities critics of the older systems (a.k.a. the "fine" arts) continue to study the work and its effects upon their own consciousnesses, the social science critics of the newer systems (especially television) choose to study the work's effects upon its receivers (i.e., the audience). A story told in print is greeted or rejected as an aesthetic event, while a story told on a TV screen reaches the world of learning as a sociological event. This petty little turf deal goes a long way in explaining the educational system's incompetence in dealing with the mass media or with a population that has been "unduly" shaped by it.[25]

To be effective, the educational system—from a child's earliest exposure to day care through postgraduate degrees—must accommodate a balance of the languages of media and the languages of myth and classical understanding. Neil Postman says (and he has a lot of company on this subject) that "we must not overestimate the capability of schools to provide coherence in the face of a culture in which almost all coherence seems to have disappeared."[26]

Christopher Lasch started that drumbeat in the late 1970s when he attacked "the deterioration of the school system and the consequent spread of stupidity." Calling it "the atrophy of competence," Lasch lashed out in *The Culture of Narcissism:*

> Mass education, which began as a promising attempt to democratize the higher culture of the privileged classes, has ended by stupefying the privileged themselves. Modern society has achieved unprecedented rates of formal literacy, but at the same time it has produced new forms of illiteracy. People increasingly find themselves unable to use language with ease and precision, to recall the basic facts of their country's history, to make logical deductions, to understand any but the most rudimentary written texts, or even grasp their constitutional rights.[27]

The impression, Lasch said, is that ordinary competence in any field lies beyond the reach of the layman. E.D. Hirsch Jr. also writes that the schools have let us down. Schools have our children for six or seven hours a day, five days a week, and they should have a significant impact. However, they don't:

> Cafeteria-style education, combined with the unwillingness of our schools to place demands on students, has resulted in a steady diminishment of commonly shared information between generations and between young people themselves. Those who graduate from the same school have often studied different subjects, and those who graduate from different schools have often studied different material even when their courses have carried the same titles. The inevitable consequence of the shopping mall high school is a lack of shared knowledge across and within schools. It would be hard to invent a more effective recipe for cultural fragmentation.[28]

Hirsch is the man who made the phrase "cultural literacy" famous. In a book of that title, he created a long list of facts that each of us should know to exhibit our grasp of America and the world around us. Dates like 1066, 1492, 1776, and the date spans of major U.S. wars. Phrases from A to Z, "abbreviation" to "Zurich," with "abolitionism" and "What will be will be" somewhere in between, for a total of more than 2,300 entries.

Hirsch's remedy is basic knowledge. His list was applauded for calling attention to the gaps in public education. At the same time, it was criticized (by Postman, among others) for concentrating on the need to memorize facts, rather than assimilation of fact and understanding. As Postman says, knowledge requires coherence, too. However, to dismiss Hirsch as calling for the memorization of a list is to misread him. Hirsch himself argued, "Any educational movement that avoids coming to terms with the specific contents of literate education or evades the responsibility of conveying them to all citizens is committing a fundamental error."

At the university level, there's what David Marc calls a "literacy charade." Professors ask their nonreading and nonwriting students to read books and to write about what they've read.

> Perhaps the worst consequence of the spiritually based fixation of university education on reading and writing is that it prevents the true functions of literacy in the modern communications market from being determined. What does print actually do best? How can reading and writing be integrated into the emerging patterns of normal communication in contemporary society? We are not likely to find out if we keep making believe in school that literacy stands apart from, and above, all other forms of human communication.[29]

There's a way to get it wrong, too. A good example is "character ed." Well-intentioned, but process-oriented schools are trying to inoculate kids with values of civility and integrity, to counter the runaway influence of popular culture.[30]

Let's put this in perspective: The average school now teaches kids how to choose a balanced diet, how to drive, how to make entries in a checkbook, how to have sex (in sex education classes), and how not to have sex (in abstinence programs). Too bad there's no time left for reading, 'riting, and 'rithmetic, but we've been a long way from the three Rs for some time now. The schools have been charged with the child-rearing lessons once the responsibilities of parents. But then parents are so busy these days, just look at their planning calendars for evidence.

It was inevitable that schools would be called on to teach our kids to be decent human beings, too: thus the new trend toward "character education" programs. Given the memories of school shootings in Littleton, Colorado, and Jonesboro, Arkansas, and evidence of character-in-decline, schools had to impose themselves.

Unfortunately, it's not as simple as reintroducing the Ten Commandments. As *Time* magazine describes it, the Ten Commandments would have to be translated into modern educationese: "Thou shalt model caring behaviors in interactive relationships with thy peer group." Commandments, after all, are judgmental. Character, on the other hand, can be built on universally accepted values, "bleached of any sectarian contamination," as *Time* puts it.

In one classroom, students assemble in groups to recite the traits that make good citizens. Being a good citizen, for example, means "to have character," says one first grader. "What does it mean to be a person of character?" the teacher asks. The boy responds with "caring, respectful, trustworthy" and another few traits from his list.

Posters in the hallways and T-shirts on the kids reinforce platitudes like "Where Character Counts!" *Time* describes the "cheerful paraphernalia that makes the modern American classroom seem like a Maoist re-education camp run by Barney the dinosaur."

Where are the busy parents? Complaining about the quality of the schools instead of trying to stop silly sloganeering that the schools use to take the place of character building. Happy talk becomes philosophy. Sounds familiar, doesn't it?

What Huxley Knew

In the brave new world of Aldous Huxley's fable, there is no whiskey, no tobacco, no illegal drugs. People do not smoke. They do not drink. They do not give themselves injections. Anyone who feels depressed or below par swallows a tablet or two of a compound called "soma." In small doses, soma brings a sense of bliss. A larger dose makes you see visions. With three tablets, you drop into a few minutes of refreshing sleep. None of this causes any mental or physical problems.

Soma is not a private vice. It is a political institution. It is the essence of life, liberty, and the pursuit of happiness, a chemical Bill of Rights. It is the brave new world's insurance policy against personal maladjustment and—most important—social unrest. Karl Marx called religion the opiate of the people. In *Brave New World*, it is just the opposite: soma is the religion of the people.

"Like religion," Huxley wrote in *Brave New World Revisited*, "the drug had the power to console and compensate, it called up visions of another, better world, it offered hope, strengthened faith and promoted charity." In 1958 Huxley wrote a real-world review and update of his dystopian satire. In it he also reviewed the real-world sources of smiling countenance, the drugs of choice that had been on the street since soma had soothed the citizen survivors of the Nine Years' War.[31]

He considers peyote and its derivatives—hashish, bhang, kif, and marijuana—declaring them "not a menace" to society nor a menace to those who indulge in the drugs, rather "merely a nuisance." He examines highly publicized tranquilizers (Miltown was the big brand name when he wrote his review, as Valium is today) and shows an understanding of their effectiveness "not in curing mental illnesses, but at least in temporarily abolishing their more distressing symptoms."

Of the perception- and vision-enhancer LSD-25, Huxley says it is "physiologically speaking, almost costless." He also talks in terms of doses of fifty millionths of a gram, not the large doses that would bring the drug notoriety in the sixties.

Huxley concludes, "We see then that, though soma does not yet exist (and will probably never exist), fairly good substitutes for the various aspects of soma have already been discovered." If a dictator wanted to control us, Huxley surmises, he could make use of all these drugs for political purposes: "He could use tranquilizers to calm the excited, stimulants to arouse enthusiasm in the indifferent, hallucinants to distract the attention of the wretched from their miseries."

How would the dictator get his subjects to take the pills? Huxley points to the use of tobacco and alcohol ("People spend considerably more on these very unsatisfactory euphorics, pseudostimulants and sedatives than they are ready to spend on the education of their children"). He also refers to the millions of prescriptions for tranquilizers that provided billions of individual tranquilizer pills (remember, he wrote in the 1950s, so his numbers pale against today).

Think of what Huxley would find if he could revisit *Brave New World* today. First, he would discover that soma exists! He would also understand almost immediately that his projections of the future were accurate—he had simply mislabeled them.

Soma is not Ritalin or the other chemicals being fed to grammar school children to balance or lengthen their attention spans. Soma is not the Ecstasy that makes teenagers at rave parties massage each other into sensual but giggling heaps. Soma is neither the smiling evenness of Prozac nor the products advertised on television suggesting that the slightest sneeze requires prescription medication.

The drug of choice in America's brave new world is not a chemical derivative, neither a modern concoction nor an allusion to a long-extinct plant from the period of the Aryan invasion of India (the source of Huxley's word "soma").

Soma is television.

Television and our television-inspired entertainment economy that prompts Neil Postman to tell us we are amusing ourselves to death. Television commercials create the same sense of bliss that soma creates. As the commercials repeat, the message intensifies into visions, like a double dose of soma. Prolonged viewing of television induces sleep, just like soma, although not as refreshing as the sleep Huxley describes. And television levels everything. The most urgent or vital report is reduced to filler between commercials.

During the lives of Americans born during or since World War II, there have been two underlying threats to the culture, each described in popular novels. The first was George Orwell's view: culture as prison. Orwell's parables, *1984* and *Animal Farm*, offer a blueprint for thought-control. The culture is shriveled by the spiritual devastation of tyranny. American children growing up in the 1960s feared the steady approach of the year 1984, which arrived with a whimper and no Big Brother watching us.

The second cultural threat was Huxley's approach: culture as burlesque. Huxley took advancing technology into account and used his parable to say that spiritual devastation would come from an enemy with a smiling face. As Neil Postman describes *Brave New World*, "Big Brother does not watch us, by his choice. We watch him, by ours. There is no need for wardens or gates or Ministries of Truth."

Postman bases his *Amusing Ourselves to Death* on the premise that Huxley's warning was right and that television is the proof:

> When a population becomes distracted by trivia, when cultural life is redefined as a perpetual round of entertainment, when serious public conversation becomes a form of baby-talk, when, in short, a people become an audience and their public business a vaudeville act, then a nation finds itself at risk; culture-death is a clear possibility.

In America, Orwell's prophecies are irrelevant. We dismiss them because they don't seem to have the possibility of coming true. Huxley's, however, are well on the way toward being realized. Postman said it first, and he says it best:

> For America is engaged in the world's most ambitious experiment to accommodate itself to the technological distractions made possible by the electric plug. This is an experiment that began slowly and modestly in the mid-nineteenth century and has now, in the latter half of the twentieth, reached a perverse maturity in America's consuming love affair with television. As nowhere else in the world, Americans have moved far and fast in bringing to a close the age of the slow moving printed word, and have granted to television sovereignty over all of their institutions. By ushering in the Age of Television, America has given the world the clearest available glimpse of the Huxleyan future.[32]

What Huxley was trying to tell us in *Brave New World* was not that people were laughing instead of thinking, but that they didn't know what they were laughing about or why they had stopped thinking. Some of them, of course, were never taught to think. That's the situation we find ourselves in today.

Feeling Sociable

One image of the interactive future is the specter of our offspring hunkered over their keyboards staring into glowing screens and "socializing" with anonymous hermits somewhere halfway around the world. Lonely hearts and empty lives playing out in sweet isolation. Fortunately, that doesn't have to be our only image. As Umberto Eco says, "There is an objective difference between downloading the works of Chaucer and goggling the Playmate of the Month."[33]

In spite of the dark portents of disconnectivity demonstrated in this volume and in so many more, there are positive glimmers from new media, especially from the new interactive uses of the Internet.

The Pew Center, which measures media usage each month and provides the television and newspaper industries with real-world views of their users, recently began the Pew Internet and American Life Project to break through the largely anecdotal and self-serving "research" that Internet companies use for promotion of their products.

The initial Pew Center survey indicates that the more involved people are with the Net, the more likely they are to enjoy other forms of social interaction, too. This must be good news for Harvard's Robert Putnam, whose theory, discussed in Chapter Four, is that television undermines civic discourse and civil interaction. Newspaper readers, Professor Putnam says, are more likely to maintain social capital than television users. He makes a compelling case.

More recent research on Internet users from the Pew Center indicates that they are more print-oriented than initially believed. They read e-mail as their first activity. Eye tracking studies show that they're more likely to gravitate to text on screen than to photos or graphics. If this is the case, then Internet users may fit more into Putnam's newspaper category than into the television category.

The most dramatic finding of the new Pew Center study is a surge in online activity by women. It is the first indication of gender parity of the Internet. Women of all ages report that they highly value the ability to use the Net to strengthen bonds with family, neighbors, and community. E-mail, the women say, helps them feel an improved connection to parents, siblings, and children.

Reporting on the latest Pew study in *The Industry Standard*, James Fallows says that "real world experience suggests that if you didn't drop that brief 'How are you doing?' e-mail to the retired parents who have already gone to bed in a different time zone or to the college student still out on a date, in fact you wouldn't reach them on the phone."

Women are way ahead of men in using the Internet for social applications. Nonetheless, the strong message of the Pew Center survey is that men and women alike see the Net as a broadening tool, giving them more ways to connect with life around them, not cutting it off. Compared to people who have never used the Internet, veteran Net users are more likely to say they have a large number of friends to turn to when they need help. They are more likely to have met or talked with a real human being on the previous day. They are more likely to have telephoned someone "just to talk."

Conversations with Internet pioneers show the same hope for positive connectivity, not the anonymous disconnect of the "lonely crowd." Many people in the Internet community socialize all the time on the Net. They have emotional relationships within their social communities. They simply define their community differently from the traditional geographic base.

As James Fallows concludes after reading the Pew Center study:

> No matter how pessimistic you may be, if you are honest you have to see this new evidence as a sign that the Net is following the path of previous technological revolutions. Like the printing press, the telephone, the airplane and the car, it is helping to fulfill the basic human desires to communicate and connect, rather than thwarting or distorting these needs.[34]

Let's hope so. We can't afford to let it happen without close scrutiny and a lesson learned from the disconnect caused by television. Shrinking attention spans and lack of historical consciousness parallel television's development. They plague our media, our education system, and our cultural exchanges. Our task is to use this all-too-brief interim before new and old media converge into their final application. For what? For grasping a sense of who we are and what we want the next wave of media to reflect.

When Umberto Eco pronounced the end of mass media, he also offered a next step: "We have to start again from the beginning, asking each other what's going on." That requires reconnection, and that's the best news we can take to the future.

The End

Marshall McLuhan concluded that when mass media triumph, Gutenberg man dies, and a new person is born. Eco remarked that we don't know if this new arrival is better off or not, but we do know he is new. Now disconnecting mass media will be subsumed by connected man. The communities are small. A community needs no more than two. The media are new and the ways they are received are new. This creates new challenges for us, since mass media man faces the same fate that befell Gutenberg man.

McLuhan was an English professor by trade, not a philosopher. In retrospect, we should call him a sociologist with a flair for trend spotting. His personal literary tastes ran to James Joyce and T.S. Eliot, and his doctoral thesis at Cambridge was on the Elizabethan writer Thomas Nashe.

If he were writing today, McLuhan would probably contradict many of the things he said. Before he died, he told an interviewer how wrong his predictions had been in one of his early works, *The Mechanical Bride*. On the other hand, he would be enormously surprised at how accurate he had been in some of his anticipations.

Given his background of serious academic study, he was asked why he enlarged his scope to include mass communications. His answer: "I find most pop culture monstrous and sickening. I study it for my own survival."

So must we all.

Notes

Chapter 1. The Illusion of Connectivity

1. The quotation is from the version of *Phaedrus* online as "Plato on Writing" at the University of Calgary, www.acs.ucalgary.ca.

2. Ed Shane, *Selling Electronic Media* (Boston: Focal Press, 1999), p. 19.

3. Neil Postman, *Amusing Ourselves to Death* (New York: Penguin Books, 1985), p. 78.

4. "The Verdict: Little Work Got Done as the Jury Spoke," *Wall Street Journal*, October 4, 1995, pp. B-1, B-3.

5. Rebecca Quick, "Television Ratings Get Strong Boost from O.J.'s Verdict," *Wall Street Journal*, October 5, 1995, p. A-9.

6. Quoted in Jib Fowles, *Television Viewers vs. Media Snobs* (New York: Stein and Day, 1982), p. 160.

7. Postman, *Amusing Ourselves to Death*, p. 78.

8. Marshall McLuhan, *The Gutenberg Galaxy: The Making of Typographic Man* (New York: Mentor Books, 1969), p. 298.

9. Ibid., p. 7.

10. Postman, *Amusing Ourselves to Death*, p. 32.

11. Ibid., p. 30.

12. Taylor Latham, "The Incredible Shrinking Movie Hero," *Swing*, November, 1994, pp. 99–100.

13. Neal Gabler, *Life the Movie* (New York: Alfred A. Knopf, 1999), p. 46.

14. Matt K. Matsuda, *The Memory of the Modern* (New York: Oxford University Press, 1996), p. 169.

15. Ibid., pp. 166–167.

16. Ibid., p. 167.

17. Quoted in Gabler, *Life the Movie*, p. 54.

18. Ibid., p. 6.

19. Ibid., p. 4.

20. Ibid., p. 5.

21. Alvin Toffler, *The Third Wave* (New York: William Morrow, 1980), p. 172.

22. Walter Truett Anderson, *Reality Isn't What It Used to Be* (San Francisco: Harper & Row, 1990), p. 6.

23. Michael J. Wolf, *The Entertainment Economy: How Mega-Media Forces Are Transforming Our Lives* (New York: Times Books, 1999), p. 72.

24. Bill McKibben, *The Age of Missing Information* (New York: Plume, 1993), p. 17.

25. Toffler, *The Third Wave*, p. 172.

26. Persistence of vision was explained by Albert Kim in a special edition of *Entertainment Weekly* dedicated to the 100 Greatest Moments in Television, February 19–26, 1999.

27. Rudolf Arnheim, *Visual Thinking* (Berkeley: University of California Press, 1969), pp. 23–24.

28. Mark Edmundson, "McLuhan: It's All Going According to Marshall's Plan," *Channels*, May-June, 1984, pp. 49–54.

29. Franklynn Peterson, "Marshall McLuhan Is Still Doin,'" *Houston Chronicle*, September 22, 1974, p. 7.

30. Edmundson, "McLuhan: It's All Going According to Marshall's Plan."

31. The phrase "virtual abandonment" was used in *The Kiplinger Washington Letter*, September 18, 1998. Additional, specific information about family law practice and Internet abuse was provided by *Kiplinger* Associate Editor, Elizabeth Kelleher.

32. "Study offers early look at how Internet is changing daily life" was the headline for the press release about the study by the Stanford Institute for the Quantitative Study of Society, Stanford University, February 16, 2000.

33. Jeff Donn, "Can't Resist the Online Pull." An Associated Press story distributed by ABC News at www.abcnews.go.com, August 23, 1999.

34. Quoted in Al Vecchione, "Unplug the TV," *Houston Chronicle*, September 14, 1997, p. C-1.

35. Stanley Cloud and Lynne Olson, *The Murrow Boys: Pioneers on the Front Lines of Broadcast Journalism* (Boston: Houghton Mifflin, 1996), p. 337.

36. George N. Gordon and Irving A. Falk, *TV Covers the Action* (New York: Julian Messner, 1968).

37. Jib Fowles, *Television Viewers vs. Media Snobs*, p. 23.

38. Ibid., p. 24.

39. David Grossman wrote an op-ed piece titled "No Denying TV's Teaching Our Children to Kill," which was printed in the *Houston Chronicle*, among other papers, as Congress wrestled with a juvenile justice bill. Grossman and DeGaetano's book, *Stop Teaching Our Kids to Kill,* was published in 1998 by Random House.

40. Robynn Tysver, "Blame It on MTV," *Houston Chronicle*, June 23, 1996, p. 10A.

41. Theodore Dalrymple, "Parental (Not Expert) Guidance Suggested," *Wall Street Journal*, August 6, 1999.

42. Fowles, *Television Viewers vs. Media Snobs*, p. 81.

43. Jerry Mander, *Four Arguments for the Elimination of Television* (New York: Quill, 1978), p. 264.

44. Fowles, *Television Viewers vs. Media Snobs*, p. 62.

45. Jane Gregory, "Parents Find Kids Don't Suffer When Deprived of Television," *Houston Chronicle*, October 24, 1981.

46. "Heavy Diet of TV May Give Children Mean View of World," *Houston Chronicle*, May 21, 1981.

47. Joan Anderson Wilkins, "A Four-Week Program to Turn Off the Tube," *Family Circle*, April 22, 1980, pp. 20–24.

48. Nancy Shulins, "Author Still Touts Joys of Pulling Plug," *Houston Chronicle*, November 9, 1987.

49. The examples are taken from the sources cited in the text: "Each Family Should Make TV Decision," *Houston Chronicle*, July 5, 1981; Peggy Charren and Martin Sandler, "Is TV Turning Off Our Children?" *Redbook*, October, 1982; "50 Families Seeking Life After Television," *Houston Post*, November 8, 1981; Patricia Skalka, "For Your Child's Creativity, Take Control of Your TV," *Friendly Exchange*, Spring, 1983; and Dennis Meredith, "TV or Not TV?" *Sundancer*, May 1980.

50. "Lear: People Watch Too Much TV," *Adweek*, October 12, 1981, p. 84.

51. Vecchione, "Unplug the TV."

52. John Perry Barlow, "The Powers That Were," *Wired*, September 1996, p. 53.

53. McKibben, *The Age of Missing Information,* p. 189.

54. "Studies Assert Television Leaves Viewers Tense and Passive," National Association of Broadcasters, *Highlights*, May 7, 1990.

55. This material was originally prepared for the Burns Media Seminars conducted from 1978 through 1982 by media consultant George A. Burns. Bettelheim's quotation comes from *Surviving and Other Essays* (New York: Vintage, 1980).

56. Michael S. Gazzaniga, "The Split Brain in Man," *Scientific American,* August 1967, pp. 24–29.

57. Also see Gazzaniga, "The Social Brain," *Psychology Today,* November 1985, pp. 29–38, and Robert E. Ornstein, *The Psychology of Consciousness,* 2nd ed. (New York: Harcourt Brace Jovanovich, 1977), p. 24.

58. Frank Mankiewicz and Joel Swerdlow, *Remote Control* (New York: Ballantine Books, 1978), p. 48.

59. Ibid., pp. 217–218.

60. Ibid., pp. 276–277.

61. Ibid., p. 12.

Chapter 2. The Attention Economy

1. The material on "triggering" and "positioning" is adapted from "Radio's Bumper Sticker Mentality," a paper delivered by the author to the Popular Culture Association, San Antonio, Texas, March 28, 1997.

2. Al Ries and Jack Trout, *Positioning: The Battle for Your Mind* (New York: McGraw-Hill, 1981), p. 3.

3. Ibid., p. 40.

4. Michael J. Wolf, *The Entertainment Economy: How Mega-Media Forces Are Transforming Our Lives* (New York: Times Books, 1999), p. 224.

5. Richard Saul Wurman, *Information Anxiety* (New York: Bantam Books, 1990), p. 35.

6. "Radio's Bumper Sticker Mentality."

7. Cathy Olofson, "Just the Meaningful Facts," *American Way*, February 1, 2000, p. 64.

8. Seth Godin, *Permission Marketing* (New York: Simon & Schuster, 1999), p. 42.

9. "Information Technology Revolution: Boon or Bane?" *The Futurist*, January–February 1997, pp. 10–15.

10. Michael H. Goldhaber, "Attention Shoppers!" *Wired*, December 1997, pp. 182–185.

11. David Ogilvy, *Confessions of an Advertising Man* (New York: Dell, 1963), p. 75.

12. David M. Potter's speech, "Advertising: The Institution of Abundance," was originally printed in the *Yale Review*, Autumn 1953, then collected in the book *Advertising in America*, edited by Poyntz Tyler (New York: H.W. Wilson, 1959).

13. Neil Postman, *Amusing Ourselves to Death* (New York: Penguin Books, 1985), p. 126.

14. Ibid., p. 128.

15. Jennifer Harrison, "Advertising Joins the Journey of the Soul," *American Demographics*, June 1997, p. 28.

16. Ibid., p. 22.

17. Michael Schrage, with Don Peppers, Martha Rogers, and Robert D. Shapiro, "Is Advertising Finally Dead?" *Wired*, February 1994, p. 71.

18. Ed Shane, *Selling Electronic Media* (Boston: Focal Press, 1999), p. 168.

19. Joseph Turow, "Breaking Up America: The Dark Side of Target Marketing," *American Demographics*, November 1997, pp. 51–54.

20. James B. Twitchell, *For Shame: The Loss of Common Decency in American Culture* (New York: St. Martin's Press, 1997), p. 85.

21. Wolf, *The Entertainment Economy*, p. 89.

22. Edward Cornish, "Television: The Great Time-Eating Machine," *The Futurist*, January–February 1998, pp. 60–61.

23. Alan Joch, "Stress Out Your Site," *Forbes Small Business*, Spring 2000, p. 33.

24. David Marc, *Bonfire of the Humanities* (Syracuse, NY: Syracuse University Press, 1995), pp. 30–34.

25. Alvin Toffler, *The Third Wave* (New York: William Morrow, 1980), p. 174.

26. Wolf, *The Entertainment Economy*, pp. 40–41.

27. The Las Vegas Hotel ads were collected from a variety of airline magazines in 1999.

28. James Poniewozik, "Bride Idea," *Time*, February 28, 2000, p. 86.

29. Lisa de Moraes, "For Darva and Rick, Separate Talk Shows," *Washington Post*, February 25, 2000, p. C-7.

30. Peter Johnson, "Media Darling Darva Keeps Viewers Engaged," *USA Today*, March 16, 2000.

31. Craig Wilson, "Why People Will Do Almost Anything to Get on TV," *USA Today*, February 25–27, 2000, p. 1A.

32. Howard Kurtz, *Hot Air: All Talk, All the Time* (New York: Basic Books, 1996), p. 222.

33. James Fallows, *Breaking the News* (New York: Vintage Books, 1997), p. 122.

34. Randall Rothenberg, "Oh, Daddy! Puff-ery Gets New Meaning in Sean Combs' Hands," *Advertising Age*, February 15, 1999, p. 22.

35. Bill Richards, "If Human Dartboards Thrill You, Be Sure to Catch This Show," *Wall Street Journal*, December 8, 1993, p. 1.

36. With thanks to Robert Hughes.

37. Paul M. Barrett, "Author Who Sued Over Scornful Review Is Now Scorned by the Publishing World," *Wall Street Journal*, April 7, 1994, p. B-1.

38. Andrea Gerlin, "How a Jury Decided That a Coffee Spill Is Worth $2.9 Million," *Wall Street Journal*, September 1, 1994, p. 1.

39. Catherine Yang, "The Disabilities Act Is a Godsend—For Lawyers," *Business Week*, August 17, 1992, p. 25.

40. Marilyn Geewax, "We're Becoming a Nation of Crybabies, Wearing Victimhood Like a Badge," *Houston Chronicle*, June 12, 1994.

41. Patricia Joyner Priest, *Self-Disclosure on Television: The Counter-Hegemonic Struggle of Marginalized Groups on* Donohue (Ph.D. diss., University of Georgia, 1992).

42. Robert Hughes, *Culture of Complaint: The Fraying of America* (New York: Oxford University Press, 1993), p. 17.

43. Meg Greenfield, "The No-Fault Confession," *Newsweek*, June 15, 1987.

44. Using the Northern Light search engine at *www.northernlight.com*.

45. Goldhaber, "Attention Shoppers!" p. 188.

46. Ibid, p. 186.

47. Chris Taylor, "Inside the Geekosystem," *Time Digital*, November 29, 1999, p. 40.

48. Godin, *Permission Marketing*, p. 30.

Chapter 3. The Bias Against Understanding

1. The ideas here—except for the true/false premise—were inspired by "HypeAmerica: What If They Announced a Trend and Nobody Came?" a presentation by Eric Miller, editor of *Research Alert*, to the Media Research Directors Association, New York, November 28, 1990.

2. Morton Winsberg, "Crime in the Suburbs: Fact and Fiction," *American Demographics*, April 1994, p. 11.

3. Cheryl Russell, "True Crime," *American Demographics*, August 1995, pp. 22–31.

4. If you want to check, see John Naisbitt and Patricia Aburdene's *Megatrends 2000* (New York: William Morrow, 1990), p. 64. The mistake shouldn't be held against them, except by us baseball fans.

5. Richard Saul Wurman, *Information Anxiety* (New York: Bantam Books, 1990), p. 32.

6. Bill Kovach and Tom Rosenstiel. *Warp Speed: America in the Age of Mixed Media* (New York: The Century Foundation Press, 1999), p. 44.

7. Jon Katz, "Technotragedies," *Wired*, February, 1998, p. 61.

8. Notes from a Shane Media report for KSDO Radio in San Diego, 1992.

9. Daniel Pearl and Glenn Burkins, "Journalists Who Flocked to the Gulf Discover They Have No War to Cover," *Wall Street Journal*, February 24, 1998.

10. Peter W. Kaplan, "Does TV Lens Distort Networks' Coverage of the Political Conventions?" *New York Times*, August 24, 1984, p. 22.

11. Peter A. Brown, "White House Stages the News to Get Its Message Across," *Houston Chronicle*, April 28, 1985, p. 26.

12. John Tebbel and Sarah Miles Watts, "Starring the President," *Channels*, January–February 1986. The article was excerpted from their book, *The Press and the Presidency* (New York: Oxford University Press, 1985), p. 75.

13. Walter Truett Anderson, *Reality Isn't What It Used to Be* (San Francisco, CA: Harper & Row, 1990), p. 168.

14. Frank Greve, "Bite-Sized Statements Key to Television News," *Houston Post*, May 6, 1984, p. 22A.

15. James Fallows, *Breaking the News* (New York: Vintage Books, 1997), p. 52.

16. Jay Rosen, "In the Air: The President Who Wasn't There," *Channels*, January–February 1986, p. 13.

17. Alan Bernstein, "Politics an Also-Ran in Local TV Coverage," *Houston Chronicle*, November 22, 1998, p. 1.

18. Eric Effron, "Seeing Double," *Brill's Content,* February, 1999, p. 44.

19. Rance Crain, "Food Lion Injured, Panel Says, but Journalism Takes Bigger Hit," *Advertising Age*, May 12, 1997.

20. Chuck Ross, "Welch's Grape Juice Squeezes into Plot Line of Pax TV Show," *Advertising Age*, November 15, 1999, p. 76.

21. "This Just In: Disney Ad Not What It Seems," *Houston Chronicle*, July 10, 1994. (Credited by the *Chronicle* to the *Washington Post*.)

22. Michael J. Wolf, *The Entertainment Economy: How Mega-Media Forces Are Transforming Our Lives* (New York: Times Books, 1999), p. 231.

23. A. Kent MacDougall, *Ninety Seconds to Tell It All* (Homewood, IL: Dow Jones-Irwin, 1981), p. 133.

24. Scott Donaton, "Media's Hunger for Gimmicks Makes It Play in the Hype Game," *Advertising Age*, April 3, 2000, p. 42.

25. John Heilemann, "Ad Nauseum," *Wired*, May 1996, p. 68.

26. Michael D. Mosettig, "Ninety Seconds over the Economy," *Channels*, December 1981–January 1982, p. 3.

27. Beth Belton, "Credit Card Data May Be Misleading," *USA Today*, March 18, 1986.

28. See "John Naisbitt's Trend Letter," April 11, 1996, pp. 6–7, for a discussion on measuring wealth vs. income.

29. James Fallows, *Breaking the News* (New York: Vintage Books, 1997), p. 139.

30. Ibid., p. 199.

31. Ibid., p. 141.

32. Mort Rosenblum, *Who Stole the News?* (New York: John Wiley & Sons, 1993), p. 17.

33. The Pew Center study, "TV News Viewership Declines," was released May 13, 1996. This analysis was prepared for clients of Shane Media Services and delivered in a memorandum report June 6, 1996.

34. American Women in Radio and Television, "News & Views by Fax," December 22, 1998.

35. S. Robert Lichter, Linda S. Lichter, and Stanley Rothman, "From Lucy to Lacey: TV's Dream Girls," *Public Opinion*, September–October 1986, pp. 16–19.

36. Joanne M. Lisosky, "Where the Girls Aren't: Children's Perceptions of TV Gender Representations,"*Feedback*, Winter 1995, p. 11.

37. Gayle Vassar Melvin, "Study Reveals Media Gender Bias," *Houston Chronicle*, May 4, 1997.

38. Susan J. Douglas, "Mixed Signals: The Messages TV Sends to Girls," *TV Guide*, October 25, 1997, p. 24.

39. A full-page ad from The Parents Television Council appeared with Allen's endorsement in *USA Today*, November 17, 1999. An earlier ad in *Advertising Age* and other industry publications listed Allen and Shirley Jones as "Honorary Co-Chairpersons."

40. Ed Shane, *Cutting Through: Strategies and Tactics for Radio* (Houston: Shane Media Services, 1991), p. 4.

41. "Lies, Damn Lies, and…" *Reputation Management*, July–August 1995, p. 39.

42. Fred Barnes, "How to Rig a Poll," *Wall Street Journal*, June 14, 1995.

43. Your mailbox may be full of these so-called polls, too. Because ours is a media household, we tend to read the junk mail, too.

44. Robert Tucker, "America's Fortune Teller," *Republic Scene*, September 1982, pp. 65–70.

45. Jeff Greenfield, "Watch Out for Those Trendaholics," *Houston Post*, November 1, 1993.

46. Kovach and Rosenstiel, *Warp Speed,* pp. 6–8.

47. Ibid., pp. 28–29.

48. A headline in *TV Guide* from the 1970s inspired this chapter. "There is a bias in television journalism," wrote John Birt of London Weekend Television. "It is not against any particular party or point of view—it is a bias against *understanding*," *TV Guide* August 9, 1975, pp. 3–7.

49. Kovach and Rosenstiel, *Warp Speed,* p. 28.

50. Beth Snyder and Ann Marie Kerwin, "'Clintern' Story Raises Issues for Cyberjournalism," *Advertising Age*, February 2, 1998, p. 32.

51. Julia Keller, "Truth Is, Research Group's Mission Is to Clear the Net of 'Cybergoofs,'" *Houston Chronicle*, December 20, 1998, p. 14A.

52. "Oops. In Cyberspace, News Often Jumps the Gun," *Wall Street Journal*, November 6, 1998, p. B-1.

53. Mike Godwin, "Daily Planet," *Wired*, July 1996, p. 101.

54. B.G. Yovovich, "Alvin Toffler Sees Advantage for Old Media in New York," *Editor & Publisher Interactive*, July 14, 1999.

Chapter 4. Seeds of Disconnect

1. Chris Taylor, "The Fight of Your Life," *Time Digital*, November 29, 1999, p. 65.

2. Nathan Cobb, "Kinetic Aesthetics," *Houston Chronicle*, July 20, 1997, p. 10.

3. Taylor, "The Fight of Your Life," p. 66.

4. Cobb, "Kinetic Aesthetics," p. 10.

5. Jared Sandberg, "The Gamer," *Wall Street Journal*, December 8, 1997, p. R4.

6. Dean Takahaski, "Golf and Football Widows, Unite! Just Create Your Own Web Site," *Wall Street Journal*, October 12, 1998, p. B-1.

7. Rebecca Quick, "On-Line Chat Can Be Safe—If You Know What to Say," *Wall Street Journal*, January 8, 1998.

8. Michael J. Wolf, *The Entertainment Economy: How Mega-Media Forces Are Transforming Our Lives* (New York: Times Books, 1999), p. 170.

9. Robert Wright, "Will We Ever Log Off?" *Time*, February 21, 2000, p. 56.

10. Ibid.

11. "Erotica Booms in a Dangerous Era," *American Demographics*, November 1993, p. 14.

12. Daryll Fogal, "Real Fake," *Wired*, June 1996, p. 156.

13. Robert D. Putnam, "The Strange Disappearance of Civic America," *The American Prospect*, no. 24 (Winter 1996), http://epn.org/prospect/24/24putn.html.

14. Sue Halpern, "Alone Again, Unnaturally," *Details*, October 1996, pp. 140–141. Also see Robert D. Putnam, "Bowling Alone: America's Declining Social Capital," *Journal of Democracy* 6, no. 1 (January 1995): 65–78; and "Robert Putnam Responds," *The American Prospect,* no. 25 (March–April 1996): 26–28.

15. Ben Steelman, "Talking Dirty in Public Becoming More Common, Studies Reveal," *Houston Chronicle*, September 13, 1999, p. 38A.

16. In 1969 and 1970, the Bistro, a comedy and folk music club in Atlanta, posted a sign in the dressing room: "One 'shit' per show." Young comedians playing the club would carefully craft their routines to take maximum advantage.

188 NOTES TO CHAPTER 4

17. Jeff Greenfield, "Turn On TV and Drop Your Jaw," *Houston Post*, January 17, 1995.

18. George F. Will, "Today, Rodman, Tomorrow, 'Whatever,'" *Houston Chronicle*, December 29, 1996, p. 3C.

19. Scott Donaton, "No Laughing Matter: 'Frat-Boy' Humor Spreads into Advertising," *Advertising Age*, November 15, 1999, p. 36.

20. Anthony Vagnoni, "'Something About' This Advertising," *Advertising Age*, February 6, 1999, p. 30.

21. Melissa Fletcher Stoeltje, "My, How Times Have Changed: In Pop Culture, Crude Is In, Baby," *Houston Chronicle*, July 4, 1999, p. 1F.

22. Ibid., p. 1F.

23. Joshua Meyrowitz, "How Television Has Reshaped the Social Landscape," *Feedback*, Fall 1989, pp. 16–22.

24. Digby Anderson, "Civility Under Siege," *Wall Street Journal*, October 2, 1998, p. W14.

25. James B. Twitchell, *For Shame: The Loss of Common Decency in American Culture* (New York: St. Martin's Press, 1997), p. 15.

26. Matt K. Matsuda, *The Memory of the Modern* (New York: Oxford University Press, 1996), p. 170.

27. Robert Basler, "New Book Details Lifestyles of Rich and Shameless," *Houston Post*, November 28, 1986.

28. Ellen Goodman, "What Happens When Beauty Meets the Net?" *Houston Chronicle,* October 31, 1999, p. 6C.

29. Mark Smith, "Internet Now Presents Auction of the Macabre," *Houston Chronicle*, December 5, 1999, p. 1A.

30. Patrick O'Driscoll and Tom Kenworthy, "Massacre Over Within Minutes," *USA Today*, May 16, 2000, p. 3A.

31. Kliebold's note appeared in *USA Today,* but his handwriting is shaky and difficult to decipher.

32. Stanley Edgar Hyman, literary critic for *The New Leader,* claimed that Burgess's book could not be read without a glossary, so he developed one that he said was "unauthorized" and "guesswork." It was published as the Afterword to the Ballentine paperback edition. Anthony Burgess, *A Clockwork Orange* (New York: Ballantine, 1965), pp. 177–190.

33. Jack I. Biles, *Talk: Conversations with William Golding* (New York: Harcourt Brace Jovanovich, 1970), p. 12.

34. John Stossel reporting on ABC-TV's *20/20,* March 23, 2000.

35. Christopher Lasch, *The Minimal Self: Psychic Survival in Troubled Times* (New York: W.W. Norton, 1984), pp. 186–187.

36. Ibid., p. 188.

37. Jeff Kunerth, "Trust, Privacy Endangered," reprinted from the *Orlando Sentinel* in *Houston Chronicle*, August 22, 1999, p. 16A.

38. See *American Demographics*, February 1999, for information on American millionaires, and Paul Davidson, "So, How Much Money Does It Take to Be Rich?" *USA Today*, June 20, 1997.

39. Robert H. Bork, *Slouching Towards Gomorrah* (New York: Regan Books, 1996), p. 9.

Chapter 5. The Community of Me

1. The classic myth of Narcissus is retold in many books about mythology. I used *Bullfinch's Mythology* (London: Spring Books, 1964), p. 74.

2. For more on the mythology of today, see Rollo May, *The Cry for Myth* (New York: W.W. Norton, 1991), and Joseph Campbell, with Bill Moyers, *The Power of Myth* (New York: Doubleday, 1988).

3. Idries Shah, "The Teaching Story: Observations on the Folklore of 'Modern' Thought," in *The Nature of Human Consciousness*, ed. Robert E. Ornstein (New York: Viking Press, 1974), p. 289.

4. Neal Gabler, *Life the Movie* (New York: Alfred A. Knopf, 1999), p. 23.

5. Walter Truett Anderson, *Reality Isn't What It Used to Be* (San Francisco, CA: Harper & Row, 1990), pp. 107–108.

6. Rob Walker, "That's Entertainment: Graduating from Beer Cans to Cocktails," *Forbes Small Business*, May–June 2000, p. 147.

7. Gabler, *Life the Movie*, p. 210.

8. Delia M. Rios, "Full Disclosure: Why Do Some Women Finding Notoriety Choose to Pose Nude?" *Houston Chronicle*, February 16, 1997, p. 12A.

9. Downloaded from 1st Books Library, www.1stbooks.com

10. Similar announcements dot papers everywhere. These were all from the *Houston Chronicle*. Shea's fiftieth birthday announcement was May 23, 1982; the engagement on October 22, 1995; the memorial (for Mary Newell Becker), September 9, 1999; and the "Elvis wedding," September 10, 1995.

11. Dan Robrish, "Writing a Life Story in 60 Seconds," *Houston Chronicle*, October 24, 1999, p. 14A.

12. Hilary Stout, "Historians-for-Hire Chronicle Lives of Ordinary Folks," *Wall Street Journal*, December 29, 1998, p. B-1.

13. "Police Baffled by Punk Story," *Houston Chronicle*, April 27, 1982.

14. Jean Caldwell, "Gruesome Rumors Salve for Society's Ills," *Boston Globe*, November 23, 1983, p. 10, section 7.

15. Dianne Hunt, "Smurf Scare Spreads in Schools," *Houston Chronicle*, January 20, 1983, p. 1.

16. Eric Brazil, "'Phantom Flood' Haunts River Town," *USA Today*, September 28, 1983.

17. The story began with a petition to the FCC—but not by O'Hair. Filed on December 1, 1974, by Jeremy Lansman and Lorenzo Milam, the petition asked for a freeze on applications for TV and radio stations by religious institutions. It was dismissed by the commission on August 1, 1975. Somehow, O'Hair's name was associated and the rumor began. In 1985 and again in 1991, the National Association of Broadcasters tried to help the FCC get the word out.

18. The 1938 broadcast of *The War of the Worlds* has stirred social psychologists since the nation panicked in the wake of events that had no existence except in the imagination. Canby's article is but one reflection on the power of radio at the time. Howard Koch, who contributed to the script, also wrote his memories of the events for Murray Hill Records in a 1976 rerelease of the audio of the broadcast.

19. Headlines in *Advertising Age* tell the story of the Procter & Gamble rumor: "Rumor Returns to Bedevil P&G," October 22, 1984, p. 1; "Devil Rumor Still Hounds

P&G," April 22, 1985; "After Devil of Fight, P&G Gives Up," April 29, 1985, p. 1; "New Logo Will Solve P&G Rumor Trouble," May 9, 1985; "P&G Goes into Court on Rumors," May 27, 1985.

20. The weatherman's apology was in a United Press International story, August 13, 1982.

21. A UPI story on January 23, 1982, referred to McDonald's problems.

22. Judith Kleinfeld, "The Best Defense Against Rumors Is a Good Offense," *The Houston Post*, April 7, 1992, p. D-1.

23. Caldwell, "Gruesome Rumors Salve for Society's Ills."

24. Darrell Sifford, "Rumors Are Easy to Start, Harder to Stop, Author Says," *Houston Chronicle*, March 31, 1985.

25. Anita Manning, "Spreading Legends on a Global Scale," *USA Today*, November 16, 1990, p. 1D.

26. Ibid., p. 2D.

27. The visions and miracles described in this section were originally collected in the early 1980s for the Burns Media Seminars. The "signs and wonders" were part of a seminar track on human perception.

28. Shah, "The Teaching Story," p. 306.

29. Christopher Lasch, *The Minimal Self: Psychic Survival in Troubled Times* (New York: W.W. Norton, 1984), pp. 29–30.

30. Gabler, *Life the Movie,* p. 8.

31. Ibid., p. 168.

32. May, *The Cry for Myth,* pp. 15–16.

33. Anderson, *Reality Isn't What It Used to Be,* p. 6.

34. Campbell, with Bill Moyers, *The Power of Myth,* p. 3.

35. Ibid., p. 13.

36. John Cloud, "It's All the Rave," *Time*, March 13, 2000, pp. 64–66.

37. Christopher Lasch, *The Culture of Narcissism* (New York: W.W. Norton, 1978), p. 87.

38. Patricia Braus, "Boomers Against Gravity," *American Demographics*, February 1995, pp. 50–57.

39. Bonnie Gangelhoff, "Doctor, Make Me a '10,'" *Houston Post*, April 9, 1989, p. F-1.

40. "Keeping Americans Beautiful Endorsed by Most," news release from The Merit Report: A Public Opinion Survey, September 19, 1983.

41. Lucinda Harper, "Good Looks Can Mean a Pretty Penny on the Job, and 'Ugly' Men Are Affected More Than Women," *Wall Street Journal*, November 23, 1993, p. B-1.

42. Rita Freeman, "New Mind/Body Basics," *Vogue*, April 1987, p. 355.

43. Robert Hughes, *Culture of Complaint: The Fraying of America* (New York: Oxford University Press, 1993), p. 17.

44. Dennis Prager, "*Everybody* Has a Support Group These Days," *Wall Street Journal*, May 7, 1998.

45. James B. Twitchell, *For Shame: The Loss of Common Decency in American Culture* (New York: St. Martin's Press, 1997), p. 117.

46. "David Sohn Interviews Jerzy Kosinski: A Nation of Videots," in *Television: The Critical View*, ed. Horace Newcomb (New York: Oxford University Press, 1976), p. 147.

Chapter 6. Context Free

1. James Brady, "The Historic China Trip . . . and a Historic Date Forgotten," *Advertising Age*, July 6, 1998, p. 12.
2. Bill McKibben, *The Age of Missing Information* (New York: Plume, 1993), p. 53.
3. The story from the film is retold in David Marc's *Bonfire of the Humanities* (Syracuse, NY: Syracuse University Press, 1995), pp. 61–62.
4. Umberto Eco, *Travels in Hyperreality* (San Diego: Harcourt Brace Jovanovich, 1986), pp. 145–146.
5. McKibben, *The Age of Missing Information,* p. 55.
6. George W.S. Trow, *Within the Context of No Context* (New York: Atlantic Monthly Press, 1997), p. 45.
7. Curt McCray, "Kaptain Kronkite: The Myth of the Eternal Frame," in *Television: The Critical View*, ed. Horace Newcomb (New York: Oxford University Press, 1976), p. 159.
8. Trow, *Within the Context of No Context,* p. 46.
9. Joseph Campbell, with Bill Moyers, *The Power of Myth* (New York: Doubleday, 1988), p. xiii.
10. Rollo May, *The Cry for Myth* (New York: W.W. Norton, 1991), p. 293.
11. Caren James, "Just Like You and Me, Only More So," *Houston Chronicle*, June 30, 1999, p. 3D.
12. James B. Twitchell, *For Shame: The Loss of Common Decency in American Culture* (New York: St. Martin's Press, 1997), p. 116.
13. Joshua Meyrowitz, "How Television Has Reshaped the Social Landscape," *Feedback*, Fall 1999, pp. 16–22.
14. Jacquelyn Mitchard, " 'Anastasia' Ignores Grim Reality of History," *Houston Chronicle*, November 23, 1997, p. 3C.
15. David Andrew Pierce, "The Real Pocahontas," *Wall Street Journal*, June 13, 1995.
16. Hal Crowther, "Disney's America and Warhol's Art," *Folio Weekly*, June 14, 1994, p. 45.
17. Michael J. Wolf, *The Entertainment Economy: How Mega-Media Forces Are Transforming Our Lives* (New York: Times Books, 1999), p. 10.
18. Charles R. Warner, "It's a Faux, Faux World: Reflections on Disneyfication, Themed Environments, and the Search for Authenticity," *Feedback*, Winter 2000, pp. 32–38. (Another version of Warner's paper was presented at the 1998 Popular Culture Association Annual Conference, Orlando, Florida.)
19. McKibben, *The Age of Missing Information*, p. 220.
20. Regis Philbin appeared on *This Week with Sam Donaldson and Cokie Roberts* on April 30, 2000. Elizabeth Vargas's remarks were made on *Good Morning America*, January 8, 1997. The Fox baseball broadcast was July 3, 1999. Complaints to the Memphis TV station were reported by WOGY Radio, January 17, 1999.
21. McKibben, *The Age of Missing Information,* p. 117.
22. Alice Z. Cuneo, "SegaSoft Online Games Tap into Cultlike Mind-Set," *Advertising Age*, April 7, 1997, p. 3.
23. Neil Postman, *Technopoly* (New York: Vintage Books, 1993), p. 15.
24. Bruce Anderson, "Losing Time: An Essay That Ticks Off the Reasons Why Analog Is Better Than Digital," *Attaché*, March 1998, p. 67.

25. Martin Miller, "From Top 10 Lists to 10k Races, Americans Fixated on Numbers," *Houston Chronicle*, May 2, 1999, p. 12F.

Chapter 7. The End of Mass Media

1. Umberto Eco, *Travels in Hyperreality* (San Diego: Harcourt Brace Jovanovich, 1986), p. 150.
2. Neil Postman, *Amusing Ourselves to Death* (New York: Penguin Books, 1985), p. 11.
3. Ed Shane, *2020 Visions: Trends and Population Projections to the Year 2020* (Houston: Shane Media Services, 1997), p. 5.
4. Eco, *Travels in Hyperreality,* p. 148.
5. Dan Ruby, "Our Circuits Are Jammed," *NewMedia*, April 14, 1997, p. 16.
6. "What Have They Been Smoking?" *Wired*, September 1997, pp. 53–56.
7. Jared Sandberg, "Immorality Play: Acclaiming Hackers as Heroes," *Wall Street Journal*, February 27, 1995, p. B-1.
8. The phrase "interactive interim" was coined by the National Association of Broadcasters to promote the association's 1998 convention. Robert L. Lindstrom wrote an article headlined "Living in the Interactive Interim" for an NAB publication called *On the Verge.*
9. Rebecca Quick, "Private Web Sites Keep Out Those Who Don't Belong," *Wall Street Journal*, December 22, 1997.
10. Robert L. Hilliard and Michael C. Keith, *Waves of Rancor* (Armonk, NY: M.E. Sharpe, 1999), pp. 124–126.
11. "www.Vonnegut.Hoax.Com," *Wall Street Journal*, August 7, 1997.
12. Ibid.
13. Mark Dery, "Tales of the Disinformation Highway: In the Era of the Big Lie, It's the Little Lies That Tell the Truth," *The Web*, April 1997, pp. 22–23.
14. "Interview: Neil Postman," *Spin*, January 1994, p. 67.
15. Marshall McLuhan, "Laws of the Media," *Et cetera*, June 1977, p. 173.
16. Neal Gabler, *Life the Movie* (New York: Alfred A. Knopf, 1999), p. 9.
17. Neil Postman, *Technopoly* (New York: Vintage Books, 1993), p. 182.
18. James B. Twitchell, *For Shame: The Loss of Common Decency in American Culture* (New York: St. Martin's Press, 1997), p. 212.
19. Ibid.
20. Robert H. Bork, *Slouching Towards Gomorrah* (New York: Regan Books, 1996), p. 123.
21. Ibid., p. 8.
22. Polak is quoted in Nell Eurich, "The Humanities Face Tomorrow," in *Learning for Tomorrow: The Role of the Future in Education,* ed. Alvin Toffler (New York: Vintage Books, 1974), p. 149.
23. Ibid., p. 150.
24. David Marc, *Bonfire of the Humanities* (Syracuse, NY: Syracuse University Press, 1995), p. 22.
25. Ibid., p. 38.
26. Postman, *Technopoly,* p. 186.
27. Christopher Lasch, *The Culture of Narcissism* (New York: W.W. Norton, 1978), pp. 127–128.

28. E.D. Hirsch, Jr., *Cultural Literacy: What Every American Needs to Know* (Boston: Houghton Mifflin, 1987), pp. 20–21.

29. Marc, *Bonfire of the Humanities*, p. 42.

30. Andrew Ferguson, "Character Goes Back to School," *Time*, May 24, 1999, p. 68.

31. Aldous Huxley, *Brave New World Revisited* (New York: Bantam Books, 1960), pp. 66–74.

32. Postman, *Amusing Ourselves to Death,* p. 156.

33. Lee Marshall, "The World According to Eco," *Wired*, March 1997, p. 144.

34. James Fallows, "Feeling Sociable," *The Industry Standard*, May 22, 2000, pp. 51–52.

Index

About the Author

Ed Shane is broadcast adviser and founder of Shane Media Services, which provides management, programming, and research consultation to electronic media organizations. He is the author of several books, including *Selling Electronic Media,* a textbook for undergraduate media courses. Two of Shane's earlier books were radio industry best-sellers: *Cutting Through: Strategies and Tactics for Radio* and *Programming Dynamics: Radio's Management Guide.*